POSTCARDS THROUGH HELL

Alan Chiasson & Edward Ford

Moonshine Cove Publishing, LLC
Abbeville, South Carolina U.S.A.
First Moonshine Cove Edition OCT 2022

ISBN: 9781952439438

Library of Congress LCCN: 2022917652

© Copyright 2022 by Alan Chiasson & Edward Ford

All rights reserved. No part of this book may be reproduced in whole or in part without written permission from the publisher except by reviewers who may quote brief excerpts in connection with a review in a newspaper, magazine or electronic publication; nor may any part of this book be reproduced, stored in a retrieval system or transmitted in any form or by any means electronic, mechanical, photocopying, recording or any other means, without written permission from the publisher.

This book shall not be lent, resold, hired out or otherwise circulated without the publisher's prior consent in any form of binding or cover other than that in which it is published. For information about permission to reproduce selections from this book, write to Moonshine Cove Publishing, 150 Willow Pt, Abbeville, SC 29620

Cover images from the authors' original photographs; cover and interior design by Moonshine Cove staff.

POSTCARDS THROUGH HELL IS A TRUE TALE OF HEROISM AND SACRIFICE THAT TAKES READERS ONTO THE DEADLY ROADS OF AFGHANISTAN AS BRAVE SECURITY CONTRACTORS RISK THEIR LIVES TO DELIVER THE US MAIL TO OUR MILITARY WARRIORS ENGAGED IN A BLOODY WAR.

Early Praise

"Postcards Through Hell rings with an authenticity that only comes from personal experience. Contracting is a different world from the military, one that has little recognition yet was no less dangerous. In fact, it was even more dangerous, as these men did not have air or fire support. Only the bravest and most dedicated men would embark upon such missions. It stands to reason that they are part of the newest 'greatest generation.'"—**Colin D. Heaton, Author and Historian**

"Postcards Through Hell is a riveting journey through war-torn Afghanistan that shares the brave and daring ride of private military contractors as they fight their way through unforgiving territory day in and day out to deliver the US mail."—*Scott Huesing, USMC (ret)* **Bestselling Author, Echo in Ramadi**

"Their story is the incredible account of courage, heroism, and brotherhood overcoming fears that everyone experiences. These are the unsung heroes of America's longest war in the Middle East. This is a must-read non-fiction account for all those seeking to go beyond their perceived limitations."—*Fred Galvin, USMC (ret)* **Bestselling Author, A Few Bad Men**

"This firsthand account takes you on an amazing journey to deliver the US mail and other critical supplies to our deployed troops in some of the most remote and dangerous outposts along the infamous Ring Road in

Afghanistan. Risking everything to fulfill their mission, Alan and Ed share their incredible story of sacrifice and survival in Postcards Through Hell."—***Amy Forsythe, USN/USMC PAO Bestselling Author, Heroes Live Here***

"In Postcards Through Hell, the men of the Pony Express are true patriots who risked life and limb to provide our military their only real connection to home, the US Mail. They are all heroes in my eyes, and I truly thank them for a job well done."—***Patrick R. Donahoe, Former Postmaster General US Postal Service***

"As a former Green Beret with multiple deployments to Afghanistan, the austere nature of our work forced us to rely heavily on resupply. I became very familiar with the importance of supply lines, logistics, and yes... the delivery of mail from thousands of miles away that offered the rare moment of respite and human connection beyond the corrosive cauldron of combat. But, I never gave much thought to the modern-day warriors who resupplied Green Berets and other Special Operators in Afghanistan...until now. This book is a legacy story to the men who did the heavy lifting behind the scenes, to keep us all in the fight. We owe them a debt of gratitude. De Oppresso Liber."--***Scott Mann, NYT Best-Selling Author of Operation Pineapple Express and Creator of "Last Out - Elegy of a Green Beret"***

"In the hellfire of ear cracking IED blasts, waves of burning shrapnel, and singed skin, we always held on to each other. Through countless snowfalls of ash and endless nights, some of us endured by kneeling over our beds in prayer while others knelt over toilet seats, the entrails of a goat "lamb-wich" looking back at them. We all held on. Bonded for life..."

Authors Note:

This book is a work of non-fiction. *Postcards Through Hell* is written in first person perspective and aspires to present a vast political and corporate sector picture of conflict in extraordinarily intimate terms.

The war in Afghanistan is arguably one of the most gruesome and long-lasting wars in human history. Afghanistan is a nation of tribes, separated by language, dialect or often varied customs. The only thing these tribes have in common is their faith, Islam which as amorphic, and subject to interpretation as lines in the sand. Afghanistan has Sunni, Shia and even the random Wahabist. There is no uniform Islam, but there is the tribe. The tribal configuration is the oldest form of local governance and social identity in human history. Long before kings sat on thrones, or the ancient Greeks created the concept of democracy, or Rome the republican form of government, the tribal chief was the lord and the law.

Whether you are in Asia or Africa, indigenous people identify more with their "tribe" than with their nation, which is unlike a majority of the United States. This is what makes places like Somalia, Iraq and Afghanistan so dangerous. In America you can drive from Portland, Maine to San Diego, California and not have any issues, you are in the same great nation. The road signs are in the same language, the rules are the same, the culture is not that different, or at least not totally alien.

In Afghanistan you can cross a dry riverbed and still be in Afghanistan but enter an entirely different and unfriendly world. This is the world in which contractors operate, and if you are unaware and distracted, it is unforgiving; it is a world in which the distracted are rewarded with injury and death.

This book explains why. Perhaps the most telling fact that emerges in the work is that these operators, who often work as support for military operations, do not always have the on-call support themselves when things become tenuous. Assets such as on call air support/strikes, indirect fire support, relief force in reserves, are prioritized for military concerns. The contractors are often left out in the open, all alone. They must be self-sufficient and self-reliant, and each man is an irreplaceable and a critical component in the overall effectiveness and survival of the group. Being alive after performing a highway run to write an after-action report is often considered a small miracle.

This work also details those times when things went badly, further increasing the realities on the ground, and highlighting the bravery of those men who risk it all to continue serving their country. What is also important is the lack of public information regarding the corporate side of war. This book serves to offer historical information about private military operations in the Middle East and dispel public perception concerning the government security contractor. The objective is to familiarize the reader to the world of security contracting that is not well-known outside of the PMC community. The world of the security contractor is best described as murky at best, and as a result is understandably not well understood by the general-public. Misinformation, conjecture, myth and obscurity perhaps define what little knowledge is available to the public regarding this type of employment, which is undoubtedly one of the most dangerous of all professions.

This book explores the personal and emotional journey of the men who dared venture into the unknown and the impact of those experiences on their daily lives. The story is a compelling, enjoyable read that you will find hard to put down – a firsthand account of the most remarkable US mail service in Afghanistan, *The Pony Express*. It focuses primarily on the psychological hardships of Ed Ford, call sign "Hammer" who must come to grips with his own personal struggles serving as team leader and operations manager with *The Pony Express*, delivering **Postcards Through Hell** in a war-ravaged nation.

FOREWORD
Major General James E. Livingston, USMC (Retired)
Medal of Honor Recipient, Vietnam

In combat, as in military life in general, there are always unforgettable moments that stay with us. Many are funny and nostalgic, while others are tragic, provoking long moments of thought as we lose comrades, bringing home the realization that we work in a very dangerous occupation.

In this extremely informative and readable book, Postcards Through Hell, Ed Ford and Alan Chiasson provide a succinct view about the world of contracting, which carries many of the same dangers as serving in frontline combat units.

This project educated me on what I was not familiar, yet also triggered memories that I experienced as a leader of Marines and a combat veteran. The reader will enjoy the operational details and methods, while also learning about a world that is not well-known outside the operators themselves.

People considering military service in general, and military support contracting in particular, should read this book—which is written from combat veterans. Being well-informed prior to making such life-altering decisions is not just wise; it is expected of the true professional.

Many of us may leave the service and take off the uniform, but we never stop being patriotic Americans. These men who served on active duty then decided to serve our nation further as part of The Pony Express did so at great risk. We can be proud of their service and their dedication. God bless them all.

Table of Contents

Lost But Not Forgotten	262
Acknowledgments	263
About the Authors	267
Appendix One – Maps	269
Appendix Two – SOC Operational Orders	272
Appendix Three – Convoy Configurations	276
Appendix Four – Medical Force Protection	279
Appendix Five – Abbreviations	283
Appendix Six – Bibliography	286

Postcards Through Hell

CHAPTER ONE
Contact!

DATE: 2009

MISSION: To carry US mail consisting of care packages and sensitive, classified cargo to American Forward Operating Bases (FOBs) and coalition forces in Afghanistan.

LOCATION: Kandahar, Kandahar Province

If the slogan, "Neither rain nor snow, nor heat or gloom of night" was synonymous with the United States Post Office, then our slogan was "Neither AK-47 nor PKM, nor IED or the Taliban" would keep us from our appointed rounds. We were security contractors known as *The Pony Express*. Our exploits led us along the most dangerous road in the world — "Ring Road" in Afghanistan.

Our convoy was nine vehicles deep as we made our way from Kabul to FOB Gecko, a firebase in dire need of supplies, approximately 460 kilometers (285 miles) away. I was in vehicle number five. Our three gun trucks, all Ford F-550s, had Level-VII armor made of TS 400 steel. Although it was considered impenetrable from multiple weapon strikes, we were still extremely vulnerable. The gun trucks separated three Mitsubishi cargo trucks.

Then it happened.

"Contact! Contact! Contact! VIC-1 taking small arms fire from the right!"

The message issued from the lead gun truck in semi-garbled radio chatter that only men familiar with the plastic feel of communication equipment are fluent in. Out of context, my next commands could have easily been mistaken for a frantic nurse's aide in a hospital delivery room.

"Push! Push! Push!" I hollered.

Only instead of a fetus being delivered into a harsh-lighted world, I was delivering our collective asses from becoming disabled. If we choked the column, we became a stationary target. If that happened, we could kiss next year's deep-sea fishing trip goodbye. I had no intention of letting that happen.

Many of us had learned during our time in various militaries that survival meant fighting through the ambush, without hesitation. There was no time to consider our options or seek input from others. There was only right now, this very instant, and my trained response.

I called up for a situation report. "Everyone okay?"

The lead vehicle replied, "Roger that, ineffective SAF."

SAF referred to small arms fire. As the team leader and vehicle commander of VIC-2, I had to check-in, take charge, ease the unrest. It was a post dedicated to keeping my men and their minds focused by putting into practice the old adage: *Calm breeds calm.*

It didn't matter that my heart was racing as adrenaline rushed through my veins or that fear wanted to consume my every thought. My brothers were depending on me.

"No damage here." Called back the vehicle commander from the lead gun truck. "Just a lot of noise."

Just then, "Cease fire!" blistered across the radio from the vehicle commander in the lead vehicle.

I stopped. *Hold the applause. Somebody's mic is still hot.*

I heard the dull clatter of both top gunners laying down cover fire to an unseen enemy. Our medic was in the rear gun truck and hadn't responded. I activated my panic button, sending a GPS ping to signal our location and keyed in my mobile radio. "Doc! What's your status?"

Radio squelch followed. It was only a few seconds, but in that moment, a sour taste filled my mouth as I silently waited for a response. *Come on, Doc. Come on...*

The trail vehicle finally replied, "Follow's up, Hammer."

Relief was instantaneous, but there was no time to relax.

We needed to get out of there. "Roger that," I said. "Keep moving."

Not two seconds later, another voice shouted, "Contact! RP...."

The "G" was cut off. The lead vehicle veered hard to the right. A huge cloud of smoke and dust billowed before us. The voice shot through again. "PKMs firing indiscriminately!

Contact left! Contact left!"

Two of the box trucks behind me stopped on a dime. The third mail truck began a futile effort to reverse out. My eyes fixed on the rear-view mirror. I couldn't believe what I was seeing. The trail vehicle's passenger door popped wide open, spitting Doc out like yesterday's lunch.

Was he bailing out? What the hell?

I radioed, "Doc! Get back in the fucking truck and get off the X!" The cargo trucks were beginning to reverse out. The only way to communicate to them was to disembark on foot and direct them to continue forward.

With that done, Doc scrambled back into the rig's mouth as quickly as he'd come out, repeating his earlier response, "Follow's up."

The only people who spoke on the radio were the three expat vehicle commanders and the local national interpreter who ran on a separate tactical channel to provide instructions to our top gunners. Everything else was either communicated by cell phone when there was a signal or face-to-face. Hell, we even had sign language.

The attack lasted through two kilometers of broken highway that was littered on both sides with huge blast holes and burnt-out tankers, buses and flatbeds. All damaged from previous roadside bombs and attacks. These shells of transportation had all seen better days but were now confined to their roles as dusty relics of death. A dismal reminder of what could be. We, looked at them and pushed past, fighting our way through the real-life river Styx to remain in the land of the living.

We survived that run from Kabul to FOB Gecko intact and many similar missions. But all of us, either individually or collectively, suffered losses in one form or another in the days, weeks, and months to come on the infamous Ring Road. Better known as "The Road of Death."

CHAPTER TWO
Ring Road

"Where the roads end in Afghanistan, the Taliban begin. Roads promote enterprise. Enterprise promotes hope. Hope is what defeats this ideology of darkness."

~*President George H.W. Bush*

Ring Road had many names: Highway One, Route A01, National Highway 01 (NH01).

To us, it was simply "The Road of Death." The ancient two-lane road stretched an amazing 2,200km (1,400mi) through vast expanses of barren desert, and rising up through impressive mountains. The highway stretches south from Kabul, to Kandahar, and curving east on to Herat, topping out at Mazar-i-Sharif in the north, eventually winding its way back to Kabul.

Originally built in the fourth century during the reign of Chandragupta Maurya, it continued to serve as the lifeline to the Afghan people. It was often in disrepair but was never completely abandoned. The natural wonder and beauty of the land hid the insidious enemy determined to stop our mission at all costs.

For the men of *The Pony Express*, traveling on Ring Road was often like traveling straight into the fires of hell.

Our mission was to deliver the US mail, messages, care packages, classified information, and critical supplies, equipment, guns, and ammo to US military and coalition forces throughout war-torn Afghanistan over the worst that Ring Road might throw at us.

Some of our missions took days. It wasn't uncommon for *The Pony Express* to be on the road for twelve to eighteen hours at a time.

When running convoys on Ring Road, we felt like drifters in a post-apocalyptic neo- western world. Like a continual river of asphalt baked under a cruel unrelenting sun, it stretched into the horizon in front of us and behind us, as far as the eye could see.

Desolate and somber, this partially paved, once-black tarmac was at times gray with dust, battle-torn and enemy-hardened. Remnants of war. As the topography began to change, it draped over the mountains like a black ribbon that fell off into the distance where tattered earth met the sky.

Due to poor construction and misappropriation of funds, the Kabul-Kandahar section of Ring Road deteriorated badly due to overweight trucks and armored vehicles, leaving clearly visible tire tracks in the asphalt. However, the brutal landscape and poor infrastructure were only part of the problem. Extreme weather conditions, local militias acting as traffic police, and countless ambushes were what made Ring Road the most dangerous road in the world.

We knew the road would not carry us home like a welcomed friend. Instead, it beat on our gun trucks and bodies with every mile, the silent monotonous path leading us to the inevitable.

The Taliban. Their Militia and insurgents attacked with frequency using roadside bombs, mortars, RPGs, and small arms fire.

Ring Road never failed to kill when instructed to do so by those who intended to do evil. It didn't know what it was to be human or what it neutralized on charged orders. It didn't suffer from PTSD. It had no compassion or shame. Yet it was given the status of artificial life by the enemy.

How could something so inanimate come alive?

The road that was black in the day, melted into the darkness of night. Only the wind kept our top gunner's company. Using GPS to map the terrain, we traveled by moonlight, without headlights, to minimize our position, but the thundering of tires and the rattling of our mechanical horses broadcast a distinct sound signature to our presence.

Our instincts served as radar, always switched on to maximum sensitivity, but as we approached a village, our senses were heightened even more. With a third of Afghanistan's population living within 50km (30mi) of the road, it wasn't uncommon to come in contact with the Afghan people. The road snaked directly through Taliban territory, splitting villages in half.

Contrary to the bustle of life in the day, this villages stood empty at nightfall. Once the sun set, no one left their earthen homes unless it was absolutely necessary. No one walked the dusty streets. Gone were the food vendors and the women in their burkas haggling loudly over handmade goods from carts and baskets. Gone were the children who played stick games amongst the trash that lined Ring Road. Only closed shops with cracked steps and small ditches that carried feces and waste away from the town were visible.

In this village, barely any lodging bordered the street. The ones that had once provided shelter to weary travelers were torn apart and abandoned. Shattered windows seemed to house the souls of the deceased.

Dim streetlights were scattered along the road, some bent and broken, others old and rusty. The glow these lights gave off was eerie, almost supernatural, flickering at the slightest hint of movement. The absence of people did nothing to ease our minds. We remained vigilant, kept driving, and watched closely, hoping not to be engaged. Once in a great while, a harried person moved quickly with intense purpose, his shadow filling the empty street like a ghost.

Silence surrounded us. The only serenade was the ever-present rumble from our gun trucks that pounded the highway to dark and dusty fragments. We had entered the fatal funnel. It felt as if there was no way out. No exit. No escape.

We kept moving and moving and moving...wondering when

the road would eat us alive.

Alongside the road, we saw burnt out tankers and the shells of reefers and flatbeds laid waste by insurgents, evidence of a particular form of ambush. An attack solely designed to create a choke point to swallow a column of trucks carrying much-needed fuel and supplies to coalition forces staged at strategic locations further on.

The Pony Express was one such column.

We cleared the town without incident and again began to pick up speed. As the lights faded, another dark area appeared, darker and dirtier than the last stretch of Ring Road.

The road was still. It turned slightly to reveal a dead tree at the end of the curve with a boarded-up hut next to it. Martyred flags blew in the chilling breeze. The hut was surrounded by a rock wall with broken mud patches that looked like chipped and fractured headstones.

The gun truck shook loudly as we rolled over another culvert. Relief replaced fear as we traversed the conduit without harm. A lone rig came thundering down the hill in our direction, high beams on, signaling our position. It was swallowed by the darkness as it passed. We let go of the collective breath we held and pressed on.

As dawn approached, intermittent rays broke through the clouds and the gloomy mist to touch the landscape with hopeful light. Such a wicked façade.

The brown water that ran in the "Jui" or bayou, on the right side of the highway, had a dreary look, like it was contaminated with chemicals and biohazards. A single tribesman was seen squatting on the side, brushing his teeth with the end of a chewed twig called a miswak. A harsh reminder of third-world life in Afghanistan.

We neared our destination, Firebase Gecko. We survived another day. Another mission. Another man fighting. Another journey of the soul. Yet here we were, too numb to even care.

The smell of death lingered in the air. We rode past it, into Firebase Gecko. Rock powder dusted our faces. Our fatigued bodies were trashed.

We had conquered Ring Road and delivered the goods with no lives lost. This time.

CHAPTER THREE
Boots on the Ground

At the height of the war in Iraq, the country was deemed the most dangerous place to work as a security contractor. Afghanistan was a different animal and even more dangerous. Dodging IEDs and explosively formed projectiles in Iraq was a walk in the park compared to fighting the Taliban. I knew we had our work cut out for us. We had to be ready when we set boots-on-the-ground.

Afghanistan was no place for anyone who didn't have thick skin. Operation Enduring Freedom was already well underway. Because of the Diplomatic and Anti-Terrorism Act of 1986, the US Department of State's Bureau of Diplomatic Security created a new sub-agency called Worldwide Personal Protective Service. WPPS worked under the Office of High Threat Protection. The goal was to recruit, evaluate, and train US operatives and third-country nationals. Their mission: protect personnel and military facilities or FOB's, both domestic and abroad.

In order to get the job done, WPPS hired private military companies as security contractors. Later on, one such company was created by former Special Forces operatives—the Special Operations Consulting-Security Management Group (SOC-SMG).

We secured lucrative contracts during Operation Iraqi Freedom in Baghdad, Iraq. Based on our experience...we taught protective security procedures and how to conduct protective security operations overseas. We provided security for short or long-term special domestic security situations.

The US Embassy's regional security office used trained WPPS contractors for added protection. WPPS handled all movements, including moving high-ranking civilian personnel from the US Embassy. SOC escorted representatives of the United States Agency for International Development, USAID, for infrastructure building, agriculture, and schools from different FOB's (Forward Operating Bases) in Iraq to worksites and venues throughout the area of operations.

In Iraq, we developed a solid reputation for providing reliable, lucrative, and static security services to several military FOBs. This included combat and security training to foreign guard force personnel and personal security detail—protection services for government VIPs, corporate CEOs, and humanitarian Non-Government Organizations. Security consultation and threat assessments were available for other governments and private entities all over the world.

Day & Zimmermann Inc. purchased the SOC company in 2008. They kept the acronym but changed its meaning from "Special Operations Consulting" to "Securing Our Country."

Although SOC was still committed to pre-existing contracts, they were spread thin. The drawdown of US troops in Iraq was accelerating, so the SOC Mobile Operations program in Afghanistan was born.

In April of 2008, I attended and graduated from the High Desert Special Operators Center for pre-deployment in Minden, Nevada, an ideal location for training. It sat at the base of the Sierra Mountains, and the surrounding desert closely resembled the terrain in Afghanistan.

It was a good vetting course since I had already been contracting overseas for four years.

Training consisted of sub-skills like protective operations in high-risk areas, explosives recognition, and improvised roadside bomb attacks. They also covered intermediate and advanced weapons and marksmanship, vehicle convoy security and protection, advanced vehicle immediate counter actions, and combat lifesaver.

Eric Roubinek, an old buddy of mine from 1st Force Recon, was an instructor there. He was able to vouch for me, and that put me on the fast track for deployment to Iraq.

In Iraq—starting out at ASP Michigan, west of Ramadi, then moving to Bayjii—I became an assistant team leader and security specialist, responsible for the security of Tetra-Tech Unexploded Ordnance (UXO) personnel during demining and clearing operations. We provided blocking positions when the teams did their demo shots for the ordnance found on the site.

Saddam Hussein was a member of the Arab Socialist Ba'ath Party and President of Iraq from 16 July 1979 until 9 April 2003. During his presidency, he amassed an unprecedented quantity of bombs and ammunition which included Scud missiles, rockets, mortars, and mines. The ammo dumpsites had since been bombed by the United States during Operation Desert Storm and Operation Iraqi Freedom.

But lone ammo was often found. That's where we came in.

On this particular day, we found two sites that were old ammunition dumps from the Saddam days. Using standard military demolition, the explosive ordnance disposal techs prepped the site. They dug a huge hole and put the unexploded ordnance and demolition for the charges in it.

SOC cleared the area one more time. We pulled security on all four points for a 360- degree overwatch to ensure no herders or kids wandered into the area. Then the EOD guys blew the shot. Afterward, they cleared the hole to make sure there were no remnants nearby.

Overall, the Tetra-Tech UXO program was not a bad gig considering the conditions we lived in. I met and worked with some really good guys, some of which would be with me later in Afghanistan. When we weren't blowing shit up, we were assigned personal security detail (PSD) missions to Ramadi or Baghdad that included motorcade, personal protection, and assisting in site security for our base of operations.

After the Tetra-Tech UXO program shut down, I was redeployed in December of 2008 and assigned to the Joint Intelligence Center at Camp Slayer in Baghdad, Iraq.

The work was routine. Twelve hours on, twelve hours off. We checked IDs and Civilian Access Cards, so I was afforded a lot of workout time. Hitting the iron became more than a hobby and wasn't strictly about physical survival either.

Working out became that safe-haven that kept my mind from totally cracking up and going inside out, to say the least. If I hadn't hit the gym at least five times a week, I would've gone nuts. Everyone knew the benefits of working out, but staying in shape here meant staying alive mentally, and being physically capable.

Due to my security clearance and background, I was assigned to a PSD team in the international zone located in Baghdad with seven others. From the start, we were focused operators. Our common ground: we were US Marines, but our diverse backgrounds and experiences produced an interesting mix of shooters. Learning each other's idiosyncrasies, habits, and motivations was crucial for our own safety and peace of mind.

In the field, each man had his areas of expertise. As we got to know the lay of the land, we found a rhythm to living and working together to take care of the client, but it went much deeper than that. When risking your life to accomplish the task at hand, it was extremely important to know who stepped up to the plate when the time came for action, not words. We had to be in sync, coordinate duties, and have each other's backs on and off a mission.

On the "home front" we worked out together and took turns in the kitchen. When I made breakfast for the guys, they cleaned up. Everyone liked bacon, eggs, and potatoes, but pork was hard to come by in the land of Islam. Instead, I used turkey bacon and spiced up the potatoes with some caramelized onions. The more I cooked, the less I cleaned. All was fair, and we settled into our routines without much complaint, learning the best and worst about each other.

That is where I met Chris Rector and several other contractors who eventually became part of the mobile teams in Afghanistan. I also met Mike Hearty. Everybody called him "Money" because he was always working the gigs to make the client happy and to bring in more clients.

Hence, more money. I personally think it was because he was always talking about getting paid.

He was a salty Marine known for his love of rice and beans. He spent twelve years in the Marine Corps as an Ammo Tech, four years at 3rd Battalion 4th Marine Regiment, a few years at Force Service Support Group, and a few other billets before getting out. He then worked as a narcotics officer for a few years stateside before being deployed to Kosovo with DynCorp International. He looked like the actor Michael Chiklis who played Vic Mackey in the TV series *The Shield*. His head was clean-shaven, and he was fairly stocky. I liked him from the get-go.

Rob Cook, "Cookie," was another Marine who served in Air Naval Gunfire Liaison Company and was a drill instructor before getting out and becoming a peace officer.

We had a Marine mentality and caliber of work ethic that guided us and bonded us on each mission.

Thankfully, the missions were in the international zone, so the threat level was semi- permissive and relatively low. But there was a slight problem we had to deal with.

The personal security detail was set up rather backward. All the operators with any WPPS training and qualifications were in subordinate positions. All untrained personnel were in leadership roles.

This created friction on the team. Upper management focused on cutting corners, cost savings, operational expenses, and budget issues. They were called pencil necks for a reason.

As operators, we knew that wasn't the correct way to operate in a combat zone. We looked at timings, patterns of predictability, procedures, tactics, and techniques. If it meant burning more fuel or wasting a few extra bullets downrange to get things right, then we did it to stay focused and sharp. Everyone wanted to be an operator until it came time to do operator shit.

They wanted us to run on a regular schedule or roll with fewer shooters.

That was just plain wrong. Being time-and-place-predictable meant the enemy knew when and where we were going to be.

Shit like that could easily get someone killed.

The issues were never resolved. The program managers told us what to do and how to operate, but once we left the wire, we did our own thing and moved accordingly to the way we were trained.

In March 2009, I was called up to go to Afghanistan and given my own team. My assignment was to provide site security for a construction job at Camp Chapman. This was the start of growing my own thick skin to deal with Afghanistan, but I had the advantage of being backed up by a good bunch of knowledgeable guys, a solid team who made all the difference in the world when it came to operating in a high-threat environment.

We were as ready as we could be. Boots-on-the-ground and frosty as hell.

CHAPTER FOUR
Camp Chapman
DATE: March 02, 2009
MISSION: Static security at Camp Chapman for C-1 construction project
LOCATION: Khost Province

With boots on my feet and my feet on the ground, I finally arrived at Camp Chapman, a US military base located at the site of a former Afghan Army installation. Occupied by the CIA, it was located in Khost Province, on an airstrip just two miles east of the city of Khost. The camp bore the name of Sergeant 1st Class Nathan Chapman, the first US soldier killed by enemy fire during the Afghanistan War, on January 4, 2002.

Chapman was directing troop movements from the back of a flatbed truck when he was shot. He did not die instantly from the attack, but on May 18, 2015, the CIA acknowledged Chapman had been detailed to a six-man CIA unit known as "Team Hotel" and unveiled a star on their memorial wall in his honor. He was posthumously awarded the Purple Heart and the Bronze Star.

The first American CIA operative to be killed in combat was Marine veteran Johnny Michael "Mike" Spann, a paramilitary operations officer in the CIA's Special Activities Division. He died at the Qala-i-Jangi fortress outside of Mazar-e-Sharif during a prisoner uprising, while interrogating Taliban prisoners in 2001.

Spann had interviewed John Walker Lindh, the "American Taliban," when a riot broke out in the prison. According to witnesses, Spann was interviewing several prisoners in the general population when they surrounded him and threatened to kill him. Spann drew his pistol, killing three attackers before being overtaken by those Taliban fighters. They launched themselves at

Spann, grabbing at his flesh with their hands, kicking and beating him. Spann killed seven more with his pistol before he disappeared under the crush.

Camp Chapman was one of the most secretive and highly guarded locations in Afghanistan. It evolved into a major counterterrorism hub of the CIA's paramilitary Special Activities Division. Used for joint operations of the CIA, military special operations forces, and Afghan allies, they had a housing compound for US intelligence officers. Because of this, there was always a threat of attack. As secretive as the CIA was, it was no secret that covert operations were being orchestrated from the camp.

After a seven-hour layover in Dubai, I finally made it to Afghanistan. I began conducting security operations as a site security manager and convoy operations team leader. Our mission was to escort convoys for a specific client and the Department of Defense throughout the area of operation.

At first, I was sent to Khost province to work as the security liaison between the construction team from CTI, a Turkish construction company, Client code name, C-1.

It was a small contract for our SOC Mobile Operations Program. Forty to fifty of us worked together at any given time. The whole team was made up of local national Afghans with one interpreter. These missions were tedious. Most of the time, they took several days because we delivered supplies to multiple C-1 pick-up and drop-off sites on the outlying FOBs.

Getting to Chapman was interesting because we ran missions in a convoy of "thin- skinned" or low-profile sport utility vehicles. Regular vehicles with no armor plating or protection, such as bulletproof glass, were said to be thin-skinned.

These vehicles were readily available, but they left us vulnerable to injury or death if we were attacked, yet it was the only option we had. This made for long days. Construction on the road between Gardez and Khost was heavy, but we arrived at

FOB Salerno, our first stop, without incident.

My next mission was to provide close protection and transport for two US supervisors and one Turkish supervisor for the C-1 construction project. The terminology and deliverables written in the scope of work made for a rather restrictive job. It dictated how we were to operate, where we were allowed to go and not go, and what we could and could not do.

All our weapons needed to be checked in and out with the Blackwater security team for safekeeping. The Blackwater guys were called "Cobras," and consisted mostly of ex-military Special Forces Operatives.

We spent a few nights at FOB Salerno. I drove them to and from Camp Chapman until the initial main camp was established. Then we lived at Camp Chapman for the duration of the contract. This was standard procedure for many projects and programs.

We were supposed to be totally independent and self-sufficient from our clients, who had base access and privileges, but we were on our own and had to rely on the Turks for our meals because we didn't have access the base dining facility (DFAC). While most Turkish people and culture were compatible with Western society, the Turks on this contract were not at all hygienic when it came to food preparation and handling. That was partially due to the austere conditions of the camp. The countertops were not washed, no matter how many times we complained. We fell victim to several gastrointestinal issues.

The other folks in the camp, mostly the BW Cobras, helped out whenever possible by bringing us plates from the chow hall. Unfortunately, we still got sick quite a few times. Take a bite. Puke it out. Repeat.

We tried to keep ourselves sane by incorporating workouts into our routine. I ran the perimeter fence of the construction site, did calisthenics, and cross-fit physical fitness training. I leaned up quite a bit during my stay at Chapman, dropping damn near thirty pounds as stomach upset and fatigue finally took its toll on me.

When I went home for my first vacation in July of 2009, no one was pleased with my appearance. My ex-wife barely recognized me. My brother Patrick commented on a photo he had seen of me and said I looked like I had AIDS.

My relief back at camp, B.J. Tooker, was a former convoy guy from Iraq and had moved up the ladder to the SOC corporate office. A former police officer, he was one of the few guys cleared for the C-1 site by the client. He made a deal with the camp commander at Chapman that allowed us to eat at the chow hall and work out at the Morale, Welfare, and Recreation with state-of-the-art gym equipment.

When I returned to the hell of Afghanistan and was awaiting transport back to Chapman, I got to run on a couple of missions to assist the convoy teams. Although I was assigned as the Site Security Manager at Camp Chapman, a lot of times our PSD team worked in tandem with the mobile operations team. Because we were all working for SOC, we did whatever we could to help each other out. It was a brotherhood, and we always had each other's back.

The two expats on the team were Mark Mattson, aka "Matty," a US Navy SEAL who spent a majority of his twenty-two years with SEAL Team Ten, and Drew Babbitt. Drew may have been short in stature, around five foot six, but he was a real powerhouse when it came to lifting weights, and strength and endurance exercises. Molded in the Marine Corps, Drew worked out relentlessly to stay fit and healthy. He could bench press three times his weight, which was about 480 pounds.

The first mission was to recover a couple of vehicles and personnel that had been ambushed by the Taliban while escorting a convoy to the Polish FOB in Ghazni, located south of Kabul about a quarter of the way to Kandahar. They made it out OK, but their vehicles were all shot up in the complex attack.

Matty and Drew said it was pretty bad. Their vehicle ended up being towed by the cargo truck they were escorting. The second escort vehicle, full of Afghan security guards, had fallen back and taken refuge in another town. Some speculated they held back intentionally and left the American vehicles on their own. Others knew they often ran away in the heat of battle.

When I finally caught up with Matty and Drew, I asked "What the fuck happened?" Matty said, "They pulled multiple ambushes on us and had us dead to rights."

"What happened to the LN vehicle?" I inquired. Part of my job was to determine how, why, and what could have been done differently to produce an alternate outcome. The local nationals' behavior and actions had to be assessed.

"They fell back, and we lost them," Matty said.

Falling back, away from the rest of the convoy, sparked all sorts of other questions. I asked, "Did they get hit or did they bail?"

Drew said, "The fuckers bailed on us."

"Yeah?" I said.

Matty agreed. "It's totally fucked up that we have to rely on these mother-fuckers." He was pissed, and rightly so. The fact that they were still alive to have this conversation meant they had beat the odds. Unfortunately, what they were describing was bound to happen again, sooner than later, unless some drastic changes were made.

"Maybe we need to keep an American in the vehicle with them," I suggested.

Matty replied, "Yeah, it may come to that—or we run all expat teams."

We ran many different types of missions on a regular basis. Some were simple cargo drops consisting of fuel, food, and miscellaneous supplies. Other times, the cargo was classified and the only information we received was a date, time, and route with no manifest. Depending on the client, we even conducted recon and venue advances to help pave the way for future operations.

Still, it was clear from the beginning, we were in a dangerous world, doing a dangerous job.

The next run was an uneventful C-1 mission to Kandahar and Spin Boldak. Our billeting was at a hotel in Kandahar that always seemed like it would be an ideal target of a suicide bomber or vehicle-borne improvised explosive device, (VBIED). We used the opportunity to conduct an advance on the hotel to use it as a possible safe-haven if necessary.

On the way back to Kabul, south of Ghazni, near Qalat, we got hit with small arms fire and RPGs. The RPGs went high and one of the vehicles took a few bullets. Other than that, no one was injured. The damage was minimal.

This area proved to be problematic for future convoys.

We informed Matty when we returned to our home-base at the SOC villa in Kabul. This way he could build a template of where most of the attacks were expected to be.

Ryan Bennett, the acting Program Manager, already had a map on the wall with pushpins indicating attack sites. He color-coded them to differentiate between SAF, RPG's, IED's, complex ambushes, and roadblocks. Walking into his office and seeing the map on the wall, inundated with push pins, told a story all its own.

There were many unrecognizable Taliban agents along the asphalt strip, looking out for targets, alerting the fighters, and carrying out attacks. According to locals, they were shopkeepers, youngsters idly strolling, men perched on walls drinking tea, or fruit sellers. We didn't know who to trust, who was safe. These "invisible forces" produced an uneasy feeling, particularly during our downtime while waiting on another mission.

During the SOC contract period from 2009 to 2012, the death toll in Afghanistan tripled.

It was officially labeled the most dangerous place in the world to be, with the highest US casualty rate.

Those statistics didn't include private security contractors. The US Labor Department, under the Defense Base Act, confirmed the numbers. The year 2010 proved to be the deadliest of them all.

According to the Afghanistan Index, the number of Afghan civilians killed as a result of fighting between pro-government forces and armed opposition groups rose between 2,500-3,000 deaths per year. The worst months were from May to October during the three-year contract period.

During that time frame, we took a beating but continued to run missions despite the dangerous outcomes. Every day was a battle that brought us closer together. Failure wasn't an option. We had a job to do. Sounds simple, but that is what it boiled down to.

I hate using clichés like "ordinary men under extraordinary circumstances," but sharing life-altering, intense experiences—like bearing the brunt of enemy fire—was what began to bond us together. It was a tribe mentality.

In the hellfire of ear cracking IED blasts, waves of burning shrapnel, and singed skin, we always held on to each other. Through countless snowfalls of ash and endless nights, some of us endured by kneeling over our beds in prayer while others knelt over toilet seats, the entrails of a goat "lamb-wich" looking back at them. We all held on. Bonded for life.

As I struggled against the constant expectation that tomorrow could bring someone else's turn to meet their maker, or perhaps even my own, I came to believe, "No one gets to Heaven without first going through Hell."

And with each mission, it became apparent. That's exactly where we were. From that moment on, I always made it a point to say "Welcome to Hell" at the beginning of all my mission briefs.

CHAPTER FIVE
Mission Brief

In Afghanistan, mission briefs were designated by the highest threat level. An enormous amount of work went into putting together a mission to escort cargo from a starting point to a release point. A private military company was paramilitary in concept and nature. Once SOC received a movement request—operational orders—from a client, it was passed down to the director of operations who delegated tasks to his subordinates.

As a contractor, understanding the meat and potatoes of preparing an effective mission brief was paramount to mission success. It wasn't something any Tom, Dick, or Harry could do without knowledge, experience, and training. As a Recon Marine, I was fortunate to have that knowledge and experience. However, there were times when I received information from my superiors who didn't have the basic concept of disseminating critical intel, which made my job even harder.

The primary function of the mission brief was to make sure everyone was on the same page with the objectives of the mission. It was extremely detailed and labor-intensive. At this point, the mission was deemed classified. Some areas of operation were semi-permissible like the SOC villa. Once outside the wire, the convoy was on its own, completely isolated and exposed.

Aside from mapping the routes, we coordinated with government and military personnel to determine the best course of action along the route, we identified rally points and safe havens, listed any known checkpoints, and developed contingency plans in case the shit hit the fan.

Each SOC employee was responsible for preparing for the mission. The operations officer gathered intelligence. The team leader prepared the mission brief. The assistant team leader coordinated various team members to perform certain jobs. Drivers conducted all the vehicle maintenance. Gunners serviced weapons and ammo. The medic ensured there were ample medical supplies available for each team member, and plans were made for any evacuation, if necessary, during the mission.

I wanted to make sure all team members always had their heads on a swivel, so I included threat intensity levels in all my briefs. A low threat meant highly dispersed, thinly concentrated enemy forces and assets with a limited ability to reconstitute. A medium threat was a significant threat requiring passive and active measures to avoid or degrade the threat and prevent subsequent engagement. The highest threat level meant hostile forces over a wide area of coverage, densely concentrated and capable of rapid reconstitution and mobility.

From a gunner's perspective, the objective was to maintain situational awareness and provide suppressive cover fire in the event of an attack. From a driver's point of view, the objective was to know the route including the distances between checkpoints, fueling stations, and rally points. The medic's responsibility was to know the location of every Battalion Aid Station, Forward Surgical Teams, and Combat Surgical Hospital along the route, as well as MEDEVAC services and their capabilities in terms of flight radius, to include the military's 9-line procedures. 9-line is a term used for calling in MEDEVAC when there is an injury sustained in combat. The team leader and assistant team leader had to know grids and comms, as well as actions on contact, and evasive maneuvers in the presence of an ambush.

We were responsible for a shitload of information. Technically, it was much more detailed than that.

We shared with the team general convoy organization, order of march, timing, speed, and distancing. We had contingencies for accidents, breakdowns, tactical tire changes, separation from convoy, and attacks. We needed to know everything from cover, camouflage, dispersion, radio silence, blackout, and other protective measures against enemy attack, signaling, and air support in case the need arose for a MEDEVAC.

We, of course, were also responsible for the cargo. messing and billeting, radio frequencies, and call signs. We handled all operational funds, including obtaining receipts, maintaining the correct balance, and documenting everything. We served as the liaison between the Afghan National Army (ANA) and the Afghan National Police (ANP) personnel and local nationals—vendors, village elders, and citizens.

Effective communication was critical to mission survival and success. The need for a reliable translator was absolutely essential and greatly appreciated.

A good interpreter made things a hell of a lot easier for everyone. They negotiated passing through checkpoints. They communicated with our local national partners and team members. They were familiar with the terrain and knew the lay of the land, local customs and traditions.

A large portion of SOC's success was due to the fact that we had guys who were wired tight and had their shit together.

Having personnel with prior military training was a benefit, but it was even more advantageous to have guys on the team with prior personal security detail and convoy operations experience. Although it took a few missions for everyone to get to know each other's idiosyncrasies, it didn't take long to figure out who made for good team continuity and cohesion and who was a pain in the ass to work with.

At least the mission briefs kept us on the same page. With each task defined, we kept our eye on the bigger picture. We needed that team continuity to stay alive.

CHAPTER SIX
The Footlocker

After being at Chapman for a while, I began to accumulate a lot of gear, so I bought a footlocker called a Gorilla Box. Made of top quality, molded, polypropylene resin, it was a tough, durable container designed for transporting tactical gear and equipment through any environment. It had a label with a gorilla slapped on it.

The boxes were black and measured about thirty-two inches long, fifteen inches wide, and thirteen inches deep. They had a reinforced padlock hole, molded hinges, and a handle so we could carry them like a suitcase. Most of the guys had them. We liked using them because they kept our personal effects secure with tie-down brackets on each end and two heavy-duty locking latches. You could also stack the boxes, which was convenient when living out of a small *CHU* or Container Housing Unit.

Back at Camp Chapman, I put MOLLE attachable pouches and additional first aid supplies in the box. I saved memorabilia, gifts, and keepsakes. I also carried most of my gun cleaning equipment and put in a few books and magazines that were lying around for those restless nights, and believe me, there were a lot of those, mostly in between assignments and missions.

After surviving several ambushes and complex attacks, I wrote "War Chest" in bold letters on the side of my footlocker and started filling it with the remnants of combat.

Everything familiar to me was in that box, items that summoned both pleasant and painful memories. I safely preserved macabre souvenirs, strangely spectral talismans, war trophies from my first enemy battle, and other memories that would come to shape me as a human being.

What I didn't know then was that it would begin to accumulate bad memories more than good. Eventually, it became a sad reminder of the turmoil my brothers and I faced together, of the death and destruction we witnessed.

Their struggles for survival flashed back in a bloody shemagh, a name tag, a patched flag, a broken flashlight, a heart-shaped stone, a piece of clothing.

There it sat in the corner of my *CHU*, a black ghost. It taunted me. As long as the box remained closed, I was okay. I only opened it long enough to place whatever it was I found lying around after an attack. But sometimes I spent vulnerable moments digging through the objects, as if they were favorite old movies. It became a necessary evil to me, something that I strangely treasured, something I needed, as well as something I loathed.

To this day, I don't know why I collected those items, or kept the box. Was it because I wanted to be reminded of my time with SOC in Afghanistan? To be reminded of all the missions? Was I paying some kind of tribute to my brothers, so I wouldn't forget their sacrifices?

I think that in reality, it went much deeper than that. It became a portal into my mind and my soul, barely keeping my demons at bay.

CHAPTER SEVEN
The Big Dogs
DATE: August 15, 2009
MISSION: First C-1 supply mission to Shkin
LOCATION: Shkin, Paktika Province

Everything we'd accomplished and endured in our missions up to this point had only brought us to the starting gate. The real race was coming, and it was time to prove our readiness—or bow out of the race.

The mission that awaited us was crucial to establishing whether we were ready to run with the big dogs in the business. It would determine whether we stayed in Afghanistan or went home.

Late in the evening on August 14, 2009, Money and Cookie were assigned a crucial and very dangerous mission to Shkin, located in Gomal Province and bordered eastern Pakistan. It was wrought with enemy activity and was a major focal point for insurgents who brought weapons and supplies from Pakistan. The base they were delivering supplies to, suffered attacks on a daily basis. Money's team finished getting all their vehicles ready for the perilous trip. They received $10,000 USD op funds from Ryan Bennett, our program manager who was a former 19-D Cavalry Scout with the 2nd Armored Cavalry Regiment assigned to the VII Corps in Europe.

We usually carried that amount of cash for a three-day mission to cover fuel, hotel, meals, breakdowns, checkpoint bribes, and get-out-of-jail fees. American dollars talked and could easily mean the difference between living and dying.

Money took a call from the president and vice president of SOC, who wished the team good luck from corporate headquarters in Minden, Nevada. Many people were counting on them and would be watching their run, the first with Money as team leader.

The next morning, Money briefed the team to make sure they understood how important the run was, and to make sure everyone was wired tight.

The convoy was stacked. The lead vehicle, an armored B-6 Toyota Landcruiser, was driven by Cappy, a Macedonian, and commanded by Rob Cook, aka "Cookie," who also functioned as the assistant team leader and navigator for the route. The team translator rode in the backseat of the lead vehicle, which was followed by four cargo trucks. The middle vehicle was loaded with four Afghan gunners and was also followed by four more cargo trucks. The trail vehicle was driven by Wolfe, who was also Macedonian and Money rode shotgun.

They moved out early to get a jump on any hostile enemy forces. The operational orders were to stop at Orgun-E to make contact with the C-1 clients and check the load on the trucks.

Money gave Cookie half the cash—$5,000—just in case he rolled up on any trouble in the front and needed to pay their way through. Cookie never needed to worry about it because every time the convoy stopped; Money ran to the front to see what was going on anyway.

The locals knew that Americans had cash. Money always tried to talk his way around a jam, bartering for the lowest payout. He looked for the person wearing the most medals on his chest—that was the one to bribe or pay a highway tax to. If a situation grew dire and they needed to jet, Money slammed a wad of rolled-up one-dollar bills in their hand. It worked. They stood there trying to count it. The team took off.

This pissed off Ryan and Jon, but Money would rather give up $50 here and there, to save time and bullets. And their lives.

Once they arrived at Orgun-E, the C-1 client advised them that the fuel tankers had been sitting for a week but needed to get to Shkin. Within twenty minutes they lined up all the trucks and departed.

With the addition of the two fuel tankers, the convoy stack was now 1:5: A lead vehicle, five cargo trucks, a gun truck, five more cargo trucks, and finally the trail vehicle.

Running fuel tankers made the mission more perilous because their presence increased the likelihood of an attack. Convoys rolled only as fast as their slowest truck, and fuel tankers were both notoriously heavy and slow. And of course, a blown-up fuel tanker left a huge footprint in terms of thick black smoke and fire. If the Taliban couldn't hijack the fuel tanker, then blowing it up was an acceptable alternative. Their mantra was, "If we can't have it, then neither can you."

They weren't two minutes out before one of the trucks pulled off to the side of the road. It was starting to act up and the driver needed a few hours to work on it. Since they were still near the camp, they left him there to deal with it.

The convoy set up was now a four to five mix.

The translator told them they needed to be extra careful around Kilo Marker 24.

Everyone needed to have eyes up and be ready for anything. If they made it to Kilo Marker 26 without being hit, they were good to go for the rest of the trip.

Cookie gave Money a *Are you fucking kidding me?* look. Granted, they always had their heads on a swivel outside the wire, so they were ready for anything—and pushed towards Shkin and Kilo Marker 24.

Cookie scanned the area and advised Money that a guy driving a blue sport utility vehicle (SUV) was trailing them from the hills. Close to Kilo Marker 23, it was slow going because the convoy had to cross a few dried-up riverbeds. They tried to keep the convoy tight, but the drivers moved at a snail's pace, and it created too much distance for a signal.

Someone on the radio said it was clear, but Money couldn't always hear everything from the front.

When the lead vehicle reached the Kilo 24 Marker, Cookie advised Money again about the "voice" on the radio. Two SUVs now trailed them on the right side.

Once the convoy was completely together at the Kilo 24 Marker, Money wanted to get out to make sure everyone was ready to move. Wolfe asked him not to. It was as if he knew the dangers waiting for them out there.

Cookie came across the radio, "Which way do we go?"

They had decided earlier this was going to be their "all or nothing" spot. Money knew how much was riding on his team getting the cargo and fuel to their destination. Not only was a huge contract in the works, but the guys in the Special Forces Operational Detachment-Alpha, also known as an "A-Team," were running out of fuel and chow—and were depending on them to bring their supplies.

The A-Team was the primary fighting force of the Green Berets. Their composition consisted of up to twelve men, each with a separate military occupational specialty and cross- training in other specialties.

Under normal conditions, they would have received supplies via air delivery. But now the rotary-winged birds weren't making any drops because they had been fired on with RPGs and crew-served weapons on their last few flights.

Money ordered Cookie to roll. As the convoy began to move, the hairs on the back of his neck stood up and his Spidey senses kicked in. He knew them all too well. When Money was in Baghdad, Iraq (2004-2005), he was the team leader of Templar 17 PSD, working for DynCorp International. They were assigned to protect American personnel for the State Department.

More than once when he felt something was wrong, he told his assistant team leader, Ty Wool, to change routes. Ty didn't ask any questions. He knew from past experience that Money's intuition was right most of the time, and so they made the adjustment. Within a few minutes, they received a report from the tactical operations center that their "green route" had been compromised and an attack or ambush had occurred on it.

On this day, the team didn't have any other choice. The option to change the route simply didn't exist. That was one of the things Money hated about Afghanistan. Once they drove outside the city of Kabul, they didn't have a choice but to drive on Ring Road.

By the time Money's vehicle made it to Kilo Marker 24, he saw only three of the cargo trucks because the road made a dogleg turn to the right.

Cookie's voice came across the radio, "Contact front! Contact front!"

Money's heart dropped and dead silence followed. He tried to radio Cookie when his own vehicle hit an IED on the right side. They'd been ambushed.

The driver in the lead vehicle sped up and lost control on the gravel surface. The vehicle rolled over at Kilo Marker 24. They were a sitting target.

It was a complex attack. More than two distinct classes of weapons—indirect fire, direct fire, SAF, IED, RPG—were fired against the target. Against them.

Wolfe did a great job keeping his B-6 on the road and moving forward. Money looked at the time—12:27. He wrote it on his pant leg, something he had always done—noting the time they were ambushed or attacked.

As they pushed forward, they were hit with ineffective small arms fire. AK-47 and PKM rounds plinked off the ground, onto the right side of his vehicle. Money was still unable to make contact with Cookie or his Afghan gunners in the middle vehicle. His concern for Cookie was distracting but quickly dissipated.

Two rocket-propelled grenades hit the cargo truck in front of them and it burst into flames.

In those moments, everything happened so fast, and yet they saw the explosion and destruction in slow motion detail. They heard the sounds and felt the heat of the flames as they rose and covered the vehicle.

And then they ricocheted back to the present.

Driving past the cargo truck fully engulfed in flames, they looked for anything that might be salvaged, cognizant of the dangers that lay ahead.

Money suddenly saw the driver jump out of the cab and yelling, "Stop the vehicle!"

Wolfe applied the brakes. Even as their bodies jerked backward, Money was opening the left rear door. The LN driver stood there frozen, with a deer-in-the-headlights look on his face.

Money instructed an Afghan gunner in the vehicle to tell the driver that if he didn't come with them, they were going to leave him behind. The driver ran as fast as he could and jumped into the backseat. Wolfe kept moving forward, passing the burning fuel tanker and looking around to make sure they didn't leave any of their guys behind. The heat of the flames and the burning fumes of oil and fuel were strong, overpowering, radiating from what remained of the sizzling and melting metal.

When they made the dogleg right turn, they noticed a vehicle off the side of the road that was turned upside down.

At first, it didn't even look like the lead vehicle because there was so little left of it. Then Money saw the large eagle sticker on the back window. His heart fell. One of his guys had fallen.

Small arms fire still came from the right, so Money had Wolfe backed up as close as possible on the left side of their lead vehicle without going over the cliff. It was tight.

Money needed to see if any of our guys were still inside. Telling Wolfe to hang tight, he took a deep breath, exited the vehicle, and rolled into the lead.

The roof was caved in, and all the windows were blown out. That made it easy for him to get inside. Money drew his pistol for protection. He expected to find bodies, hopefully still alive, but to his amazement, there was only a lot of blood in the vehicle, No bodies.

A few rounds of 7.62mm stitched the ground near him. There was no time to think about the empty vehicle.

He rolled back out of the burning wreck and returned to the trail vehicle. Taking a quick scan, he froze. A Taliban fighter aimed an RPG right at them.

Money dropped to one knee just as the Tango fired a round in his direction. Tango was a term we used to identify the Taliban. The impact of the RPG threw him back. He landed by the front of the follow-vehicle, slightly dazed from the sudden blinding flash, followed by a muffled roar. The fury of shock waves peppered debris and dust everywhere. A black funnel of smoke rose from the ground and obscured Money's vision. He got up quickly and fired a few rounds back with his AK-47 before lunging for the open door, and into the vehicle.

Money yelled at Wolfe, "Push! Push! Push!"

They rolled out at high speed, dirt and debris flying out from beneath the wheels. One of the fuel trucks got hit on the right side with multiple AK-47's. The local national driver had his nine-year-old son with him. He shifted the truck to a low gear and slowed down, and then, incredibly, he jumped out, and went running into the woods.

"What in the hell? Where's he going?" Money couldn't believe it.

Almost as soon as the question was asked, they watched the driver come running back, his hands full of branches. The truck was still slowly moving forward, and they assumed the man's son was steering the heavy vehicle.

The LN ran up to the truck and pushed the branches into the bullet holes, plugging them up to stop the loss of fuel.

It was like nothing they had ever witnessed before. That crazy fucker did that while they were still under attack. Then he jumped back into his truck, shifted it into a higher gear, and drove on.

As soon as they made it outside the kill zone, the attack subsided. Money looked at his watch. 12:57. Only thirty minutes had elapsed from the start of the ambush. Still, that short span felt like a lifetime.

They continued forward. The first SUV Cookie had spotted earlier was trailing them again. Not wanting to give the Taliban another chance to hit them, Money knew something had to be done. When they made the next right turn, Money told Wolfe, "Slow down on this curve."

Wolfe did so and Money opened the door and rolled out of the follow-vehicle, his AK held tightly to his body. He hid in the ditch. Money kept his eyes trained on the SUV. As the SUV came around the turn, two shooters were hanging out the windows with AK-47s. They aimed at Wolfe.

Money unloaded a magazine of 7.62mm, shooting across the hood from left to right and back again. The SUV came to a screeching halt. The driver put the vehicle in reverse and backed into the side of a hill. Since the road was completely blocked by the Taliban, Money climbed back into his B-6 and they drove for another fifteen minutes, all the while trying to make contact with anyone to get a QRF moving.

With the onslaught of attacks, Money hadn't taken time until then to consider the empty lead vehicle. Going back to look for Cookie and the others wasn't an option. The thought that his teammate might still be back there in the kill zone was unbearable. Minutes went by, and they moved farther and farther away.

He'd been unsuccessful in contacting anyone, meaning they were on their own for the moment. His heart was heavy, but the mission wasn't over yet and there was no time to grieve. He had to remain on alert.

As they came over the hill, they couldn't believe what they saw. There stood Cookie and the guys from the lead vehicle! It was a welcome sight. Holy shit!

"Stop!" Money yelled.

Wolfe slammed on the brakes and Money bounded out of the vehicle, his AK at the ready as he rounded the front of the vehicle. Cookie had a makeshift bandage on his head. Cappy and the terp also had a few bumps and bruises but were in pretty good shape overall. Money was relieved to see his Assistant Team Leader (ATL), his friend, his brother, still alive.

"Man, we're glad to see you," Cookie told him. "How did you guys get here?" Wolfe asked.

"The vehicle rolled. We were taking heavy small arms fire, so we had to get out. The tanker truck was dumping its load of diesel fuel, so we ran up and jumped on the sides. Once we were away from the kill zone, we made the decision to get off the X." Cookie touched the bandage at his head as blood began to seep from beneath it. Money grabbed the med-kit and fit a better functioning bandage on his head.

"We need to move," Wolfe called out. The gunners had been keeping watch on the horizon, but everyone could sense the urgency to get the trucks moving. They weren't sure how much time they had until the Taliban cleared the road and came after them.

One of the truck drivers said he knew how to get to Shkin. Money had one of his Afghan gunners get in with him and translate. If he went the wrong way, he would be dead before they were. As another motivator, he also promised if they got to the camp, he would give him $500 USD.

Amazingly, they made their way to Shkin without any other incidents.

The C-1 client and (ODA) operational detachment-Alpha guys asked Money how many men were lost.

Money said, "Three men were injured but were still able to walk away. We lost one truck, but no lives."

"I can't believe it," the client said. "With everything you guys got hit with, it's amazing no one was killed."

What Money didn't tell the client was that he'd been determined to survive the mission.

There was no way in hell he was going to end up getting killed. It was his daughter Taylor's birthday.

Money and I discussed the (SIR) Serious Incident Report shortly after the debrief. The ambush was confirmed by satellite imagery from the tactical operations center in Shkin. Everyone made it out okay. Cookie and the tanker driver's son got the worst of it. Cookie suffered a traumatic brain injury and was sent home to recover, but later rejoined the teams.

They were damn lucky.

On the tech side, the mission set a precedent for future operations. We understood the need for better intel, weapons, vehicles, and medics.

For Money and Cookie, the mission sealed their bond for a lifetime. To say it was a small miracle they survived the ambush was an understatement. They got their cherries popped and were no longer the new kids on the block. They had passed the test.

It was time to run with the big dogs.

CHAPTER EIGHT
Shark Teams

We needed a solid team medic. We'd had too many close calls. After the mission to Shkin, we realized how fortunate we were not to have suffered any casualties or major injuries. Since SOC's footprint was becoming more established and the missions were becoming more dangerous, a concrete, workable medical program had to be put in place. Our choice needed to fit the team mold.

Money and I referred Alan Chiasson, call sign "Chase," to the acting program manager, Ryan Bennett. Money and Chase had worked together in Iraq, at FOB Echo in Ad Diwaniyah, just east of Najaf. I met Chase in 2006 when I conducted crucible training with Kroll Inc. for DynCorp International in Baghdad, Iraq and vouched for him.

He was there with the elite Shark Teams I was training and evaluating. Shark Teams conducted close protection for the International Police Liaison Officers (IPLO) who, in turn, were tasked with training local law enforcement such as the Iraqi police.

Named after a South African rugby team, the Shark Teams were responsible for transporting the trainers to different sites, including the Baghdad Police Academy and several prisons throughout Baghdad, where several insurgents were held for major crimes and acts of terrorism.

There were ten teams, and they were not pussies. The mix of US expats and third-country nationals made vetting difficult, but most of the members had prior military service. A few had law enforcement backgrounds. They hunkered down at the Al Sadeer and Baghdad Hotels.

The missions they ran were extremely dangerous. Like them, DynCorp contracted with civilian police (CIVPOL), the Adnan Palace, the Iraqi Embassy and the Ministry of Justice. We lost several good men to attacks during their short tenure. Kyle Kaczynski died in December 2005 during an evaluation of the Shark Teams. He and a South African named Janni Strauss were killed by an explosively formed projectile.

This was an eye-opener for me and my introduction to the realities of contracting in a war zone. I learned how civilian corporations dealt with these situations.

What I knew to be true was this: Shark Teams were well-trained and mission oriented.

I was teaching the best. Crucible training consisted of Protective Operations in High-Risk Areas, Principal Briefings, Surveillance Detection and Countermeasures, Explosives Recognition and Improvised Roadside Bomb Attacks, Combat Life Saver, Intermediate and Advanced Weapons, Force on Force scenarios and live-fire evolutions.

They mastered all of these. We rolled out with them and IPLO teams to get a feel for their missions and team dynamics. The IPLO's used a civilian police academy training doctrine to teach arrest procedures, checkpoints, and investigation techniques.

It was a win-win.

At that time, the senior man for CIVPOL in Iraq was Col. Lucius E "Ed" Delk (Ret.), aka "Papa-1." Papa-1 was the third highest-ranking civilian in Iraq. As a retired military police commander, he was considered the "Father" of the Shark Teams and their prime principal/client. As an icon with the 18th Military Police Brigade, he exemplified the caliber of Shark Team members.

His word was gold. Everything he said was based on a lifetime of knowledge and experience and was never questioned. He was the man in charge.

Well-known for his leadership and his slogan: "First on the ground and last to leave," Col. Delk commanded the brigade that was instrumental in providing security for the MP headquarters camp, Kurdish refugee camps, and convoy security. The brigade was the last unit to leave the area at the conclusion of Operation Provide Comfort. Several members received the Soldier's Medal for heroic acts after assisting in the MEDEVAC of a wounded Iraqi national from a minefield near the river, not far from the MP Headquarters camp.

Whenever Papa 1 moved anywhere, he used the Shark Teams. Even if the military was on a joint mission, Col. Delk insisted on bringing the Sharks to the party. He was the client and although he was a retired Colonel with the MP Brigade, he trusted the Shark Teams over the Army to provide close protection. Chase was Delk's personal protection officer on a few of the missions as well.

Chase and I became acquainted at that crucible training in 2006. He sought my advice on motorcade operations for an article he was writing titled "TEMS in the Red Zone." He'd been published several times in magazines like EMS and SWAT.

Assigned to Shark Team 5 as a personal protection officer and team medic, I knew Chase had his shit together as a medic, but like all teams, you're only as strong as your weakest link.

Although he was well-versed in tactical/combat medicine and rode with the Shark Teams for a couple of years, he had not yet been exposed to convoy operations and would require a lot of additional training.

I was okay with that.

With a strong endorsement from Brent Kunzler, PA-C (18-Delta), SOC's medical manager in Iraq, it was decided to bring Chase on board as the team's senior medic. According to Brent, Chase was one of the top medics working for SOC in-country.

On the day he arrived in Kabul, Money and I were doing a vehicle recovery on the B-6 SUV that was hit on a previous mission. No one was at the airport to pick him up, so he hopped in a cab, told the driver to head towards the neighborhood of Shahr-e-Naw on the northwest side of Kabul. and rode to the SOC villa alone.

He was outside his element and got lost. All he remembered was that we were in district four. Chase worried the cab driver was going to take him directly to Taliban headquarters.

They drove around the Shahr-e-Naw neighborhood for five or six hours. By a stroke of luck, he spotted a local national guard wearing a SOC uniform shirt, standing outside the SOC villa gate. Money said it was trial by fire and Chase had passed the test.

The taxi bill totaled $3,000 AFN–approximately $40 USD. I'm not sure if he ever got reimbursed, but I highly doubt it. His training on the Shark Teams may have paid off, even though he stood there looking like a fish out of water. We both laughed out loud at the irony of the metaphor.

We bumped shoulder to shoulder and went to work getting him settled in. It was a relief to have him on board as our team medic. The Shark Team mentality and training were exactly what we needed for the missions ahead.

CHAPTER NINE
Payout
DATE: September 06, 2009
MISSION: Convoy Security for C-1 client
LOCATION: Ghazni Province

We ran multiple missions at a time. Requests for movements were sporadic. Sometimes operational orders came in all at once, followed by a lull in business. It was feast or famine.

In either case, it was not always about the mission or being combat-ready. It was *always* about watching your brother's six. Many times, though, we had to sit back and say, "What the hell?" when our guys' safety was compromised.

Extortion payouts were a good example. It was not unusual to fork out cash if our convoy was in a traffic accident. We tried to make the payout before the Afghan National Police arrived because then the amount of money would increase substantially—and it always ended up being the fault of the Americans.

Sam Samano was assigned a team to haul cargo down south to Kandahar. A retired Master Sergeant with the US Army Special Forces and a Ranger with the 75th Regiment, he had been outside the wire with a few of the teams and had a wealth of knowledge to share with us.

Going outside the wire meant leaving our secured compound. High walls adorned by Concertina razor wire formed a barrier and elevated guard posts on the corners. Anything outside the wire exponentially increased the potential for attack.

He knew the drill, but this was his first mission as team leader. At Sam's request, Money ran support for and commanded a fourth gun truck. It ran solo behind the trail vehicle. Just south of Ghazni, near a village called Moqor, one of the cargo drivers hit a bus loaded with Afghans. The convoy halted because both the cargo truck and the bus had extensive damage. Worse, more than half the forty travelers on the bus were injured.

Some of them were thrown under seats and had to crawl on the bloody floor to reach the exit. Others were thrown on top of fellow passengers. Outside the bus, people were limping around holding their immobilized arms. Others held pressure on their heads to stop the bleeding from gashes received from flying luggage.

Sam remained calm but was concerned about how to mitigate the situation. He consulted with Money on the best course of action so they could get the convoy back on the road. Although the injuries were not serious, some form of intervention was necessary to avoid controversy and retribution from the bus driver and his passengers.

The bus driver demanded payment. Money instructed Sam to give him $2,000 from the op fund. It was a huge payout, but they needed to make the deal and get back on the road. Money had his terp explain to the driver that they would give him the 2K if he got back on the bus, drove away, and didn't look back. As long as he didn't mention the incident to anyone, there wouldn't be any problems.

The bus driver ferried his passengers back on the bus. Money gave the bus driver a thumbs up and they continued on their way with a broken wheel and smoke trailing behind them.

Sam learned another way to smooth out issues and how to keep the locals happy. Our drivers repaired the damage to the cargo truck while they negotiated, and so, Sam was able to keep the convoy rolling. We always looked out for one another, and this was one incident when having a brother's back literally paid off, no pun intended. Paying off the bus driver was instrumental in completing the mission. It was as simple as that.

Despite the circumstances, it was good to know we had brothers who cared about our safety and well-being. Every incident, every battle, every payout, was a lesson learned. We all did our part. What we did was all about the team because all our asses were on the line

CHAPTER TEN
The Indian Embassy Bombing
DATE: October 8, 2009
MISSION: PSD to FOB Eggers and RTB
LOCATION: Kabul

The Indian Embassy suffered the wrath of the Taliban. Civilians and soldiers alike heard the explosion from several miles away. A plume of smoke and dust rose from the center of Kabul city.

The attacker struck at approximately 0830 on the street where the Embassy and the Afghan Interior Ministry faced each other. The blast killed seventeen people. Sixty-three people were wounded, their lives changed forever. Kabul Police immediately sealed off the area.

The SOC villa was located less than three blocks away from where hell had come to call.

The blast rocked our compound, shattering glass, and delivered the rumbling shockwave that brought death.

It knocked a couple of Serbians out of bed. Everyone else at the villa jumped up, threw on gear, and grabbed their weapons, in case there was more to it, like a complex attack initiated by a mass casualty producing device.

Matty and Chase were updating the team's medical force protection plan. They had received intelligence on medical assets along Ring Road that would be beneficial to the teams if something happened along the route. Going over some maps, they had marked safe havens and rally points. Maybe they needed some of that intel here. Matty went to the TOC to account for the teams out on the road and Chase scrambled throughout the villa to make sure everyone was ok. They all knew it would not be an ordinary day—if there was such a thing in Afghanistan.

The Indian Foreign Secretary said the attackers "...came up to the outside perimeter wall of the Embassy with a car crammed full of explosives, obviously with the aim of targeting the Embassy."

The bombing was the same intensity as the 2008 Indian Embassy bombing. However, blast walls had been built since then to deflect the force of explosions. The bomb blew out the doors and windows at the Embassy but caused no loss of life inside. Only those unfortunate to be on the outside succumbed to the devastating blast.

A couple of the SOC-A guards said it rained debris on them within seconds of the explosion, but they remained safe. There was no damage to the watchtower, no damage to chancery premises. Glass shattered in nearby buildings, but the structures remained intact.

Drew, Money, and Jon were returning from FOB Eggers when the VBIED detonated.

Less than a block from the circle that leads to the Indian Embassy gate, they were stuck in traffic for hours waiting for the road to clear. With no immediate threat to Drew's team, Money dialed up his Roshan cell and let Matty know they were safe.

It was kind of funny because Money was calling Matty, and Matty was attempting to call Drew, and Chase was calling Jon, and Jon was calling Ryan, and Ryan was calling Cecil, all at the same time. It was a cluster fuck of phone calls that took about five minutes to get through.

Early on, in the start-up phase of the mobile operations program, communications were marginal at best, but we always had a backup plan, and everyone usually carried two cell phones for situations just like this. The two major cell phone carriers in Afghanistan were Roshan and AWCC, so most of us had AWCC phones, and the team leader carried one Roshan cell for the team. The teams also carried an Iridium satellite phone on the long-range C-1 missions out of Kabul.

But the gear, in general, was an issue for the program. Stuff broke and needed to be replaced, gear continually needed updating, and heavily used foreign weapons often malfunctioned.

The vehicle platform we rolled in also needed to change if we were to expand the program and improve the survivability of the teams while conducting these high-risk missions. Hence, the Ford F-550-gun truck by Streit USA, was on order, soon to arrive.

Communication was paramount to survival. Drew let us know when all was clear. They pushed the B-6 past the traffic circle and two checkpoints to get back to the villa where the rest of the team waited for them. Looking in his rearview mirror, the Indian Embassy continued to burn.

CHAPTER ELEVEN
Gun Trucks
ATE: September 19, 2009
MISSION: Retrieve shipment of Gun Trucks from BAF & RTB
LOCATION: Parwan Province

Driving and route planning was critical to mission success because SOC needed drivers that listened, not just drove. The vehicle commander controlled the vehicle movement. He dictated the speed, distancing, and offset. He also looked for threats. Four eyes were better than two and most of the time, the vehicle commander was able to see things in a wider peripheral field of view.

When the commander ordered, "Strong left," the driver moved the vehicle left, no questions asked. The vehicle commander may have seen a dead animal or something out of place that indicated a potential hazard to the crew. Even though they also relied on the driver to take evasive action if he perceived a threat, no one ever questioned the order.

Because of the need to pivot quickly, drivers had to handle the massive gun trucks with precision, skill and quick reflexes.

After the Indian Embassy bombing, Money, Cookie, Drew, and Chase remained in Kabul on the mobile teams running long hops from Kabul to Kandahar and back using the armored B-6 Toyota Land Cruisers. Bumped up to Director of Operations, Matty handled most, if not all, of the Intel, communications, and coordination of movements for the mobile teams.

He set up our Global Positioning System (GPS) tracking devices with updated map overlays using the Military Grid Reference System to identify FOB/COB locations along each route. He also handled the deployment of any counter-assault

QRF and MEDEVAC resources if needed.

Since Matty was a Navy SEAL, he had top-secret security clearance that allowed him access to the base Tactical Operations Center and the Base Defensive Operations Center (BDOC) at Bagram Airfield. He was able to extract information from the BDOC Commander and stay abreast of enemy activity and movements within the region.

I was eventually transferred over to the SOC mobile operations team in Kabul as an Assistant Team Leader/Navigator and vehicle commander. With my previous experience in motorcade operations, I brought a great deal of experience to the table with respect to mission planning, route reconnaissance, and team briefings.

Afghanistan, however, was a steep learning curve, especially since SOC was starting to turn a profit and we were able to upgrade our defensive posture with new weapons and vehicles.

SOC had just taken possession of four Ford F-550-gun trucks made by Streit USA Armoring, LLC out of Charleston, South Carolina. Originally white, we painted them dark gray to reduce their signature at night. The 300-plus horsepower beasts were heavily armored with thick TS 400 level VII steel and bulletproof glass. The Achilles heel was the flat-bottomed chassis. If we drove over an IED, it could not divert a blast, which could rip the trucks in half. This resulted in massive blunt force trauma and lower extremity injuries or death to anyone in the vehicle.

The rear had a pillbox mounted on it with blast doors that separated the cab from the box. The boxes were outfitted with portholes on each side and one in the rear. The auxiliary fuel tank had a fuel transfer pump that was notorious for not working.

The trucks were flown to Bagram on a Russian Superliner. The drive shafts had been disassembled and reassembled to accommodate loading and off-loading the trucks on the steep-angled ramp of the cargo plane.

By then, HDSOC instructors, Dave Gengenbach and Rudy Belloc arrived from Minden, Nevada. They were there to provide off-road driver training in austere environments and foreign weapons training to the team.

Training was instrumental in enhancing our mobile operations because most of the driving was off-road and required a four-wheel drive. The course covered tactical vehicle operations, ground mobility, and 4x4 operations, as well as non-tactical 4x4's such as, Jeeps, motorcycles, and special-purpose-built security vehicles.

Dave was a former NASCAR pit-crew member and a top-notch driver and instructor with SOC in Minden. He trained Navy SEAL Team 6, aka DEVGRU, and other CAG operators such as 1st Special Forces Operational Detachment-Delta, aka Delta Force.

He knew his shit when it came to driving, and he did it well. He didn't have any combat experience, but he could drive and that's all that mattered at the time. He received weapons training with the team at Morehead. The rest was on-the-job training.

Rudy was a sniper with the 75th Ranger Battalion and a Silver Star recipient during Operation Iraqi Freedom. He worked as a team leader with Blackwater USA before coming to SOC, where he functioned as a weapons specialist and trainer.

Their first mission was to drive the trucks back to the SOC villa from Bagram Air Base, the largest US military base in Afghanistan. Someone on the flight crew had screwed up connecting the drive shafts on a few of the rigs. One truck wouldn't start, another truck started but couldn't roll, and a third truck that Money and Chase were driving dropped its drive shaft a third of the way back to Kabul.

Money and Chase put up a 360-degree security bubble on the side of the road, while Dave crawled under the rig to fix the drive shaft. I'm ninety percent sure he used a coat hanger. I'm only ten percent sure of how that thing held together. Somehow, they made it all the way back to the compound without additional problems.

He was one of the most loyal guys we could ever have asked for. No matter what, he was there to back us up and got the vehicles running right. His training was extremely valuable to the team for future mobile operations.

He was a natural—and became known as Racer Dave after that.

CHAPTER TWELVE
Firebase Gecko
DATE: October 05, 2009
MISSION: Security for C-1 convoy to Kandahar AO
LOCATION: Kandahar Province

Firebase Gecko sat isolated on the outskirts of Kandahar; a city surrounded by agricultural fields next to the Arghandab River. Due to its location, bringing in supplies took effort. No one wanted to touch the gig because the attacks on Ring Road occurred daily.

The roadway showcased all the hallmarks of a formal battlefield. Its asphalt surface was melted by charred truck carcasses lying along the roadside. Sunlight bounced off brass bullet casings. IED craters pockmarked the middle of the road.

Gecko got its name after an Operational Detachment "A" mission, code-named "Objective Gecko." US Special Operations Forces carried out a large-scale, airborne helicopter assault on the night of October 19. The next day, US Delta Force and Army Rangers carried out "Objective Rhino." The mission for both; pierce the heart of Taliban-held southern Afghanistan.

Delta's objective was to raid the large-walled compound belonging to the meritorious one-eyed Taliban leader, Mullah Mohammed Omar—and kill any Taliban inside, including Omar himself if we got lucky. They also needed to gather any intelligence found there.

The Rangers provided a security perimeter around the Delta operation. Before the troops arrived, USAF AC-130 and MH-60L DAP gunships pounded the area around the compound. A fleet of MH-60 and MH-47 helicopters then flew the Delta/Rangers assault group in.

The Rangers set up blocking positions. Delta entered the compound and began to clear it.

There were no Taliban forces inside.

As the assault force prepared to extract from Objective Gecko, a large Taliban force sprang an ambush. Armed with a large supply of rocket-propelled grenades, they attacked.

One projectile slammed into a departing helicopter, clipping a piece of its landing gear as it took off. Delta and the Rangers took heavy fire. One grenade blasted the foot off an American soldier. There were conflicting reports on whether the troops discovered any useful intelligence.

This kind of often-unreported violence formed a lasting impression of the lack of security in Afghanistan. Actual violence aside, the most disturbing times were when US troops blocked the road, forcing us to circumvent the multi-kilometer traffic jams.

Because SOC was still relatively new in Afghanistan, we needed to establish a stronger foothold in the surging market for contracts, so we stepped up to the plate. We received an operations order for the team's first big mission with the new gun trucks: deliver much-needed cargo and supplies to ODA Firebase Gecko. It was the second time we needed to prove ourselves in order to set a precedent for future mobile operations in Afghanistan.

The success of the program weighed heavily on the team. SOC's reputation was on the line. If we stood any chance of getting any further contracts, it was imperative that the mission prove successful. That was a lot of pressure to put on a group of guys who had only worked together for a short period of time, but everyone was up to the task.

Moving the cargo was like herding cats. The route, we knew, was treacherous. Many parts of Ring Road involved off-road driving. Detours allowed for road and bridge repair, mainly due to multiple roadside bombs and IEDs placed in culverts along the route. We took narrow dirt roads to bypass the blockages.

Culverts were our biggest threat since they were anywhere from 500-1,000 meters apart to allow cross drainage into farming plots. On long runs, it wasn't uncommon to cross over a thousand culverts on one mission. That translated to a 1:4 chance of getting blown to bits instantly.

Another team elsewhere on a separate mission was rolling with the same likelihood of getting whacked. It translated into a "not if, but when" situation.

The sky often went dark brown in the middle of the day, as traffic stirred up the Afghan soil. So many vehicles caused a mile-wide dirt cloud that ascended from the road. Those clouds unleashed huge amounts of static electricity, enough to knock someone down or short out an engine. Dust stuck to the windows of the gun trucks. It was so thick; we moistened rags and stuffed them into the AC vents yet buckets of ancient earth still managed to permeate the cab.

I thought of our Afghan top gunners who wore goggles and shemaghs to cover their faces, despite the blistering heat. The grime that ravaged the area could make life untenable, but they were tough as nails and were used to the conditions of their homeland.

For us, it was a process of acclimation no one wanted to endure. Yet we had a job to do, so we kept moving. Not too many people were willing to take such a huge gamble, considering the odds.

Most of the farmland in the rural areas consisted of opium fields. Afghanistan was the world's largest producer of opium, accounting for ninety percent of the global supply. The 2009 opium trade generated approximately $68 billion USD in annual revenue. It was not unusual to see hundreds of acres of pink and white flowers blooming when the poppies were in season.

With that kind of cash, how much was the Taliban making on the illicit drug trade? It turned out their take was estimated at $400 million a year. So, not only did we have to deal with a mounting insurgency; we found ourselves in the crosshairs of local drug lords who controlled much of the traffic, particularly in the southern provinces of Helmand, Kandahar, and Nimruz.

The Taliban imposed two types of taxes over their illicit drug business. The land tax was used to produce opium poppies. The road tax was levied for trafficking. The Taliban attacked military checkpoints to support passage for drug dealers. The drug dealers then provided the Taliban with weapons, vehicles, and satellite phones in exchange for safe passage and protection.

Fueling anywhere on Ring Road was a bitch. The convoy had to dominate a fuel station by placing manned gun trucks on the corners blocking the entrances and exits. Top gunners were poised behind their PKM machine guns.

As the team leader on this mission, Money handled the cash and receipts while the rest of the crew walked the perimeter with guns up. We always looked pissed off, a "Don't fuck with us!" warning.

No one was allowed in or out while we refueled. We were on lockdown until every truck rotated position and was topped off. I'm sure the owners didn't give a damn since SOC paid in cash and paid well.

A three-day mission ran around $10,000 USD. That included food, fuel, billeting, bribes, and get-out-of-jail-free assurance. Now there's an oxymoron for you. It wasn't technically free, but we weren't paying for it, SOC was.

When we finally arrived at Gecko, we were greeted by the nation's elite Green Berets.

The team leader met Matty and Drew at the gate. "Man, we're glad to see you guys! We've been waiting for weeks for supplies. How was the trip?"

"Long, but uneventful," Matty said.

"No shit? We tried getting the Army to fly stuff in, but they won't sling load and we don't have a place for them to land inside the compound."

Drew and Matty shared a look before Drew asked, "Will you be needing regular drops?"

"Most likely," the team leader replied. "Why don't you guys take a load off your feet, and we'll grill up some burgers for ya."

Those special ops guys had been waiting for weeks for their gear to arrive and were so thankful to receive their cargo, they cooked dinner for the team.

Chase hit up one of the 18-Deltas for medical supplies. "Is there any way you could hook me up with some fresh juice? I've got Hextend, but it's expired. I can keep it in case one of the nurses needs a bag or two or a fresh Tango is begging for a 14gu Kool-Aid booster."

The Delta helped him out and asked if he needed anything else. "Hell, yeah. We're the FNGs here. I'll take whatever I can get."

He was more than willing. "You guys got some brass balls making this run," he said.

With Chase squared away, Matty was able to get solid Intel from the TOC. We rolled back to Kabul empty, making the return trip much faster. Critiquing the mission and making adjustments to help streamline future missions was our next task.

Heading back through Ghazni and Wardak Province proved interesting. The fragrance of blooming oleasters, relatives of the olive tree, floated on the balmy early summer breeze, and the sight of lush roadside orchards should have made traveling that route a delight.

However, the unpleasant scenes outnumbered the pleasant ones.

More attacks occurred during our stay at Gecko. The Turks were hit near Jaldak. Just after that, insurgents ambushed a huge convoy in Qalat, which included the Four Horsemen's convoy, the notorious local nationals-owned security company (LNs). The US Army was actively engaged with the Taliban, trying to recover what was left over from the ambush.

The area was hot. The battle between the Four Horsemen and the Taliban raged incessantly, directly on Ring Road. As we rumbled past, the Four Horsemen lay prone on the right side of the highway. The enemy was concealed about 1,000 meters to the left.

Stopping the convoy was not an option. We would've been part of the ambush. It was not our fight, so we pushed through. Chase said they saw the Four Horseman on their three o'clock using the gun trucks as cover to take up better positions alongside Ring Road. I guess we served a small purpose in their defensive posture.

No one at the time knew who we were or when we were coming. But they knew one thing for sure—we were coming back on Ring Road, the only route from Kandahar to Kabul.

When the team returned safely to the SOC villa, the only thing they talked about was the compliments they received from the ODA guys at Gecko. Ryan and I were impressed with the way Money ran the mission. Matty was able to extract additional intel. Chase grabbed much needed medical supplies, and Drew was happy just to be appreciated for a job well done.

The successful mission outcome solidified the team dynamic and was the start of *The Pony Express* brotherhood.

Telamon of Arcadia, a mercenary from the fifth century, said, "It is one thing to study war and yet another to live the warriors' life."

It was true and we were living proof. Brotherhood and war went together. Our bonds would again be tested, sooner than we knew.

CHAPTER THIRTEEN
Guardian Medical

Once we survived our first mission to Gecko, we began to expand our reach. We contacted other companies like SECURO, an IT communication and GPS company specializing in location-based and communication solutions.

The software they used was PDT300i systems and Track-24, which was similar to the military's version of Blue Force Tracker, but without the need for a top security clearance to access the program. We also used Google Maps overlays to pinpoint our positions throughout the theater of operations.

SECURO sub-contracted and coordinated MEDEVAC services through Guardian Medical. We toured the birds and facility at KAM Air, a leading Afghan airline, and got a feel for their capabilities based on information provided by the SECURO rep.

All we knew about the company was they flew stripped-down Russian MI-8s. The pilots in Guardian Medical's birds were ex-Russian military. It certainly helped that they knew the territory. They had flown sorties during the Russian invasion of Afghanistan from 1979-1989.

The word on the ground was that most of them had a bottle of vodka lying next to their control sticks, so they had some hair of the dog before taking off. That seemed wrong on so many levels. Who knew if it was true? We had more important issues to worry about, like figuring out the communications protocol for Guardian Medical and identifying dead zones along the route.

Guardian Medical was controlled by KAM Air and flew out of Kabul International Airport on the domestic side of the airport. If we needed MEDEVAC services, the better choice for take-off and landing was at Bagram because the Craig Joint Theater Hospital was located there.

The Combat Surgical Hospital, or CASH as we called it, was staffed by the 455th Expeditionary Medical Group, the Air Force component for Task Force MED-East. This included the 349th CASH at FOB Salerno in Khost province. Both provided combat medical/surgical support services to US and coalition forces throughout eastern Afghanistan.

If we got hit anywhere along Ring Road south of Ghazni, we were screwed. The helicopters never flew more than 150 kilometers one way. Their distances had to accommodate start-up, load time/winch ops, return, and shut down.

The task of developing standard operating procedures for medical assistance included a protocol for Guardian Medical to land at Bagram Airfield. Chase handled that. It was a huge undertaking since working with Task Force Med Helicopter-operations for grid references required a security clearance.

Matty stepped in to help out. They obtained grid references to every Forward Surgical Team along Ring Road, which was a tremendous accomplishment. That kind of medical intel made our missions much easier. We knew which locations on our routes were covered by MEDEVAC services.

The worst part of Ring Road was that it was located in an area where no MEDEVAC services were available. That included the US military. Knowing that Guardian Medical had limitations, all the teams came to rely heavily on their medics.

The medics on *The Pony Express* teams needed to be highly skilled and self-sufficient. As Force Recon Marines, many were required to take a battlefield trauma course as part of our training. They had to have the ability to keep wounded men alive for longer periods of time, perhaps even days depending on the circumstances.

Chase explained the mission of a Forward Surgical Team (FST); to provide surgical capability at Role II and provide quality care for patients unable to survive MEDEVAC to Role III hospital care. Surgeons performed damage control surgery on combat casualties within the "golden hour" of injury whenever possible. Casualties were then packaged for medical evacuation to a higher level of care.

The FST consisted of 20 people: three general surgeons, one orthopedic surgeon, two nurse anesthetists, three nurses, plus army medics, and other support personnel. Each FST was equipped to move directly behind troops and establish a functioning hospital with four ventilator-equipped beds and two operating tables within sixty minutes of arrival at a location.

Matty and Chase integrated our maps with locations of each FST. They calculated the maximum flight distance from FOB to Rally Point and return for the US military's Sikorsky UH- 60 Black Hawk Helicopter. They estimated a five-minute engine start, forty-minute flight time including dust-off or winch ops and return, and a five-minute shutdown procedure. The timeframe helped determine the maximum distance—360 degrees from the point of takeoff—and created perimeters of MEDEVAC coverage areas on our maps.

I was impressed to say the least and appreciated the work they did to ensure the health and safety of the teams. I also took comfort in the fact that they took care of us.

Many team guys never knew Chase went that extra mile to ensure our well-being. He kept a constant eye on the weather. He stayed abreast of the environment, plants and animals. He was always on everyone's ass to stay hydrated and developed medical profile cards with all our pertinent information such as blood type, medications, and allergies, in case anyone was injured and couldn't provide the information themselves. We carried them on our vests for easy access.

A free-spirited, no filter kind of guy, everyone liked having Chase around. He was not under-appreciated. It was just that the guys had more important things to worry about. They expected that level of commitment from a good team medic.

Having a contracted air-evac resource may have been comforting to some, but Chase and I had yet to use their services and were somewhat uncomfortable in their abilities to get the job done. We decided to maintain the status quo of our current medical response posture. Missions to Kandahar required a lot of preparation, medical supplies, and a great deal of confidence in the expertise of our medics to keep us alive.

When we made it to Kandahar, it was time to rest and recharge our batteries. When taking a long trip in the real world, most people have the opportunity to stop, stretch their legs, get a cold drink or snack, and take in the sights.

We, on the other hand, never stopped, never rested, never let our guard down. We constantly scanned the area around us for threats. Shit like that took a toll on mind and body. We headed to the Kandahar Hotel. It afforded us a small break, but we remained tense and ready, considering we had targets on our backs.

CHAPTER FOURTEEN
The Kandahar Hotel
DATE: October 09, 2009
MISSION: Multiple drops in the Kandahar AO
LOCATION: Kandahar Province

SOC was growing and acquiring larger contracts since we now had a solid reputation for getting the job done. Even though more guys came into the country to work with us, the original crew was solid with Cookie, Money, Matty, Drew, Mark King, Ryan Bennett, Ryan Buytenhuys, Phil Chatum, and Chase.

Still, the missions were always more than intense. We needed down time more than we cared to admit.

The Kandahar Hotel was not even close to being a two-star hotel by American standards, but it was the best the city had to offer in terms of comfort and amenities. Since a large number of our missions were doing multiple drops in the southern provinces, it was the only option we had.

The problem was operational security. It wasn't easy to roll into Kandahar driving three loud-as-hell Ford F-550 turbo-powered gun trucks. We stuck out like a turd in a punchbowl.

Everyone saw us coming and knew where we were staying.

After a hard day's run, we returned to the SOC villa and were finally given a couple days off. We spent a majority of the time during the day training and gathering supplies for our next push. One night, eight of us loaded up in two B-6 limos (Toyota Land Cruisers) and headed out to a private villa about twelve blocks away for some much-needed R&R, local cuisine and a few cold ones. Money, Chase, Ryan Buytenhuys, and I were in one vehicle. Ryan Bennett, Matty, Drew, and Cecil were in another.

We reconnoitered the compound and considered it secure.

One guard stood watch at the gate and two others were positioned on the corners.

Once we checked in, we gathered around an open pit bonfire, smoked Drew Estate Kahlua cigars and drank Tuborg Near-Beer. The restaurant had a bar and a grill that served pretty good rice, goat, and lamb.

After dinner, the hotel owner handed me a white napkin his wife had made as a gift. It was embroidered in red with a Pashtun symbol which meant "peace." Although I appreciated the gesture, I somehow suspected there were a couple hundred more mass-produced napkins lying around somewhere. Yet I saved it for my footlocker, a token of my visit there.

We headed back to Kandahar Province and made multiple drops and pickups through south Afghanistan. The mission took us to four different locations, and we completed all the movements and drops without incident. It was time for another break.

Money contacted his connection at the Kandahar Hotel to see if they had any vacancies. We talked at great length about staying there. I voiced my concerns about the footprint we were leaving, and the need to avoid being time-and-place predictable.

It wasn't a question of "if" we were going to get hit, but "when," considering all the attacks and ambushes that often waited for us. The missions we ran had some insane conditions and unsettling situations—and ruffled feathers.

The team leaders, expats, and third-country nationals thought Money was taking a big chance staying there. Everyone understood the risks of heading to the hotel, but our options were extremely limited, and the guys needed to get their batteries recharged for the trip back to Kabul.

At the Kandahar, everyone felt like warriors returning from battle. It was truly an oasis that brought some light in the middle of a very dark place.

The entire team was able to kick back to relax for a while. The white stone walls of the hotel offered a welcome respite from the missions we'd just completed.

The place was moderately secure, with one guard at the gate and two others positioned on high-top corners. The rooms were clean and fairly quaint. We had IT connections, a small fridge, and an AC that worked. The expats stayed in rooms that surrounded the courtyard and the LNs stayed in rooms that surrounded the inside parking area.

Outside our rooms, there was a manicured lawn. The grass was hand-cut with scissors and leaves were picked up by hand. There were bountiful grapevines, so we ate grapes right off the vine when in season. We made sure our teams ate together and it was always a huge feast. The way we figured it, we might be eating our last meal.

We ate like kings. Our dinner together was served at an ancient table that looked like it was built for the Last Supper. Served Afghan-style, the food was really good. No custom burgers and fries, but lamb, chicken, and goat were readily available. Our hosts also served Kabuli Palau, Afghanistan's national dish, created with caramelized carrots, plump raisins, and coveted nuts in rice.

We never drank alcohol on missions because everyone needed to be focused on the task at hand at all times. All the expats slept with one eye open and rose before dawn. The LNs prepped the trucks and rotated guards for inner security. Additional security inside the compound was supposed to benefit the team because it meant the overall responsibility for our protection fell on our top gunners, but I doubt if any of them ever stayed awake.

Late one night, the smell of a disagreeably damp and musty-smelling herb invaded the air, a moist pungent aroma, much like the smell of dank hash. It was a smell we recognized and was not one I welcomed.

We had received reports that some of the Afghan truck drivers were scoring hash from Kandahar because of its reputation of being the best in Afghanistan. It was also a lot cheaper. Bringing it back to Kabul meant extra money in their pockets.

My concern was what might happen to us if we got stopped at a checkpoint and the ANP decided to search for contraband. Although not illegal, we didn't want to take any chances.

SOC's policy was no narcotics.

Before we left Kandahar, we had all the drivers come up to Money's truck for a quick safety check. The translator informed them to get rid of any hash or anything questionable. We told them no one was going to get in trouble for having anything illegal if they tossed it. Some went to their trucks and got rid of a few items.

As a former narcotics officer, Money knew most of the standard hiding places and went to work conducting searches on the trucks. One of the drivers had a softball-size amount of hash hidden in his seat. He said he needed it to make enough money to feed his family and could get five times more for it in Kabul.

We told the driver he wasn't getting anything for it and to get back in his truck. If he didn't stop bitching, he could roll back to Kabul by himself.

We decided to send a message to the drivers. Once all of the trucks had been checked, Money walked around, tossing the big ball of hash up in the air and catching it like it was a baseball. Then he took the ball of hash and slowly crumbled it up, letting it fly away into the wind.

Our return to Kabul, tensions ran high, despite having the down time. The guys seemed on edge. I'm not sure if it had anything to do with the disconnect between the drivers and the gun crew, or if it was just plain old intuition for what was coming next.

Not long after we left Kandahar, we found out the Kandahar Hotel had been bombed.

CHAPTER FIFTEEN
In Trust and Sickness
DATE: October 15, 2009, **MISSION:** RTB to Kabul (dry run)
LOCATION: Ghazni Province

The bombing of the Kandahar Hotel left everyone with an uneasy feeling. Were we the targets? Had we had barely escaped? I was relieved knowing our guys were okay, but questions and concerns about our safety and the employees of the hotel plagued me.

The topic of billeting was tabled for a later discussion. We had other pressing issues to think about, including an increase in our operational tempo. Drew Babbitt and his crew joined us to add a layer of protection. They had been running a PSD mission in Herat and instructed the team to hang back and make sure we were clear from behind. This reduced the size of the convoy.

Everything was cool. We were making good time since all the trucks were empty. We were on Ring Road for four hours and needed to refuel for the last half of the journey. Aside from setting up a 360-degree security bubble, we also took the convoy truck drivers' cell phones. We couldn't let them make any phone calls that might give our position away.

Everyone at SOC was properly vetted. However, at SOC-A, the drivers were hired by contract companies. Background checks were minuscule at best and not to our liking or up to security standards.

One of the drivers saw Money walking towards him, and quickly shoved something in his pocket.

Money had a way with words with no filter at all. "Yo! Pedro, Abdul, Mohammed! What's in the bag?"

"What bag, Suh?" The driver spoke broken English. He shrugged and a look of fear and bewilderment shadowed his face.

"You know what I'm talking about, dumbass! Don't make me ask you again!" Money wasted no time in approaching the man, his irritation evident in his actions and on his face.

The driver stood there motionless as Money frisked him like he'd done a thousand times before as a street cop in Meridian, Mississippi's south side.

Money found the bag stashed in the driver's front pocket. Inside there was a ball of hash and a cell phone. The driver grabbed for it, but Money slapped it away from him.

Money was pissed. Drew joined him and asked, "Problem?"

Money tossed him the bag. Drew shook his head, dumped the contents of the bag out on the ground and then stomped on it. Those items did not just disrespect us. They were a potential security risk.

After fueling up, we prepared to head out, but one of Drew's guys got really sick and couldn't stop shitting. We couldn't leave him behind and we couldn't wait for him to get better, so we handed him a bucket in case he needed to take a dump while we were on the road.

Night fell, and we started rolling through an area with overhanging cliffs, where the military had been ambushed quite often in the past. Large bomb craters littered the road. It made movement extremely slow. What was worse, one of the gun trucks went down with a blown Turbocharger. This had happened before when we first took possession of the new F-550s, but there was no time to do repairs on the road, so we hooked up the gun truck to another gun truck to tow.

Everyone was on edge.

Once we got everything set up, we started to push again. We advised our guys to be especially ready and alert. If the Taliban saw us towing a vehicle, they might think we were a softer target to hit.

We had just passed Ghazni and were rolling next to a few mud huts sitting close to the roadside. Suddenly an IED slammed the right side of Money's gun truck.

He yelled into the radio, "Push! Push! Push!" They needed to escape the attack.

Two Taliban knelt next to a wall on the driver's side. One of the black hats shouldered an RPG ready to fire. Money yelled to his top gunner, Blade, "Left side fire!"

Blade swung the PKM to the left and opened fire, cutting the insurgents down like weeds.

Once we got off the X, Drew's teammate, the one who was sick, apparently couldn't hold it anymore. His bucket was full and there was no place to go. I felt sorry for Drew. The cab of the gun truck must have smelled like, well, like shit!

They only had two cargo trucks between them, but he had to get out of the truck. The Taliban hit us again.

Money couldn't believe what he was seeing. That dude jumped out of the only safe place on the planet and leaned up against one of the Ford-550s. Safe is a relative term here. He pulled his pants down and took a shit like he'd never seen before in his life. All of this unfolded in real-time while we were still getting shot at. Then he ripped the tail off his t-shirt and used it to wipe his ass before jumping back into the truck.

This was the reality we lived with, day in and day out. It might have been one of Drew's guys this time, but the next week could easily be one of mine or even me. Welcome to the world of dysentery.

We didn't make it another two hundred yards before he radioed up that he had to go again. Luckily, by this time, the shooting had stopped. Money opened the door and the guy rolled into a mud hut that was close to the road. Within a minute, he was back in, and we kept moving.

At this point, we had been attacked three times and weren't even close to being finished.

We told all the guys to stay frosty and get their ammo straightened out.

Since we had passed Ghazni, we thought we had a chance of making it back to Kabul without getting hit again but driving on Ring Road brought the battlefield. We passed by fierce skirmishes, exploding bombs, burning oil tankers, gun-toting Afghan forces, and convoys of US forces that looked hostile to anyone. We were so used to the constant violence, we continued traveling amidst flying bullets, not bothering to wait until the fighting finished.

There were about twenty tankers that had been hit along Ring Road, a battle space of several kilometers. There were at least a dozen vehicles that had been busted up by RPGs. We could see another attack a couple of kilometers ahead of us, with at least one IED that Taliban militia had used to create a choke point.

This was a common tactic. It was very effective, especially against long convoys that lacked the ability to negotiate the roadway. Everyone knew the Four Horsemen had been whacked in this particular ambush. The casualty count and cargo losses were high. Twelve dead, two missing, and several wounded.
Money started to get a hard-on, bracing for the worst. "Get ready. We're about to get hit again!"

As soon as the words left his mouth, we got hit with everything they had, delivering pure chaos. Small arms fire, RPGs, and IEDs. There must have been a dozen Taliban on both sides of the road in a double flank ambush, complete with a PKM machine gun that was raining hot lead at us from the right.

Since I was still at the opening to the kill zone, I saw all the trucks hauling ass, hitting blast holes in the road. The flash of an RPG momentarily blinded us from the right.

I yelled at the LN gunners, "Pikka Rast!" (Dari for "PKM Right!").

One IED erupted in front of a cargo truck. The whole truck bounced ten feet into the air and landed down hard, but the driver kept bulldozing forward. It was fucking nuts and one of the strangest things I ever saw.

Our guys laid down some serious fire downrange. Everyone held their own.

The thing about war is that it's very chaotic, nasty, violent, all at the same time. It didn't matter how well the men were trained or the amount of experience or badass they brought to the table. Bombs and bullets don't discriminate.

I was working with Marines. I was proud of them for their actions under fire. There were no medals and no awards. All I could say was "Job well done," but their courage served to bolster the confidence in my crew.

People can't wrap their heads around the fact that in the middle of battles, a group of guys are willing to lay down their life for them. That will haunt them in the dark stillness of the night, well into their old age. But that's what it meant to be a brother. That was our reward and our curse.

Once we got off the X, the drivers didn't want to ride with us anymore because we were always getting attacked. To this day, we still can't believe we didn't lose any lives or vehicles that night. When we got back to the villa, Money and I fired both truck drivers for carrying contraband and for unauthorized use of a cell phone. They had compromised our operational security for a bit of money.

There was no way of telling whether one of the cargo drivers gave up our position, but it was more likely than not. The Taliban paid well for information. In some cases, when people didn't cooperate with them, family members began to disappear. It wasn't uncommon for the Taliban to extort information via threats, kidnappings, and even murder. We couldn't afford those kinds of proxy intimidations and messy mistakes, the kind that compromised our lives and missions.

Something needed to be done, but what?

I grabbed all the cell phones thinking it would be useful to determine if any stored numbers were related to the enemy. There wasn't a protocol on extracting intel from a cell phone, so I gave them to Matty to see if he could find out something that would be useful to the teams. Nothing.

Later on, sitting in my *CHU,* I stuffed one of the phones into my footlocker, a reminder of the attack. It stood out among the other mundane objects in my room. It was almost like it had an aura about it, some kind of glow, something magnetic that drew me to its existence. Perhaps it was a lifeline. A testament to all we'd had, all that was taken, and all the unknown ready to rain chaos on us again.

CHAPTER SIXTEEN
The Dust Bowl
DATE: October 18, 2009
MISSION: Phase I - Convoy Security for ODA Contingent - Classified Phase II - Vehicle Recovery COB Crazy
LOCATION: Kandahar Province/Zabul Province

Escaping by the skin of our teeth from Kandahar to Kabul brought home the reality that we had all expected but now felt down to our bones. This was war, really a war, and we were in the thick of it.

Sometimes running the roads in Afghanistan seemed like a scene out of a Mad Max movie. Every bend in the road that slowed us down was a potential ambush point. It was always a bad tactic to stop on the X. In the contracting business, movement was life. Turning back was never an option either.

Running missions in broad daylight sucked. We were at our most vulnerable then. Living by the mantra, "Another day, another dollar" had its risks.

We had painted the trucks dark gray so we could run safer at night and that helped. The F-550s were extremely loud from the sound of the turbo engine, but reducing our visual signature definitely helped give us peace of mind. Instead of seeing us coming, they only heard us. That gave us a slight advantage.

Heading south, we left early and spent another night at the Kandahar Hotel. After daybreak, the team picked up a two-pronged mission. The first was a classified load from Kandahar Airfield to be delivered to an ODA outpost in Spin Boldak. The firebase was located on the main supply route from Kandahar. It sat in the middle of a dust bowl. Convoys delivering supplies to the isolated camp threw up so much dirt that, at times, there was zero visibility.

Everything was covered in dust. The silt was so fine, we called it moon dust, much like that found in Iraq and reminiscent of the 1930's dustbowl in America. We were just trading one shithole for another. I wore an N-95 mask covered with a shemagh, but still cringed every time we had to go there simply because it was so hard to breathe.

The Taliban controlled a major portion of the road between Spin Boldak and the border by extorting toll fees from convoys bringing imports to Kandahar from Pakistan.

A small ODA contingent was responsible for area and border reconnaissance and some weapons interdiction. These guys were all hardened, bearded Pipe Hitters--the elite, special operations, direct action units of the United States Military.

All of these units were highly respectable, well-trained, and at the top of their branch as Tier I operators. But the term Pipe Hitters had also come to mean anyone who would go to the extreme to accomplish an impossible mission, so we were in good company.

The package they were waiting for included two Scorpion DPV's (Desert Patrol Vehicle) manufactured by Chenoweth Racing Company, The DPV is a dune buggy on steroids. Armed with mission specific weapons systems to include the 40mm SACO MK-19 automatic grenade launcher. the 7.62mm M60 general purpose machine gun, and two Anti-Tank Missile Launchers, these fast-attack buggies were known for their high maneuverability and speed in rough terrain and were used for long range reconnaissance and deep strike missions. Hell, if we had known that, we would have driven them there ourselves.

After Spin Boldak, the team had to do a vehicle recovery at Contingency Operating Base (COB) Crazy/Bullard because the previous team's gun truck broke down from bad diesel fuel.

Located in Shen Joy between Qalat and Ghazni, the COB was

both a fuel depot and mechanics shop divided in the middle by Hesco barriers. COB Crazy was on the left and COB Bullard was on the right.

COB Crazy housed an MRAP/Stryker Unit that was responsible for clearing Ring Road of IEDs. R-2 drivers appeared to be the only military personnel allowed to smoke in a vehicle because of the level of danger involved when clearing roads. We never knew when the IED we ran over was going be our last, so might as well light up and enjoy a smoke. I wondered if the Russian pilots with their bottles of vodka felt the same way. Every flight could have been their last.

COB Bullard had a bunch of fuel tankers next to each other that were dug in and sand-bagged fairly deep. It kept the other tankers from being compromised in case they were hit with incoming mortar rounds.

We never stopped to fuel up at the same place twice unless it was absolutely necessary. A drawback of being time-and-place predictable meant running the risk of getting bad diesel.

Since the COB was the only place that Drew was allowed access to, he had no choice but to leave the gun truck there. At least it would be guarded and kept safe. He rode back to Kabul and doubled up in the remaining B-6.

When the recovery team neared Qalat, real-time Intel from the TOC indicated the Taliban had ambushed a huge convoy of sixteen LN and third country national truck drivers about thirty minutes earlier. The complex attack killed several drivers. The Afghans used a combination of IEDs, RPGs, and small arms fire. One of the Serbian drivers quit as soon as the team returned.

A scene of total devastation remained. Nothing but silence hung over the area. A ghostly wind whistled by. The eerie images of numerous dead bodies and burnt trucks all over the road were burned into our minds.

Money figured out what occurred in the ambush by the way the vehicles were laid out.

The first truck was hit with an IED blast that crippled it on the spot. The driver was DRT—Dead Right There. The second truck in the convoy tried to go around but was also hit with an IED. Both roadside bombs had been placed at the entrance to the small hamlet, creating a choke point. There was no place for the convoy to go after that. It was obvious the next two drivers in the convoy tried to reverse out. Instead, they were annihilated by RPGs from both flanks, stopping them in their tracks.

One vehicle was jack-knifed. The other one had rolled off the side of the road. Six more vehicles that were caught up in the jam were peppered full of bullet holes. Thick columns of black smoke covered the sky and merged, blanketing the village.

Money said it was darker than shit when they rolled through the onslaught, even though it was 1000 hours. It was a well-planned attack and a strong indication that the Taliban's tactics, techniques, and procedures had improved through years of cyclic warfare.

Our team had missed the slaughter by a few kilometers, so we weaved our way through quickly and carefully.

Driving next to one of the burning tankers was an event within itself. The heat emanating from the fire was intense, and the pathway through the ambush was narrow. The gun trucks came within a few feet of the destruction.

Chase felt his skin burning as they passed by. Visibility was nil and the top gunners ducked into the pill box to avoid getting burned. The combination of diesel, burning rubber, and flesh was unmistakable and a somber reminder that life was fragile and could be taken so easily.

Those were the dangers of rolling on Ring Road. Everyone was silent as we observed the devastation, but we had to press on.

The sky grew dark with thunder clouds, promising that a storm was imminent. By the time we arrived at COB Crazy, it had started to rain heavily. The dust quickly turned to mud. Visibility was poor, so Drew flashed the gate guard a one-inch square piece of glint tape to gain access.

Glint tape/patches attached to military field and flight uniforms to provide covert combat identification. The patch reflected IR light, identifying friend or foe when viewed through night vision equipment. Once inside, we were given a tent breakfast, some hot coffee, and a quick smoke. One of the non-commissioned officers gave Chase a nickel tour.

"You guys been taking a lot of hits?" the NCO asked.

Chase shrugged. "So-so. Does anyone smoke sticks on this COB?" Chase didn't smoke cigarettes, but he was heavy into cigars.

"There's a guy over on the Bullard side who has some Swisher Sweets if that's your thing."

"Hell, I'm not picky in this weather. I have some Drew Estates back at the villa. I just need something to hold me over until we get back." We all needed a good stick to take the edge off, especially after the devastation we had just witnessed.

The NCO took Chase to see the mechanic and they met back at Crazy. We hooked up our gun truck and departed the COB. The rain kept the Taliban at bay, at least for the run back to Kabul. The Taliban didn't like to come out to play in the rain or snow, but they loved the concealment of a decent sandstorm. We were safe in the rainstorm, heading home.

CHAPTER SEVENTEEN
Chechnyan Sniper
DATE: October 21, 2009
MISSION: Resupply C-1 compounds near Ghazni
LOCATION: Ghazni Province

In addition to the weather, threats in Afghanistan took on many forms. We coped with the aftermath of major attacks like the one on the way to Qalat, but sometimes a single adversary could also wreak havoc.

In the early morning light, around 0530, the team was only a few clicks away from Ghazni when a shot rang out. The single projectile slammed into the window Money was leaning against as he looked over maps and paperwork. He moved into action. Turning to see where the shot came from, a second strike immediately hit right in front of the driver.

They both sensed the Taliban sniper was still targeting them, possibly through a scope.

They flipped him off. "Fuck you," Money said. He advised the rest of the team to stay alert. They continued moving to make their drops.

They completed their hop to Ghazni, dropped their cargo, cracked some MREs and prepared to roll back to Kabul. Aware of what had just happened, the team was apprehensive. The Taliban knew to expect a round-trip.

Normally, on an infantry recon patrol, we planned our route to the target, but never came back the way we entered. This prevented the enemy from setting up traps and ambushes. We took alternate routes on the exfiltration. Exfil was the process of removing personnel when it was considered imperative, they be immediately relocated out of a hostile environment and taken to a secure area.

Unfortunately, on convoy, we didn't have that option. Every ride one way had its dangers, but there was always an expected pucker factor on the return trip. *The Pony Express* normally ran with a lead gun truck, three cargo trucks, a center gun truck, three more cargo trucks, and a trail vehicle. Some teams preferred to push one gun truck upfront as a rabbit, followed by six cargo trucks and two follow-vehicles.

Either way, the configurations made it easy to move quickly even while loaded.

A week later, a second attack hit when Money was running with Sam's team as an augmentee in an extra gun truck. It was kind of funny because his driver, who had been with him the first time, was also with him on this run. They were actually talking about the first hit as they crested the hill going into Ghazni when it happened again.

They took a round to the top of the cab that ricocheted up, striking the top front of the box that housed our LN gunners. That's when Money named the sniper, "The Chechnyan." Special Forces briefed us that Chechnyan snipers hid in a mosque in the Qalat area.

The level VII armor on the Ford F-550s afforded some protection from armor-piercing rounds of a higher caliber such as 7.62mm, but the bullet-resistant glass was only rated at UL 752. This only provided protection against five shots of a 55-grain, 5.56mm rifle, full metal copper jacket with a lead core, traveling between 3080 and 3383 feet per second. Stats like that offered little comfort to the men knowing the enemy used 7.62 caliber weapons and above.

A second round in the same spot would undeniably penetrate the one-and-a- half-inch thick glass that surrounded the cab. In addition, our top gunners were continually fully exposed.

Lesson learned: when running missions to Qalat, never ever stop.

After that incident, there were a couple of days of downtime between gigs. We needed to come up with a plan to minimize our exposure and enhance our defense posture to effectively survive an attack that everyone knew was inevitable.

SOC was growing and they were running out of space at the villa. There were two to four guys per room, so we had to multi-task, divide, and conquer. In reality, each room was barely large enough for one person. We had to share two showers in the entire compound between sixteen men. They began to sneak off to the Safi Hotel—approximately two blocks from the villa—for rooms, showers, and the cafeteria.

The Safi Hotel was not technically labeled "off-limits." But it was considered restricted, which made it dangerous to be there. Why not enjoy a decent meal, a shit, shower, and shave? It was an opportunity to collaborate and share ideas, intel, and relax all at the same time.

Our guys didn't take any chances while getting there. They went from point-of-cover to point-of-cover to avoid detection until they arrived at the entrance to the hotel. Once there, the guard demanded they surrender their weapons, but there was no way that was going to happen. Someone in the group slipped him twenty bucks—a week's pay—to bypass the metal detector.

I believe the Safi Hotel was owned by Safi Airlines because pilots and airline crew always stayed there at night between flights. It was a welcomed respite, a place to kick back and mingle with some English-speaking patrons. Most of the Safi aircrew were South African. There was also a mix of Asian and Eastern bloc personnel, which made for some interesting conversations.

Anytime a person left the SOC Villa, a movement request was needed to document the reason for the trip (mission objective), date and time, number of personnel, types of vehicles used and more. The mission had to be approved by the Ops manager, who coordinated with the intel officer to provide updated information on enemy activity in the area. This included threats, kidnappings, proxy shootings, and snipers.

It wasn't like the potential threat was high, but it did exist, and there were several occasions when we were put on lockdown until a direct threat was mitigated, confirmed, or denied.

Sneaking off to the Safi might have been a sign of complacency, but it wasn't anything like being in Ghazni, and there weren't too many active snipers in the area of operation.

Although there were several Marines working on the SOC mobile operations program, we didn't have anyone designated as a DDM (dedicated defensive marksman). Everyone could shoot, move and communicate, but we didn't have the weapons platform or equipment to support the idea of a counter-sniper in the event of another sniper attack.

It was not practical for convoy operations. There was nothing we could do but roll the dice.

CHAPTER EIGHTEEN
Recon
DATE: October 25, 2009
MISSION: Phase I - Route reconnaissance
Phase II Conduct an advance at FOB Shank
LOCATION: Logar Province

A Taliban crap shoot meant attacks could come in the form of a single sniper's bullet—or something much more destructive such as a rocket attack. FOB Shank in Logar Province was ground zero and the target of constant rocket attacks by the Taliban.

There were two reasons for this. First, the terrain. Located sixty-five kilometers south of Kabul, Logar Province was in a large valley situated between two mountain ranges. With little command presence, the Taliban launched mortars and rockets ten or more kilometers out (roughly seven miles). There were plenty of places for them to hide.

Second, Shank was an extremely large base with a huge signature that made it easy to hit.

Some people called it a Stevie Wonder target. You could fire and hit that place blind and still have guaranteed damage.

Third, the International Security Assistance Force (ISAF) troops that actively supported and trained the Afghan National Security Forces were based there.

Logar province was also home to a mix of Pashtun, Tajik, and Hazara tribes. It appeared to be extremely commercial in terms of farming, lumber, and other local commodities. One of the things that stood out to me was the number of headstones being shaped and produced.

Memorial headstones were stacked everywhere.

It was Afghanistan, I reminded myself. There was never a

shortage of dead bodies. The Kabul-Logar-Gardez Highway ran directly across FOB Shank, splitting it in two during the early construction phase and expansion project of 2009. A larger airstrip and tarmac were added, along with accommodations for a 2,000-man camp. Their headquarters was located on the top of a hill to the right of the highway. Their operations side was situated on the left side of the road, below headquarters.

We had a lot of recon to do for our first official mission there. When the project was completed, Shank was no longer divided and the Kabul-Logar-Gardez route skirted the perimeter to the west. A larger airbase was being constructed as a touchdown point between Orgun E (Role 1 FST) and the 349th Combat Surgical Hospital (CSH) near Khost.

The trip went smoothly, although there was evidence of battle everywhere and a strong ANA presence lingered. Logar was a staging point for the Taliban and there was a moderate presence of black hats—Taliban militia—in the town. They eyed us with bad intent, and I had the feeling we were being sized up.

Guys on the teams with law enforcement backgrounds including Money, Cookie, and Chase were always the first to spot something out of the ordinary. I chalked it up to their experience as peace officers because they were trained to look out for suspicious activity and furtive movements. It was a huge plus on the teams. I appreciated their input and was thankful to have them with me.

Pulling into the city, Chase spied a black hat with a lot of facial scars who appeared to be the head honcho in Logar.

"Hammer – Chase," he radioed up. I cued the mic. "Send it."

"You see that black hat on your two o'clock? He looks like he's in charge."

"Copy that. Try and get a pic if you can." Chase replied, "Roger, I'm on it."

The black hat was surrounded by other men I suspected were members of the Taliban Militia. Most other men in town seemed gainfully employed and were working.

It's one thing to speculate, another to be paranoid, but we were astute and cautiously aware of enemy activity in the area. We knew this guy was the man. Whenever we saw him, he was standing on a brick wall or some other elevated platform conducting business.

We also saw one group of Afghan Commandos lying prone, facing west, as though they had received contact or were expecting it. One of the ANA commanders had a detonator in his hand, so they could be setting up a counter-ambush.

When we traveled to or from FOB Shank, we got an eyeful. Pressure plate IEDs targeted US troops. Pieces of asphalt catapulted through the air, landing dozens of meters away. Trucks were burned out and firefights raged over vehicles passing by.

We drove right through. There was no doubt in our minds that we crossed several culverts packed full of explosives. Whether they were intended for a harder target like the military or a target of opportunity such as *The Pony Express*, we will never know. Maybe the enemy tried to destroy us, but the IEDs failed to detonate on us.

"Must've been a dud," I said to myself more than once. But if I had to guess, our chances of getting killed by an IED on the road to Logar were about 50/50. Racer Dave told Chase he suffered from some serious pucker factor and flinched every time they rolled over a covert or a wire that crossed the road.

We often wondered what the Taliban said when a device didn't go off. Something like "Al-Akhbar Al-Ooops?" At Shank, they had a decent coffee shop and a massage parlor that provided all the luxuries of a spa, with the unfortunate exception of a happy ending. The Tajikistani women working there were of Russian/Chinese roots. In my humble opinion, the women in the Middle East—Lebanese, Jordanian, and Tajikistani—were very beautiful, unlike any I had seen before.

We took advantage of the services, from haircuts to foot

massages or a full-body back massage. We took some pictures, loaded up on PX supplies, and did our advance, heading back to Kabul before nightfall.

Shortly after that mission, we received news that the hotel we stayed at in Kandahar had been bombed a second time. We scrapped the next mission because there wasn't a contingency plan on a place to hunker down.

Rolling back to Kabul, I had mixed emotions. Part of me kept thinking about the reprieve at FOB Shank. Although it was dangerous to be rolling through what some might consider Taliban HQ, I was relieved we didn't have any enemy contacts. It was also great for the guys to stock up on supplies and catch a decent meal at the DFAC. The other thought I had was the uncertainty of our chosen billets and supply chain in Kandahar and at the China Hotel.

I knew it was just a matter of time. Hotels, or any location housing foreigners, were low hanging fruit for terrorists. The message the Taliban sent was clear: "Do not aid and abet Americans."

What made things worse was knowing I had teams hunkered down there on the occasions when I needed to run missions elsewhere. We were trained to concentrate on the immediate mission, but when my friends were in harm's way and there was nothing, anyone could do about it, I was uneasy and could not get it out of my mind.

This was the first of two hotel bombings and one shopping center bombing, a strong indication that SOC was under some kind of enemy surveillance. We always knew we were being watched, but to what degree remained the question. The Taliban is no different than any other enemy insurgency when gathering intel. They use open-source documentation, human intelligence, and active surveillance to consolidate information on their targets of interest. It was also quite possible that someone from our guard force was leaking information to the Taliban.

No one could be trusted. We found that out when Spinney's Grocery store got hit.

CHAPTER NINETEEN
Bombings and Bounties

Having spent a majority of time thinking about our exposure and predictability after our advance on FOB Shank, we soon found out the grocery store and hotel we frequented in Kabul were both bombed within a week of each other.

One of our primary modes of operation was to be as unpredictable as possible by leaving at different times, taking different routes, and staggering our arrivals and departures. But we could only do so much to avoid contact with the Taliban. We had limited choices for food supplies, not having established any solid contracts with KBR and other coalition vendors.

It was only a matter of time before a large-scale attack came at us.

Spinneys was a grocery store where we shopped for food and supplies before moving to the Kabul Program Management Office compound (KMPO) and obtaining a meal service contract with Pinnacle Group of Companies which offered hotel services in Afghanistan.

Located on the other side of Masood Circle, Spinney's was bombed on October 27, 2009, minutes after Money picked up groceries and supplies.

My initial reaction was, "Oh, shit."

A few minutes earlier and it would have been hair, teeth, and eyeballs all over the place. Once all SOC personnel were accounted for and safe, I breathed a sigh of relief. I thought for a minute we might have to go there to dig out our own.

I had the same punch to the gut when the hotel in Kandahar got hit because we had just been there. They hit the spot where we normally slept. It was a weird feeling to know we were a walking target—or a sleeping one.

I was told the Taliban had a bounty out for us, a grim reminder of where we were, what we were doing, and what was at stake. Since SOC wouldn't pay the Taliban any money, we wanted to see if the bounty would go up just to piss them off.

A week later, the China Hotel was bombed. It was only a few blocks away from Spinney's grocery store and we all began to take things a bit more personal because we knew the staff who worked and lived there. Ryan, Jon and I believed we were being targeted. Three bombings after frequenting each location was not a coincidence.

The China Hotel was managed by a beautiful Chinese woman in her late thirties who served as the hostess. She spoke English quite well, although it was heavily accented. Everyone liked her and tipped her well to keep our VIP status intact. We established a non-mission-oriented partnership with the hotel. They served an awesome dinner, catered to our Western tastes, and had a healthy supply of liquor.

Once, Drew Babbitt had found a set of skeleton keys lying around while having dinner at the restaurant there. We joked about which one of the keys went to the liquor cabinet at the hotel. Drew gave a key to each of us. They became a symbol of our friendship and made us VIP members of the China Hotel. It was one of the few good memories I stored in my footlocker.

In the aftermath of the VBIED bombing, we also found out our gracious hostess was killed. It was a somber moment for the guys. Money took it the hardest because he knew her longer than anyone else and they got along really well.

He was first to recon the China Hotel, looking for a safe-haven or an establishment that provided amenities to take care of his crew. Money always put his men first. That's what I admired about him the most. It pained him to tell the team and it pained us to see him take it personally.

Drew asked, "Hey, Money, when are we going back to the

China Hotel for some grub?"

"Not anytime soon, Bro. The Taliban leveled the place two days ago when we were in Kandahar."

"No shit!" Drew said. "What the fuck? What's the damage assessment?"

"Totally destroyed, along with everyone in it," Money responded in a low voice.

"What about your contact, the Chinese woman?"

"Gone," Money said.

Drew placed his hand on his shoulder, then turned and walked away to give Money some space.

The attack took an emotional toll on us all. Our reality became crystal clear. We were being targeted.

It was common knowledge that anyone who was not from Afghanistan had a huge target painted on their backs. We were considered even more dangerous just because of the nature of the business we were in, along with our reputation for getting the job done.

We also had no problem dropping a bad guy if it was warranted, and the locals knew it. Fear is a great motivator, but fear with respect is a decent stabilizer. It went both ways.

Don't try to harm me, and I will not reduce your world to rubble. Leave me alone and I'll leave you alone. The Golden Rule at SOC was: "Never turn your back or walk in front of any LN. Keep him in your line-of-sight at all times."

I was ready to drop a dude in a heartbeat if I thought one of them even entertained the idea of attacking, ROE be damned. I was not into that green on blue bullshit.

There were proxy shootings in Afghanistan all the time and any expat could be killed at any time. Proxy shootings and proxy bombings are the most clandestine form of attack.

The Taliban used threats of kidnapping, assault, and murder to coerce a non-combatant to commit an attack.

I was not getting killed because some pencil neck in

Washington D.C. decided we needed to be more trusting and polite, another catch-22.

Screw him. He was not there. Not at Spinney's. Not at the China Hotel. And definitely not on Ring Road.

Early on in Iraq, per the Status of Forces Agreement, anyone who crept up on you would've been neutralized in a heartbeat. In Afghanistan, the military used the Rules of Engagement (ROE) as a prelude to contact. Security contractors were bound by the Rules for the Use of Escalation of Force (RUF). They were much different.

Initially termed the "Rules for the Use of Force," the term "escalation" was added for domestic support to civil authority missions, "nonoperational" force protection, and security contractor defensive posture operations. There is no doubt that the liberal, civilian, and unproven hands of Washington, DC were all over these "requirements."

It sucked having to go through so many steps to protect the team, but the rules were considered a practical way of putting into place safeguards and measures to ensure that security contractors complied with international law. They were also meant to minimize the infliction of collateral damage.

To avoid litigation, the process consisted of an acronym known as the Five S's—Show, Shout, Shove, Shoot to Warn, and Shoot to Kill.

In convoy and PSD operations it became even more detailed. Technically, we had to use signaling devices like pen flares, spotlights, or VS-17 panels to wave at the incoming threat (Show). Next, we used warning devices such as a siren, a loud-speaker, or PA to hail any approaching vehicles or persons in case they didn't see the flares, VS-17 panels, or ignored the visual warning (Shout).

In the absence of either device, an operator could raise his weapon to demonstrate his intent to fire if the threat continued forward. He could physically use the barrel of his weapon to poke at the threat if the shooter was dismounted and the threat was on foot (Shove).

The next step was two-fold. The operator could place a few well-aimed shots to the engine block to hopefully disable the vehicle (Shoot to Warn). Finally, the operator was authorized to (Shoot to Kill). We aimed at the driver.

Regardless of the regulations and process, we weren't going to get our China Hotel back.

Spinneys recovered from the bombing, but both incidents dictated our future movements because Spinney's became off-limits for us as our safety was always the number one priority.

Our restriction felt like punishment for a crime that someone else committed. But they were big boy rules, and this was war, baby and war is hell. We had a lot to do to get ready for more attacks and get the bounty off our heads.

CHAPTER TWENTY
Train, Train, Train

The bounty on our heads got us in gear. We stayed in shape to stay alive! And trained to keep our skills sharp. At no time did we underestimate the need to stay fit. We never knew when we would need to carry a teammate. It was called sweat equity.

Guys who didn't invest in their health and work out paid the price one way or the other. For the most part, anyone with a Marine Corps background seemed much more motivated and knew the importance of maintaining a higher standard of fitness.

Since we had no place to eat out because of the bombings, we had down time on our hands. When we weren't running missions, we were training. When we weren't training, we were working out. Money, Chase, Drew, and I hit the weights hard. We worked out much more than everyone else, but the gym at the villa was rudimentary, so we used whatever we could find to stay in shape.

There were some scattered cement weights, a couple of dumbbells, some bent barbells, a pull-up bar, a kettlebell, and a tattered bench press. We made makeshift weights using five-gallon buckets of dirt and Drew found an old tractor tire from a previous mission that we hauled back to the villa to use for Cross Fit exercises.

When we ran a PSD mission to FOB Eggers, we worked out there. They had two gyms. We used the one closest to the battalion aide station because it had ample parking and was close to the gate, in case we had to leave in a hurry.

We protected ourselves in other ways. When Chase and I were in Iraq with the Shark Teams, we wore level IV ballistic protection called Dragon Skin body armor. Manufactured by

Pinnacle Armor, it had a dry weight of forty-four pounds, but there was no mechanism to attach any additional equipment, so we had to wear load-bearing vests to carry our ammo and supplies.

Wearing dragon skin body armor had benefits. It was completely flexible and encapsulated our entire chest and back. It defeated rifle rounds from 7.62 x 39mm 122 grain, steel case ammo with a velocity of 2300-2400 fps, and 5.56 x 45mm 65 grain, M855 (SS109 Green tip) ammo traveling at 3200-3300 fps. The 2000 flexible Level IV system exceeded MIL-P-46593A fragmentation specifications using high-powered rifle rounds.

The disadvantage was the excessive weight. It caused spinal compression over a short period of time. Chase was 6 foot 1 when he came into the country and lost a solid inch in height in just two years.

The other controversy associated with the body armor was the adhesive that held the ceramic discs together, hence the name Dragon Skin. According to a lawsuit filed by the US Army, the body armor could not withstand additional strikes in the same area. The adhesive failed and melted with temperatures above 118 degrees Fahrenheit. Anyone who's ever been to Iraq knows temperatures surpassed 126 degrees on many occasions.

The job was physically demanding and there were a number of mitigating factors that impacted our endurance levels. One; Kabul was somewhere around 5,876 feet above sea level, so the air was thin, which made for better aerobics. Two; our diets consisted mostly of clean protein like lamb, goat, and chicken. Since we ate food that was not mass-produced or chemically treated with preservatives, the fat content remained low. Three; the weather in Afghanistan was hotter than shit in the summer. It wasn't uncommon to sweat off a couple pounds a day while on mission.

Everyone wore a ton of kit on the long hauls. My rig weighed about sixty pounds. It consisted of two parts—chest plates and a cross-shoulder harness that held most of my ammo and necessities such as my GPS, IFAK, and radio.

Money, Cookie, Buddha, Chase, and I all wore wrap-around MOLLE vests which were Modular Lightweight Load-Carrying Equipment, with webbing. The vests held a dozen different configurations depending on how they were set up. Chase and Buddha carried extra med-kit on their vests, so their rigs weighed closer to seventy-five pounds. They also had a ripcord that could pull the vest apart to access the chest or abdomen in case of an emergency. If someone was injured or fell into deep water, he could strip the vest off cleanly, and hopefully not get dragged under from the excessive weight.

Matty and a few of the other guys strictly wore breastplates with a load-bearing vest pulled over them. They were easier to get in and out of but made things difficult for anyone who tried to do a hasty cross-deck or body drag. The vest constantly slipped up over the head because the two rigs were not connected.

In addition to the weight, we wore on our backs, everyone carried an Escape and Evasion kit or go-bag with additional mags/ammo, some basic med supplies, spare batteries, water, and MRE—meals ready to eat. Team medics also had to pack around a STOMP III surgical med-kit that was loaded to the teeth with advanced medical equipment and supplies and weighed between fifty to seventy-five pounds.

Lastly, aside from packing a shitload of weapons, ammo, and kit, we had to be able to do some physically demanding and exhausting tasks under extremes like tactical tire changes, sling and tow operations, medical evacuations and cross-decking. It was bad enough to have to pack your own weight around, let alone carry another Pony Express team member who weighed the same, if not more, and was also fully kitted up and completely immobile.

Anyone who didn't take his job seriously enough found out very quickly—the hard way—what it was really like. They either ate crow and got their shit together in a hurry or got the hell out. If they didn't leave of their own accord, then we had no problem showing them the door—and it usually came with a stiff boot up the ass, too.

When you're with a group of guys 24/7, you get to know them quickly. We ate, slept, worked out, trained, and ran missions together for months at a time, again, tribe mentality. The guy who stood out the most wasn't the leader of the pack. He was the loser, the weakling, a detriment to the team. He could be a great guy but if he couldn't hack it, he had to pack it.

Most of our weapon's training and qualifications occurred at Camp Morehead, a designated Afghan Commando base. SOC had just procured the compound static security contract to provide force protection at Morehead, so we had access to the range and other base amenities.

Everyone dreaded making the movement to Morehead, which meant braving downtown Kabul traffic. No one in Afghanistan knew how to drive, at least to Western standards.

One time, Money and Chase were driving back from FOB Eggers after working out at the gym. They turned left to take a short cut to the villa, when suddenly, an Afghan on a motorbike crashed into the right side of their SUV. The rider went airborne over the hood of the Toyota Land Cruiser. Even though they were innocent, Money yelled to Chase, "Punch it!"

He knew someone would try and lie their way into a quick pay-off, so they took off, weaving in and out of traffic. Sure enough, one of the bystanders who witnessed the accident decided to become judge, jury, and executioner. He ran after them on foot. Having the advantage of gridlock, he hopped over cars, pushed his way through pedestrians shopping on the street, and even knocked over a fruit stand just to catch up to the B-6 that got jammed up at a traffic stop.

The Afghan screamed, "Police! Police!" desperately trying to get anyone's attention.

Money opened the door and tossed out a ten-dollar bill. The Afghan dove to the ground trying to grab at the cash. It diverted his attention long enough for them to push into the gate at FOB Eggers and avoid a losing financial battle between him and the ANP.

Technically, there were no traffic laws in Afghanistan. Since the Taliban had been removed from power, there was a huge influx of vehicles into the country. Inexperienced drivers, mixed with the old school cart and donkey, a shitload of motorbikes and crappy road conditions resulted in a ton of locals making up their own rules as they crashed their way into oblivion.

Once at Morehead, we spent one day dedicated to small arms training, including weapons remediation, stoppages, and transitions. Another day was spent training on assault rifles and automatic weapons, including orientation on foreign weapons, AK-47s, and PKMs.

SOC had one truck, a purple Hilux, that killed more people than the PKM that was mounted on the back of it. Everyone said it was jinxed. Anytime the truck was driven, someone got hit or run over. It was a bad luck truck, and no one wanted to drive it, so we outfitted a pillbox in the bed of the truck and used it to rig up arm-spindles to test the fan of fire on our PKMs before mounting them on the gun trucks.

The physical work was a good way to teach the top gunners how to lead a belt-fed weapon while in motion. We even retrofitted a couple of AK-47s with 37mm grenade launchers and pumped off a few rounds of 37mm at some busted up half-tracks laid out on the mountainside.

SOC had made a black-market purchase of several Glocks and PKMs that needed to be test-fired prior to being issued to ensure their integrity. Many of the weapons malfunctioned. The magazines for the Glocks proved to be the failure point. They were imitation knockoffs that were likely smuggled into the country from Pakistan, where one of the largest weapons bazaars in the world was located. If they didn't have what someone wanted, they could get it or make it.

We wanted our money back, but Ryan Bennett informed us the arms dealer was no longer with us. We took that to mean he was taking a dirt nap somewhere, flirting with seventy-two virgins.

We didn't want to end up like that. We were in the thick of it. Working out and training could end up saving us.

CHAPTER TWENTY-ONE
The Colonel

Despite the smell, the heat, the sickness, the fact that we had targets on our backs, and our movements becoming increasingly restricted after the hotel and grocery store attacks, we resorted to colorful human resources to help smooth things out in operations. We needed them to make our missions easier. It cost us though, in more ways than one.

SOC had a retired Afghan Colonel on the payroll who had major airport connections in Kabul (who knew?). We sarcastically called him "Colonel Sanders." He was considered the liaison between SOC and the ANP and was paid a lot of money. Way more than his Afghan military paygrade. I never really trusted him, but he did come in handy at times. In that country, everyone not on your team was suspect.

When we got stuck at a gate or checkpoint and needed to get through, we called on the colonel. We had laminated pass cards with his photo ID and contact information. We also produced a letter that illustrated his relationship with SOC and our PSD missions, mostly to pick up and/or drop off clients, company personnel, and miscellaneous cargo at Kabul International Airport.

Afghanistan's main international airport was five kilometers from the city center of Kabul. It was also one of the largest military bases, capable of housing over one hundred aircraft. A number of military bases built around it were used by the United States Armed Forces and NATO's International Security Assistance Force. The Afghan Air Force also had a base there, and the ANP provided security inside the passenger terminals.

The Colonel had direct access to information and control over access. His office was directly across from the newly appointed Prime Minister's office Mohammed Hanif Atmar. He also had indirect access to the TOC.

We had far too many unanswered questions for me to feel comfortable. Who had actually vetted the Colonel? How did the relationship between the Colonel and SOC/SOC-A evolve?

Were we being set up? Were we at risk?

Some of us suspected he was being fed other forms of payment—favors, immunity, protection, or even cash—under the table from other outside sources. Technically, there was no such thing as extortion or embezzlement in the way the government functioned in Afghanistan. Neither word existed in their language. They used the term "Expedition Fee" instead.

In order for SOC, LLC to operate in Afghanistan, it needed to establish a working relationship with an Afghan company for the purpose of obtaining security and operating permits. That also helped to stimulate the Afghan economy. We paid expedition fees to have our vehicles flown into Bagram, for our vehicle registrations, for our security licenses, arming authority, and more.

The Colonel could supposedly move paperwork to the top of the pile if he was paid additional sums of money. He also had a solid connection with Afghan President Hamid Karzai and his family, specifically his half-brother, Ahmed Wali Karzai, an elder of the Popalzai tribe. Wali had formerly lived in the United States where he managed a restaurant owned by his family. He returned to Afghanistan following the removal of the Taliban government in late 2001.

Allegedly on the CIA's payroll, Wali was accused of political corruption. In October 2009, the *New York Times* reported that Wali received payments from the CIA for "a variety of services," including the recruitment of the Kandahar Strike Force, an Afghan paramilitary force run by the CIA in the Kandahar region.

It also stated he was paid for allowing the CIA and US Special Operations Forces to rent the former residence of Taliban supreme leader Mullah Omar (aka Firebase Gecko). Wali denied that allegation.

The Colonel's relationships with the Karzai family and SOC caused a lot of friction and crossed ethical boundaries. The Colonel had knowledge that could do us a lot of harm if he were so inclined.

Then there were logistical concerns. If SOC-A gave the Colonel money to pay Wali's office for expedition fees, who determined how much money would guarantee moving an application to the front? If there was a minimal amount of money required to get a job expedited, then anyone who paid more money trumped the latter.

We needed to get gun trucks into the country from Dubai and everything in Afghanistan that was imported or exported was done through Wali's office. The info he was privy to include the number of vehicles and shipments, routes we took, delivery times, the security personnel numbers and organization, and the entire Table of Organization and Equipment. We were at their mercy. At the advice of the Colonel, we paid the expedition fees.

Wali's reputation preceded him. A cable that was intercepted from the US Embassy alleged that much of the actual business of running the city of Kandahar took place "out of public sight, where Wali Karzai used state institutions to protect and enable licit and illicit enterprises."

The *New York Times* wrote that Wali may have been involved in the Afghan opium and heroin trade. President Karzai denied the allegations, calling the charges political propaganda.

Wali's dealings always put him in danger. Wali himself said he survived a total of nine assassination attempts by Taliban militants and at least two bombing attacks against his office in Kandahar—one in November 2008 and the other in April 2009.

On July 12, 2011, in the truest tradition of Julius Caesar, Wali

Karzai was assassinated by his own long-time head of security, Sardar Mohammad.

So much for one's inner circle. Trust no one in Afghanistan.

President Karzai didn't waste any time appointing Shah Wali Karzai, a brother of Ahmed Wali, as his brother's successor and newest chairman of the Kandahar Provincial Council. He reinforced family and political pre-eminence in the southern provinces. The process of expedition remained in place.

This led back to the Colonel. He had a lot of influence no matter how many ways we cut it, and SOC needed someone with clout in their corner, despite all the underhanded shit that was going on. Our concern was that information about our movements was being sold to the Taliban. Only the Colonel knew for sure.

CHAPTER TWENTY-TWO
Beggar's Alley
DATE: October 29, 2009
MISSION: Phase I - Medical Resupply Fob Eggers
Phase II - Biometrics/CAC cards FOB Phoenix
LOCATION: Kabul

We had the Colonel greasing the skids, and possibly working against us at the same time. Team members had to improvise to make sure we were covered. In order to accomplish the task at hand, we needed contacts for resupply, IDs, and a reliable point of contact (POC) in Kabul.

FOB Eggers was home to the Combined Forces Command. All US military branches, and the International Security Assistance Force used it. Getting into FOB Phoenix, a joint US-Canadian base, proved interesting. Phoenix required biometrics specific to the base in addition to having a Civilian Access Card. The process was time-consuming and inconvenient, but it was a necessary evil since we required access on a daily basis. Getting there and back was the problem.

Driving through Beggar's Alley proved difficult. If something happened to us there, it would be a while before a QRF could reach our location. Movement was extremely slow.

The road was indescribable. It was busier than an open market road but had tons of potholes. Dust was everywhere, which obscured visibility. Although it was no wider than a two-lane road, it wasn't uncommon for cars to pass cars that were passing other cars. The street was only eight blocks long, but it saw more traffic throughout the day than a major city during morning rush hour. As many runs as we made through the short hellhole, it was a miracle we were able to push through without running anyone over.

The most troublesome sight was widowed beggars wearing dirty burkas sitting in potholes in the middle of the road looking for handouts. The women fed their newborn babies with bottle caps dipped in muddy water. We couldn't believe what we were seeing, and we couldn't help but feel sorry for them. If we tried to give them any money, oftentimes, men passing by rushed into the street and took the money away from them.

I later learned that women whose husbands were killed or disappeared were often unable to claim any inheritance from the family without having to go through the courts.

In general, Afghan society considered it "shameful" for these women to try to claim their inheritance, which only equated to one-quarter of the husband's entire estate. Widows were discouraged to go through the courts as it tarnished the memory of their missing or dead husband. In addition to having no money, widows were sometimes not allowed to reside in the matrimonial home. They were subjected to sexual abuse, rape, and forced pregnancy by the husband's family and others because they lacked a male protector.

It was culturally unacceptable for a man to marry a widow or for a widow to remarry.

They were literally kicked to the curb and left to fend for themselves. In the West, we could not fathom this practice. Witnessing it made us appreciate what we had regarding laws and rights in America. This put us on edge because fights and riots easily broke out.

Once, during a PSD mission to Eggers, Ryan and Phil mixed it up with a couple of locals on Beggar's Alley. Phil leaned out of his limo and gave a twenty-dollar bill to one of the widows with a little baby. A man who witnessed the cash exchange ran into the road and grabbed the money from the widowed beggar. This pissed off Ryan. He stopped the B-6 and jumped out, grabbed the thief, and handed him some street justice, Muay Thai style.

Money and Chase also got into it with a bunch of Afghans on their return through Beggar's Alley. Luga, one of the static guard supervisors, started the fight. He was arguing with an LN on the corner of the street a block away from the SOC entrance.

Money stopped the B-6 limo near the gate and tried to separate the two Afghans, but more people started to flock around. Soon, he was outnumbered. Chase got out to help, but when he got close to the crowd, someone tried to grab his sidearm from behind. He swung around sharply and kicked him back in the chest.

Another Afghan stood there with fists clenched, ready to jump.

Chase covered the grip of his Glock. Some of the crowd started to back up. Money yelled, "Chase, get back in the limo!"

Chase pushed his way through the fringe, ran around to the passenger side, and reached over to open the driver's door.

Just when they thought the fight was over, Luga lunged back into the crowd and took another swing at his unknown opponent. More people jumped in, and guards from the villa ran out to help.

Money fired a couple of rounds in the dirt and that scared the shit out of everyone. They all scattered like a bunch of cockroaches caught in the light. Money got back into the limo, and they pushed back into the villa. No one knows what happened to Luga after that, but he was never seen in the villa again.

FOB Eggers was our greatest asset in terms of supplies, access to the MWR and the DFAC. It was a lot closer than Phoenix but getting through the gate was hardest part. They had a checkpoint that started at a busy intersection, and we were constantly exposed. Gaining access from the other side was also a bitch because they continually changed procedures. The only access for vehicles was through the intersection gate and we had to park outside the wire and walk in if we wanted to get in on the other side.

Chase was one very resourceful medic. He met with all the medical staff at the Battalion Aid Station on FOBs Eggers and Phoenix to let them know who we were. They helped each other out. It was pretty cool because every time we left the FOB, Chase had ample medical supplies to enhance our mission outcome, no matter where we were headed.

Side note: During the Stanley Cup playoffs of 2011, the Boston Bruins were playing the Vancouver Canucks. Since Camp Phoenix was a joint US-Canadian base, a bet was made between the two commands. If the Bruins won, the Canadians had to fly the Boston Bruins flag over their command post. If the Canucks won, the US Army would fly the Canucks flag over theirs. The Bruins won—and a lot of photos were taken of the Bruins' flag flying over the Canadian command post.

Regardless of the benefits, we always loathed the ride back to the villa. Beggar's alley was dangerous and unpredictable. We rolled out of Beggar's Alley, silent, as the widowed beggars watched us leave. No matter how many times we wanted to help them, we knew our efforts only served the criminal element who stole from the widows. Stopping was never an option, tossing a water bottle in their direction was the very least we could do.

CHAPTER TWENTY-THREE
Bandits
DATE: October 31, 2009
MISSION: Security for C-1 convoy to Kandahar
LOCATION: Maidan Shahar, Wardak Province

We drove our gun trucks like we stole them and parked them like we owned them. We endured the danger, the dust, and the road to safeguard America. But we also did it for one of the oldest reasons around. Money.

Contracting was a business and war always had a business side. That is a hard fact.

We were being paid to perform a service, get the job done, and to turn a profit for SOC corporate. If situations got too dangerous, we could always walk away from them and go home. On the other hand, we could also be fired at any time by the company we worked for.

Management and command made decisions for business reasons, which weren't always the best to keep the teams safe and the gear intact. If the company had to cut costs to save money, the payroll was always the first to get chopped because the gear and weapons were typically at a set price.

However, if the client required a certain level of security personnel, and the pay was cut too much, then we ran the risk of not meeting manning requirements and ended up going into default on the contract.

It was a constant balancing act. The gig at Chapman was winding down and I was glad to get back to Kabul. Business started to pick back up again, and SOC was running two full-time crews, but changes were coming.

Money was getting ready to go on leave for a month. Cookie

had just returned from injured reserve status and was assigned as the team leader on Team II, taking Money's place. And the news was Rector was coming up from Iraq to be the new program manager for the mobile operations contract.

That wasn't necessarily a good move. Rector and Chase didn't get along. There was going to be some friction.

I'm not too sure why Rector had it out for Chase, but I knew Chase got screwed over when he was hired. When he first signed up with SOC, his pay was stated on the LOA (letter of authorization) at the standard pay rate for expats. When he arrived at HDSOC headquarters for indoctrination and training, his contract was changed to a lower amount. When he arrived in country, they reduced it a third time.

It may have been due to his Canadian citizenship. SOC knew they could save some money.

Chase put up a fight because he didn't know of the changes until he arrived at Camp Slayer in Iraq. Rector put him on the spot. The only choice he had was to sign the contract or turn around and go home.

Some folks looked at him as being a possible troublemaker. But guys like Chase were needed to speak up for what was right and fair. This was not a yes man's game. We didn't want corporate to look at us as a statistic and try and walk all over us.

Chase was a good guy in addition to being a great medic and a pipe-hitter. Rector was a former US Army veteran with the 82nd Airborne Division who had worked with me on the Tetra Tech UXO gig in Iraq. When Tetra Tech ended, many of the guys wanted to stay in-country and looked for contracts.

Rector's first act as PM was to cut operational funds in half. He slowly replaced guys in Kabul with his old crew from Iraq and pushed other operators out. Money saw it coming and told Chase to watch his back.

Money and Chase worked together at SOC in Iraq and got along well. They had similar backgrounds, and both liked working with wood. Chase built furniture out of old pallets and Money refurbished old antiques as a hobby.

Money and Cookie were also good friends since they both served in the Corps, but with the incident that occurred at Kilo Marker 24, they became bonded for life. Money stayed in touch with Cookie to follow-up on his care and rehabilitation at home. He let Cookie know that he would have a stellar medic on his team when he got back in country.

After Money introduced Chase to Cookie, they became good friends. As the team medic, Chase was used to running trail. Money rolled as the tactical commander in the second vehicle. Drew was always upfront, on point.

Cookie ran his team the opposite way and maintained command and control from the rear of the convoy. His concept made it easier to dictate tactics if something happened in the front.

We'd always known that you need to learn the guy's job above you, and you need to be willing to do the guy's job below you. That really was the bottom line.

In this line of work, it was a catch-22, damned if you do, damned if you don't. SOC's policy was to hire personnel who were already vetted and trained for the mission. They provided ongoing training in perishable skill sets such as weapons, driving, and combat medicine, A SOC candidate needed to be technically proficient and cross-trained in all areas of convoy operations. There were very few exceptions.

The cards were stacked against anyone who was on point. Drew had been rolling the dice for quite some time, being in the lead vehicle on all the long hauls. It was time to mix things up.

We decided to move Chase up front. The commander of the lead vehicle was responsible for calling out threats and navigating the route. Chase voiced his concerns about being put in that position. He wasn't scared, he was just concerned for the betterment of the team with his lack of experience.

His argument made sense because if anything happened up front, it was his ass that would get shredded to pieces—and what good was he as a medic then?

My solution was to have Chase provide combat medical training to the gunners and other crew members. He wasn't a fan, but he got it done.

"Man, this sucks!" said Chase.

"It's your job," I replied. "Like it or leave it. Just don't bitch about it."

"I'm not complaining about having to train these guys. I'm just not comfortable running lead. I don't have the experience."

"You gotta take the bull by the horns sooner or later, dude. You know how to read a map?" I asked.

He did.

"You know how to work a GPS? He did. You know how to handle comms?" He did.

"Well then, you're good to go! Everyone at SOC needs to be cross-trained. That's what makes the team effective."

He took a deep breath. "Copy that, Hammer. I'm on it." I was more than glad to see that Chase got it. He was ready to step up.

Chase and Cookie's first mission to Kandahar was fucked up from the beginning.

Racer Dave had gone back to Minden to instruct another driver training course at SOC headquarters. Money had just gone on leave. I was headed south to recon another gig, and Matty was in the TOC. Ryan, Phil, and Mark were running PSD missions for the Defense Group International (DGI) contract. Team II was rolling to Kandahar for a three-day run.

On mission, Cookie was paired up with Wolfe. Drew's driver was Saso, and Chase got stuck with Dragan. They were former Serbian or Macedonian soldiers who spent their post- military careers working as mercenaries. Their English was marginal, and they had a reputation for being crazy and unpredictable.

The team left extremely early. This was the first time they had rolled before sunrise.

Although Chase was on point and knew the route, he wasn't comfortable calling out threats and making critical movement decisions.

Their first contact was a group of bandits who had taken up position on the roadway just south of Maidan Shahar in Wardak Province. Debris had been placed across the road, forming a chokepoint.

As the first gun truck crested the hill, Chase saw the blockade and three bandits standing in the middle of the road with RPGs. He keyed up his radio and yelled, "Contact front! Roadblock!"

His blast door was closed so, neither top gunner heard him except Dragan. The translator was in the trail vehicle with Cookie. Dragan punched the throttle at the same time one of the bandits leveled his RPG in their direction.

Cookie yelled "Push through!" They closed the distance between the lead and the blockade quickly. All three bandits ran for cover to the right side of the road to avoid getting hit. The last bandit dove into the gully. The convoy broke through the barrier sending debris everywhere.

Cookie called up, "Follows up Chase. Everything okay up there?" "My fucking top gunner is asleep!" Chase yelled into the radio.

Cookie radioed back, "Calm down, bro. They haven't had their morning chai. Besides, they're only bandits trying to make a quick score."

Chase double-keyed the mic to confirm receipt of the message. Cookie replied, "Don't worry brother. I got your back."

Bandits rarely engaged a superior target when they knew they were outnumbered and outgunned. They were nothing more than criminals with RPGs but could easily become deadly if they felt they had the upper hand. Seeing a massive Ford F-550 barreling down towards them at top speed must have done the trick.

No one was surprised the top gunners hadn't opened fire because everyone but Chase knew they were asleep in their sling seats inside the turret. Both gunners were jolted awake when they barreled through the debris pile, but it was too late to lay down the hate. Needless to say, Chase was pissed off for a month.

From that point on Chase always made sure his team was juiced up on coffee, tea, Red Bull, or Rip-It energy drinks prior to leaving the compound. There was no way in hell he was ever gonna let that happen again

They did their drop and again stayed at the Kandahar Hotel. It was different this time. The staff seemed rushed and uncomfortable. After the bombing, they knew we might still be a target. It made for a restless evening. Dinner wasn't the same either. There was no prep time, the service was quick, the food stale, and there was no conversation.

It seemed as though they were afraid to refuse us service, and at the same time afraid of the consequences of catering to us.

It was a catch-22 for them, as much as it was for us. The "damned if you do, damned if you don't" mantra followed us like the plague everywhere we went, including the Taliban stronghold.

CHAPTER TWENTY-FOUR
The Taliban Stronghold
DATE: November 02, 2009
MISSION: Phase I - PSD for DGI client in Herat (Team I)
Phase II - Convoy Security to Gardez for C-1 client (Team II)
LOCATION: Ring Road Kandahar to Herat

I had just arrived in Kabul and wasn't boots on the ground for more than an hour before I was instructed to meet the team at the hotel in Kandahar. Cookie was contacted by the TOC and was told the mission to return to Kabul had changed. He laid out a quick brief and the team waited for the new objective: SOC had secured another contract and needed two gun trucks to haul supplies and equipment to Gardez.

It took us six hours to get to Kandahar. Not bad, considering all the detours Drew and I had to take. When we pulled into the hotel, everyone was prepping their gear for a hasty departure. There was no breakfast or coffee available. Chase didn't have any Red Bull either, thanks to Rector, so he was chewing on coffee grounds and trying to choke them down with water.

Expenses were scrutinized more and there was a huge push to cut back on unnecessary, "frivolous" spending. That was subjective, depending on who was making the call. Red Bull was important to the teams, but headquarters thought it was excessive and more of a luxury as opposed to a necessity.

What made matters worse was when some of the guys came back from HDSOC in Minden and told us stories of the break room fridge at corporate being filled with Monsters, Red Bulls, and Rock Star energy drinks. Why were they allowed to drink them, and we were limited to water and cokes? It was our asses on the line out there. If anyone needed or deserved the caffeine-filled drinks, it was us.

At this point, Chase still had coffee grounds stuck in his teeth. He looked like he had just eaten a shit sandwich, so I figured it was a good time to let them know about the new objective.

Defense Group International was running well-head survey operations in Torghundi on the Turkmenistan border. Chase and I were tasked to push to Herat with one B-6 and a gun truck to support that mission.

Chase's jaw dropped. "What the hell?"

I replied, "How does your shit sandwich taste now?"

"Not funny," Chase said as he spat his coffee grounds in the dirt.

Cookie and Drew took the remaining two gun trucks back to Kabul to run the Gardez mission, so we all packed up and headed out.

SOC hadn't been through Helmand Province, but everyone knew all too well the dangers of rolling through the Taliban stronghold.

We still had bounties on our heads. To run a solo mission with only two expats, two TCN drivers, and two LN gunners was nuts. We were out-numbered, out-gunned, and out of our minds.

Our only saving grace was that we didn't have to escort any cargo, so we moved faster on the highway.

If we were lucky and managed not to get injured, killed, or worse—captured and tortured—then we might need to claim "Nanawatai."

Traditionally, nanawatai means "sanctuary." It is a tenet of the Pashtunwali code of the Pashtun people. It allowed a beleaguered person who came knocking at someone's door seeking refuge to enter the house and request sanctuary. The host could not refuse the request, even if it was a sworn enemy, even at the cost of the host's own life or fortune.

Some suggested that Mullah Omar's refusal to turn in Osama bin Laden was due to his having availed himself of Nanawatai.

This was also what saved Navy SEAL Marcus Luttrell, who was the subject of the book and film *Lone Survivor*.

We could be in the same country, but in a different tribal area, and it was a roll of the dice. We could be assisted or killed. It all depended on luck and just how civilized the people we rolled with were—and whether they had any Taliban or Al Qaeda sympathies. We hoped we wouldn't be in the position of needing to seek sanctuary, but it was reassuring to know it was there.

We headed southwest on Ring Road, unchartered territory for both of us. I had been to Herat by air, but this was my first ground run there. We distanced our vehicles and used my B-6 as a Rabbit, while maintaining line-of-sight and comms.

The first vehicle in front of the stick was the rabbit, also known as the point man. They distracted the main enemy firing arc towards the vehicle as the convoy moved forward. When the point man/rabbit took fire from the left or right side, then the following vehicle in the convoy instantly cleared those flanks. They offered real-time information of where the enemy was located and how many we were facing.

We weren't twenty minutes outside of Kandahar when a battle between the Taliban Militia and Big Army broke out to our south. We heard talking guns going off intermittently (mostly .50 Cal and 240 Bravos) and a lot of dust was stirred up by Mine Resistant Ambush Protected movements.

The two gunners were shitting their pants. They wanted to keep low, but we needed extras eyes on top, so I radioed Chase to stay frosty. He told me he was scared shitless.

"You wouldn't be human if you weren't," I said.

I had trained him in Iraq. He had a lot of confidence in me because of my background as a Recon Marine. I trusted him. He was a good paramedic. We rolled past Kandahar Province toward Helmand Province. I radioed back to him to mark a rally point near FOB Ramrod on his GPS. It was literally in the middle of nowhere, so if we needed to seek cover on future missions, it would be ideal.

The base was initially established, secured, and named by the 2nd Battalion, 2nd Infantry "Ramrods" in 2008. Located in Maywand District, Kandahar Province, just to the left of Ring Road, several thousand US Army soldiers were stationed there.

Ramrod became famous after making the news in 2010. A group of infantry soldiers called the "Kill Team" targeted innocent civilians and Afghan farmers in an attempt to make it look like a battle between the Army and the Taliban.

In May 2010, the military launched an investigation into the alleged use of hashish by members of Bravo Company of the 2nd Battalion, 1st Infantry Regiment. The 5th Brigade, 2nd Infantry Division uncovered what appeared to be a murder conspiracy ring. Five soldiers, aka the "Kill Team," were charged with deliberately targeting innocent civilians and killing them for sport. Body parts of the victims, such as finger bones and a skull, had been collected as war trophies.

This was the furthest thing from a "hearts and minds" campaign. The US military was passive/aggressive in their approach to defeating the Taliban. They wanted to end the war but didn't want to make additional enemies in the process. Damage to local relations was irreparable. Yet here we were.

We stopped in Farah. At the start of the Soviet invasion in December 1979, Farah was occupied by the Soviet 357th and the 66th Motorized Rifle Divisions. In 1982, the Russians established a base there to force out the Mujahideen, who had settled in the Farah area before them. The camp was turned into a patrol base, but it looked desolate and abandoned.

I entered the dilapidated fort alone. My buddy from MARSOC was supposed to be there. He wasn't. The only information I got was about a recent attack that had occurred near Delaram. We passed the remnants of that battle on the way to Farah. There was nothing we could do but press on.

All along the road, there was evidence of Taliban attacks

everywhere. Blown out bridges, burnt buses, tankers, and box trucks were scattered all over the place. Along some of the mountain beds were white-marked acres of landmines that had been previously located by EOD clearing teams.

A huge FOB called Bastion had completed road sweeps using R-2s, Mine Rollers, Buffalos, and MRAPs. The R-2s looked like converted construction graters. They had a single- man cab and a big cone-shaped blower on the front to clear debris in order to reveal exposed wires, roadside bombs, or other IED indicators.

When the Army cleared a road, the R-2s always pushed out front. Next, sapper engineers drove MRAPs with huge mine rollers. They tripped any anti-tank mines or could dismantle or blow-in-place any IEDs they found on the road. They were followed by Buffalos—MRAPs equipped with a huge articulating boom and grabber. Lastly, Hunter/Killers took up the rear.

Infantry dismounted from these MRAPs to provide security for the sappers. They also had to hunt down any Taliban that had initiated the attack.

In 2005, Bastion was the logistics hub for ISAF operations in Helmand Province. It accommodated over 32,000 people. However, from early 2006, personnel from the 39th Engineer Regiment, Royal Engineers, and various contracting firms, all under the supervision of the 62nd Works Group Royal Engineers, started to build the base with more robust facilities. The camp was four miles long and two miles wide. It had a busy airfield and a field hospital. It was situated in a remote desert area, far from population centers. Aside from the Brits, FOB Bastion was also home to Camp Leatherneck. Go Marines!

After Bastion, there wasn't much activity, only scenic countryside with mountain ranges in the backdrop, rich with iron. It was hard to believe that so much destruction could occur in a place so beautiful. It was also amazing that such a mineral-rich region was not properly managed to extract all that potential wealth. Such an enterprise, when properly conducted, could rapidly raise the standard of living for the people.

But then again, Afghanistan was one of those nations that had great natural resources and economic potential, but was unfortunately mismanaged and neglected due to the corruption of local and political leaders.

Once again, tribalism ruled.

It took us several hours before reaching Herat, but we made it there safely. We stopped in at Camp Arena, located next to the Herat Airport.

Camp Arena hosted up to 900 Italian officers and soldiers. We wanted to look up another buddy of ours whom we both worked with on the Shark Teams in Baghdad, Iraq. Bob Murray was staying on a remote training center running the Role II Enhanced Support Program for DynCorp International, as the training coordinator.

Bob had several connections on the Italian base that benefitted SOC—supplies, intel sources, and contacts for safe-havens throughout the area of operation. We sat for a while and caught up on old times, then departed to the Herat Hotel to plan for our future mission objectives to support DGI.

The Italians must have consumed a lot of booze because they had a huge PX that sold plenty of alcohol. They also had a bad reputation for paying protection money to the Taliban, so they wouldn't be attacked.

This was later confirmed when Mohammed Ishmayel, a Taliban commander, said a deal had been struck to guarantee that Italian forces would not be attacked in Herat. Afghan officials added they were aware of the protection payments being issued on behalf of Italian forces in Pakistan, as well. The protection payments came to light in August 2008, after the death of ten French soldiers, at the hands of the Taliban in the region.

The French had taken over the district from Italian troops thinking the area was quiet and safe. They were unaware of the alleged secret payments meant to stop attacks on their forces.

Ishmayel stated that under the deal it was agreed that "...neither side should attack one another. That is why we were informed at that time, that we should not attack NATO troops."

When the Italian forces left the area, the insurgents were not informed. They thought the Italians had broken the deal. Attacks increased. When the Italians returned, the attacks subsided. Every time the payments stopped the attacks increased.

This pattern affected the Pony Express because we also ran supplies on Ring Road. If the Taliban were not attacking NATO troops, *The Pony Express* now became the primary target.

An October 2009 article published in *Time* Magazine brought our dilemma to light.

> To supply nearly 100,000 troops in Afghanistan, the U.S. and its Western allies rely on road convoys with dozens of trucks to carry in everything from jet fuel to frozen pizza. But increasingly, these convoys are coming under savage attack by the Taliban. Experts say that if the ambushes get worse, it could impair NATO's efforts to keep a supply lifeline running to its troops in forts and camps scattered across the mountainous country. Often, the death of a private security contractor in Afghanistan goes unheralded; after all, they risk their lives for money, not country. Yet the drivers and guards who ride shotgun on the long convoys snaking over the mountains also suffer heavy casualties. Many have died heroically. Figures released to TIME by NATO showed that from June to September 2009 more than 145 truck drivers and guards were killed in attacks on convoys and 123 vehicles were destroyed.

Reaching the hotel in Herat was a miracle unto itself. We knew how lucky—how damn fortunate—we were.

Even though it was a welcomed place to stay, two stars above the Kandahar Hotel with great food and service, we couldn't let our guard down. But we took time to decompress and refocus.

We dropped off our gear in the rooms and went over the

details of our next mission.

Since we would be going off-grid in uncharted territory, I googled an aerial map of Torghundi and the surrounding area to get a feel for the terrain.

The map I used to navigate our solo run to Herat was laminated so it allowed me to mark rally points and MEDEVAC locations with a grease pencil using my Garmin GPS Unit. I later placed it in my footlocker for future reference—and as a memento of our perilous journeys.

This was the life we chose, the routes we ran. All along the Taliban stronghold.

CHAPTER TWENTY-FIVE
Herat
DATE: November 05, 2009
MISSION: PSD for DGI clients
LOCATION: Torghundi, Herat Province

We were tasked with running a mission to Torghundi, the second border checkpoint and crossing between Afghanistan and neighboring Turkmenistan. The mission was for DGI to search out old Russian well-heads that had been placed during the Soviet occupation. They needed to determine their precise location and whether or not the well-heads were functional for the purpose of reestablishing natural resources to the country.

We set up operations at the Herat Hotel, which was positioned on a hillside overlooking the city. Herat was the third-largest city in the northern part of Afghanistan, with a population of 436,000. The violence level was low. Growing and cultivating crops other than poppy, like wheat and saffron, helped stimulate the economy. It was linked to Mazar-i-Sharif, Kabul, and Kandahar via Ring Road.

The Russians had intentionally marked the location of the well-heads off-grid by twenty kilometers in any direction. We relied on information gathered by the village elders in the region about the whereabouts of each well. DGI engineers explained that there was a possibility that some of the well-heads were still active.

Aside from a strategic geographical location, one of the other reasons the Soviets' invaded Afghanistan was to capitalize upon and exploit the country's rich natural resources. Digging the wells afforded Soviet troops watering holes along the various routes when water tankers were not available. As far as locating these wells, it was our job to provide escort and close protection for the operation.

We had been to several locations, some of which were not passable by vehicle. Grazing and agricultural land, irrigation systems, residential areas, roads, and footpaths, in both urban and rural areas, were all danger zones until cleared by Explosive Ordnance Disposal teams.

Russian forces based in Tajikistan also mined the Tajik-Afghan border where most of the well-head sites were located. A plethora of landmines had been planted indiscriminately over most of the isolated areas.

Mines were used in all phases of the Afghan conflict—during the Soviet occupation, during the power struggle between Mujahideen commanders after the Soviet withdrawal, and during the fighting between Taliban forces and other Afghan commanders. Despite the reasons, our job was amplified to include battle area reconnaissance and landmine avoidance. The fun never ended.

Surviving a mine strike wasn't about ending up alive or dead. The amount of misery involved was staggering and long lasting. We'd seen firsthand what a mine strike did. It was devastating.

It started with the shock of the explosion, which meant a guy felt nothing for a few minutes, and then pain flooded over his body. The wait for help took forever. Lying in a minefield losing blood, the sight of shattered and jagged bones stuck out from the end of his legs. Horror and fear were evident on his teammates' faces as they tried to keep him alive. He wondered whether he would live or die. The journey to a hospital in a helicopter, or gun truck, or over somebody's shoulders warped reality. They arrived at the hospital where there may or may not be a surgeon available to treat the injury.

Then there was the scramble to raise money for an operation. The difficult task of cleaning the wounds of dirt, shrapnel, and bone made him scream or pass out. Then likely amputation. The aftershocks: the good chance that the amputation was not done properly, leaving sharp pieces of bone pushing into the stump, the lack of physiotherapy, the possibility of infection, the phantom pains following the amputation.

A second operation might be required to recut the bone in order to make it suitable for a prosthesis. But the nightmarish spiral could continue. There was the lack of mobility of a wheelchair or prosthesis; the impossibility of a disabled person finding a job; the shame of being a burden to family and community; the reduced likelihood of marriage and children.

I could go on and on. It was worse for our Afghan counterparts. Still, being in a foreign country didn't make it any easier for expats.

Having landmines on the brain was bad enough. The movement was slow, but that was to be expected. We were out on foot in Torghundi. We walked the village perimeter looking for any signs of a well-head, valve, or mechanical structure.

Anything that seemed out of place, considering the terrain and location, was a danger indicator. We were doing a grid search when we crept up on an adobe hut. I was off to the left and Cookie was about twenty-five meters to the right. All of a sudden, a huge Afghan fighting dog charged at Chase. He raised his weapon to shoot.

I thought, "Oh shit!"

And suddenly, the dog stopped in mid-attack, only a foot away.

Chase stood his ground. The dog turned around and headed back toward the hut. From where I was standing, the hair on the dog's back stood straight up. Cookie whispered on his portable, "Good job, Chase."

If he had pulled the trigger, he would've killed the dog, but it also would've made for a very bad day with the locals. The team had just established a good working relationship with the village elders. Thankfully, Chase was able to shake it off after a few minutes. Nothing like an attack dog coming for your throat at full speed.

After Torghundi, DGI subcontracted SOC on a more detailed scope of work. Several times we had to split missions up and run solo, with only two vehicle teams. Twice we had been back and forth to Herat and both times we ran screwed up missions. Our gun trucks took a beating too, since the well-heads were so isolated. The terrain was too rough for the heavy bullet magnets. We must've had to change half a dozen flat tires and got pretty good at it before it was decided to put an aerial operation together at DGI's request.

I flew back to Kabul and Cookie was instructed to bring the team and equipment and meet me there for much-needed maintenance. When they arrived at the villa, Cookie was sicker than a dog. Chase treated him for exposure to E. coli the night before. He started an IV with a Banana Bag, which contained fluids with vitamins and minerals, and gave him anti-emetics.

The bags typically contain thiamine, folic acid, and magnesium sulfate. They were usually used to correct nutritional deficiencies or chemical imbalances in the human body. The solution had a yellow color, hence the term "banana bag."

Cookie kept taking Imodium AD, but Chase told him not to. He wanted the disease to run its course, but Cookie wouldn't listen. The next day, Cookie was trashed. He had been up all night, puking his guts out, and didn't get any sleep. Chase gave him 25mg Phenergan IM for the trip and he slept in the back of the lead gun truck. It was not easily accomplished, as the eight-ton gun trucks rattled, bumped, and banged with every dip, pothole, and speed bump on the road.

Chase had the drivers dominate the center of the roadway in case the Sappers hadn't cleared the route. When the team reached Kandahar, Cookie felt better and took back command. They decided to push the rest of the way to the villa but stopped in Ghazni for fuel and a quick break. They made it back to Kabul intact just after midnight.

Although not official, Cookie's team was the first to make the run from Herat to Kabul in one trip. It was later dubbed the "1000 Kilometer Club." Technically, the distance was 883 kilometers. We racked up the odometer by going off-road, taking detours to bypass blown out bridges and avoiding hot spots, and making fuel stops along the way.

DGI seemed impressed. The guys were tasked with preparing a brief for the client that would address the well-head operations in the Herat Province. We wanted to develop the best course of action to ensure we sealed the contract.

Chase handled all the med stuff, Cookie took care of communications, and Matty provided the intel. Phil and Ryan Buytenhuys put together a PowerPoint presentation that included an aerial insert into the area of operation, and the total proposed operation. Jon coordinated their efforts.

I was glad that we were doing a presentation because it was a foot in the door for SOC, which meant a longer deployment. DGI came to fruition, but the aerial mission was scrapped due to budget restraints. SOC ate the brunt of the costs because of all the damage the gun trucks sustained off-road. The terrain was just too rough. A lot of missions were conducted on foot with no line of sight and minimal communications. Outside of delivering cargo, some of the *Pony Express* members conducted missions on horseback giving authenticity to the name, but only for recon purposes and close protection for the client

After DGI, Cookie and Chase picked up a mission to deliver supplies to FOB Delhi, a military expeditionary base occupied by the Marine Corps. Situated along the Helmand River Valley in Garmsir, just south of Lashkar Gah, the base was an old abandoned agricultural college building.

Again, we put Chase out front. This time he was comfortable and in control. Running command previously must have boosted his confidence. He was starting to enjoy the thrill.

War is gruesome and fascinating at the same time. According to Generation Kill, combat could be fun. As distasteful as that sounds, it's also true. Surviving a battle without injury was an adrenalin rush and it made us feel more than alive. What often followed was the thought that we wouldn't feel that alive again.

For Chase, it was simultaneously horrifying and thrilling. That's what made it so deceptive. For those of us who went to war, it was a peak experience. Nothing compares to shooting at the enemy and cheating death.

The road splintered off from the main route and turned into a narrow, elevated strip of asphalt and gravel. Blown up vehicles, rigs, fuel trucks, buses, and whole convoys were flipped onto their backs the entire route. The team only had one option: stay center. They must have both thought they were on a one-way mission to hell. Pictures that Chase came back with showed massive destruction everywhere.

Upon arrival, Cookie noticed one of the cargo trucks had a fresh set of bullet holes on both sides, but no one ever heard any SAF contact during the short hop. He asked the terp to speak to the cargo driver, but the Indian didn't have a clue. He just kept shrugging his shoulders and looking at all the holes in his truck. The team dropped the load and headed back. They just wanted to get the hell out of there while there was still daylight. They made one more drop in Kandahar, and then were instructed to head back to Kabul. More personnel were arriving. It looked like it was going to be one hell of a cluster fuck.

CHAPTER TWENTY-SIX
Selous Scout

Maybe they didn't know about the bad food and the menu of sicknesses that awaited them. Maybe they knew and didn't care. Maybe they needed the money. Either way, more team guys arrived, including Raffaele Di Giorgio (aka Max), John Pickett (aka Buddha), and Big Dan. Then there was Andy Langley, a Vietnam-era-veteran Marine, who had also deployed to Afghanistan during the Russian occupation back in 1985 and worked in El Salvador. He was a former Rhodesian Special Air Service and a Selous Scout.

The Selous Scouts were a counter-insurgency unit that functioned as a combat reconnaissance force, an entirely volunteer force. Their mission was to infiltrate Rhodesia's tribal population and guerrilla networks, pinpoint rebel groups, and to relay vital information back to the conventional forces earmarked to carry out the actual attacks. Members of the regiment were trained to operate in small undercover, clandestine teams, capable of working independently in the bush for weeks at a time, even passing themselves off as rebels.

Despite their reputation, they had the best kill to loss ratio and mission success rate of any special operations unit in history.

In Afghanistan, Andy's team had trained insurgent groups known collectively as the Mujahideen. During the Soviet occupation, the Mujahideen were backed primarily by the United States and Pakistan, making it a cold war. At the time, the CIA played a significant role in asserting US influence in Afghanistan by funding military operations designed to frustrate the Soviet invasion, from 1979 to 1989. Code-name: *Operation Cyclone.*

Considered one of the top five pistol shooters in the world,

Andy had a one-of-a-kind personality and was liked by everyone. Since Racer Dave was still in Minden and Money was on leave, Andy drove for Chase on the next set of missions to Khost. He helped Chase improve his shooting skills with extra range time. Chase was grateful Andy took him under his wing. I guess they got along pretty-well together since they were both older than dirt.

Andy was a walking encyclopedia and a welcomed addition to the teams. Everyone tapped into the resources and experiences he had to offer, and Andy had no problems sharing his knowledge. If we weren't actively training, just riding with him on a mission was a huge benefit. The lessons never ended, and he brought an air of confidence that only served to bolster the teams. We all felt safer when he was there and our skills improved even more.

Then we were slammed with another mission. By then, we had made a name for ourselves and SOC wasn't messing around. Andy's Selous Scout training and knowledge helped us establish a solid reputation. We left a bigger footprint with each mission. But with that came unwanted attention. The Taliban painted a larger target on our backs and put a bigger bounty on our heads.

CHAPTER TWENTY-SEVEN
The Four Horsemen
DATE: November 14, 2009
MISSION: RTB Kabul
LOCATION: Helmand Province

Although we had crossed paths with a group of Afghan contractors known as The Four Horsemen before, we never expected to try and negotiate an alliance with them in the middle of Taliban country.

As Chase kept getting more experience on Ring Road, and with a new veteran trainer on board, management began to use him on more missions. He was teamed up with Saso as his driver. Even though Chase hated driving with him because he always did weird shit, they got the job done.

They made a couple of runs with Ryan Buytenhuys as an augmentee. Ryan was a welcome addition, another Marine badass who liked mixing it up. He stood about 6 foot 5, was heavy into Muay Thai kickboxing and would square off with anyone, under any circumstances. Ryan liked to use a B-6 as a rabbit because it was powerful and could maneuver easily, pushing out front to recon the route and communicate any threats.

Once, on the way to RTB Kabul, they stopped for fuel at the intersection of Ring Road and Lash. It was a hole-in-the-wall haji shop that was lit up with neon signs. It had a quick mart and a souvenir store that sold chai. It even had semi-clean restrooms. The weirdest thing about it was that it sat in the middle of no man's land, miles from anywhere.

Ryan spotted The Four Horsemen sitting near the coffee shop.

The Four Horsemen were a local convoy security company (FHI) that ran 100 to 200 truck convoys back and forth between

Herat and Kabul. Running 100 trucks with Turkish and Punjabi drivers who were always high from smoking *khat,* a substance similar to peyote, and was probably about as safe as having Stevie Wonder drive a taxi. Moving their convoys was like nailing Jell-O to a goat.

Despite overwhelming losses of trucks and manpower, they somehow got the job done.

The Four Horsemen rolled heavy. They ran in a mixture of soft-skin SUVs with four men per truck. Some had pillboxes mounted in the truck beds, with crew-served weapons, AK-47s, PKMs, RPG 5s/7s, and Dishkas. The DShK was a Soviet heavy machine gun that fired a 12.7×108mm cartridge. It is often described as the Russian version of the M2 Browning .50 caliber, or "Ma Deuce."

Almost every major conflict that pitted Soviet proxies against Western allies involved the DShK. Asian, Middle Eastern, and Eastern European militaries were well-stocked with this powerful machine gun. Guerillas and terrorists across four continents, including the Afghan Mujahideen, found it indispensable against vehicles, armor, and even aircraft.

Ryan, Chase, and Ali, their terp, walked over to the Afghans and talked to the team leader, Majid. Ryan had Ali translate and ask Majid if he knew who we were.

The man nodded in response. He said something to Ali and a half dozen of his guys behind him began to laugh out loud.

Ali translated what Majid said: "We are the crazy Americans with big balls and little dicks who drove the Ring."

Majid leaned forward, kicked at the dirt, and asked what we wanted. Ryan said, "We've seen you come under attack by the Taliban. We know your guys have suffered casualties. We wanted to let you know that if we're in the area and the Four Horsemen are in trouble, we will help you out whenever we can."

He pointed to Chase and introduced him as a doctor.

Majid looked at him, then showed him a huge scar on his arm.

Apparently, the injury was from a recent attack. The arm was previously bandaged but in poor fashion. The wound had developed a serious infection.

Ryan told Chase, "Take a look and see what you can do." Ryan was hoping to create some goodwill between the two groups.

Chase nodded and whipped out some med-kit. He cleaned and redressed the wound, nodding to Majid when he finished.

Ryan's objective was to get the Four Horsemen to verbally commit to providing some backup in terms of weapons and manpower, should we find ourselves in the same predicament. We didn't have access to RPGs or Dishkas. That kind of firepower could turn the tide in a battle. Majid agreed, and everyone went their separate ways.

Trusting the wrong person in this line of work was a deadly business, and those we could trust we held close. SOC and FHI continued to get attacked, but nothing ever occurred when either of us were in close proximity with The Four Horsemen.

In the military, especially in grunt units, we often discussed the most morbid, absurd, and completely illogical situations during our downtime. With us contractors, it was no different. Our circumstances and experiences, as well as the information we gathered from other groups, stirred our imaginations—and made us even more aware of our environment. Since security firms were widely despised in Afghanistan, they were often blamed for fueling corruption and behaving with impunity, especially when their activities got out of hand.

Those events occurred more often than we would have liked and gave us more fodder for discussion about the "what ifs" in our world.

When we talked about The Four Horsemen, we talked about murder. In May 2009, an Australian killed one of the team leaders when he was called to assist a convoy that had been attacked. The shooter was allegedly drinking heavily and smoking hashish in a Kabul bar while assigned to QRF. When he arrived at the scene of the first attack, he ordered the convoy to move onward. The Afghan team leader refused, saying it was too dangerous. A violent argument ensued, and the Australian shot the team leader four times in the chest.

To cover up his crime, he threw a grenade into the truck containing the team leader's body. He then ordered two guards to fire bullets into the side of it, to fake a Taliban attack.

A Nepalese guard reported the shooting to Afghan police after the convoy returned to Kabul. The Australian immediately went to his bank and withdrew all his money. He was about to board a flight for Dubai when Afghan police officers arrested him. The shooter originally pleaded not guilty on grounds of diminished capacity. In court, he claimed he fired in self-defense.

In the end, he admitted to the brutal murder of his Afghan colleague and was sentenced to death. The sentence was changed to twenty years after he agreed to pay the family $100,000 USD. Under Afghan law, if the family of the victim agrees, the family of a murderer can pay compensation, known in Sharia law as "ibra" or blood money, to avert the death penalty.

I've said it before, and I'll say it again. Money talks.

Even after such a payment, the accused normally remained in prison. The Australian began serving his time in Afghanistan's notorious Poli Charki prison,

It was shit like that which gave guys like us a bad name. It didn't matter how good our intentions were, or the level of professionalism we displayed on or off duty. The general consensus was that all foreigners were dirtbags.

At SOC, we never treated anyone badly who didn't have it coming. We complied with all ROEs and legitimately established checkpoints by ANP and Army personnel. We were respectful to village elders, local national guardsmen, and other foreign military personnel. We treated the indigenous population of Afghanistan with kid gloves.

As long as no one messed with us or tried anything stupid, we got along fine. I remembered a quote from Sonny Barger, an old biker and founder the Hells Angels. "Treat us good, we'll treat you better. Treat us bad and we'll treat you worse."

Yet, there were certain procedures we came to expect. Checkpoints that were established on the entrance to city and town limits near border crossings were the norm. If we ran across a checkpoint set up in the middle of nowhere, or near an area that had recent signs of enemy engagement, then we became suspicious. Understaffed checkpoints, or those staffed with Afghans in partial or makeshift uniforms were suspect, and we never stopped for them.

It was like that in Somalia where warlords sent their militias out, usually kids barely taller than the AK-47s they carried, to set up a hastily made half-assed checkpoint. They stopped the food relief trucks and demanded a "passage payment" or they wouldn't be allowed to continue. When Americans showed up in 1985 and again in 1992-93 to cover relief operations, such payments stopped for the most part.

What also separated us from other security contractors was the fact that we never shot at anyone who didn't shoot at us first. Admittedly, we had assholes that worked for SOC, but they didn't last long on *The Pony Express*. We wouldn't tolerate rude behavior or repetitive mistakes. Everything was handled in house. If someone got out of line, we took care of it immediately.

There were no second chances.

The Four Horsemen were stand up guys for security contractors. We had more respect for the Afghan gunners of The Four Horsemen than we did for the operators who controlled them.

Those guys took the same risk, but only got paid a fraction of the money. I knew of one of their gunners who claimed he worked for the company for four years and only got paid $400 a month.

Four hundred dollars for risking his life. Granted, that was a lot of coin for an LN gunner, but we all understood the equation.

We had to ask ourselves, "How much is our life worth?" If we were willing to risk our lives, we were forever grateful for alliances like the one we had with The Four Horsemen.

CHAPTER TWENTY-EIGHT
Operational Security

How is the value of a life determined in a war-torn country? I suppose it depends on who is doing the killing, and who is doing the dying.

After the south runs were completed, the teams had a few days down time in Kabul.

Technically, there wasn't really any down time, as the guys were training, cleaning weapons, and conducting maintenance. Others were off gathering intel, picking up supplies, and prepping for the next mission. I was planning operations via Roshan or VOIP communications with Matty.

We made collective decisions based on weather, weapons, money, and miles.

Cookie's team was sent to Khost and this time, they were better prepared.

The problem with running any missions at SOC was Operational Security—OPSEC— keeping potential adversaries from discovering critical information. Success depended upon secrecy and surprise so the team could more quickly accomplish the mission. To minimize the risk, team leaders confiscated all the cell phones from the LN gunners and cargo drivers prior to the mission briefing.

SOC-A vetted their gunners, but to what extent could they be trusted? Was money the deciding factor? Was a job that paid better than the average Afghan wage good enough? Did the possibility of forced collusion with the Taliban and proxy insurgency exist? What would it take for a new hire to shift loyalties?

We had one gunner who used to work for the Taliban in the

Tora Bora region. When we asked about it, he said he liked working for us better, since we paid a lot more and paid on time. He proved his worth, especially on the Jalalabad runs, an area he was familiar with. The route was dynamic and fluid in how the Taliban conducted their ambushes.

Team IV with Matt McClure, aka "Samurai", experienced this firsthand. Matt was a Marine who served in the infantry with 2/1. He worked with me in 2008 at SOC on the Tetra Tech contract in Iraq, and then again with SOC on the Army Corps of Engineers PSD contract in Iraq from 2006-2008. He was well versed in both PSD and convoy operations.

They called him Samurai because he was raised in Okinawa, Japan, took Kendo, and was the quiet professional. Some of the team guys had watched the *Last Samurai* Starring Tom Cruise. When Matt was pushing out on a PSD mission, one of his teammates queued the radio and said, "There goes the last Samurai."

A senior UXO client overheard the comms and said, "That's what we're gonna call you from now on."

The first time Samurai got hit in Afghanistan was in the summer of 2010, in an ambush set up over several kilometers, all in the high ground. The steep angle made it impossible for the gunners to engage with their PKM machine guns, so they transitioned to their AK-47s to provide suppressive fire.

The nature of asymmetrical warfare meant tactics often changed. Like Marines, we had to improvise, adapt, and overcome.

The second time they were ambushed was in the fall of 2010. Team IV was moving to J-Bad when a vehicle swerved in front of the mail truck, and the mail truck flipped over on its side. Samurai immediately contacted the TOC and let them know what was going on. He cut the seals and began to transfer the mail from the downed mail truck to another mail truck.

The Taliban began to engage Team IV with small arms fire.

The team returned fire, suppressing the threat while trying to continue the cross load of mail. Samurai had to burn the downed mail truck because they weren't able to complete the mail transfer and the info could not fall into enemy hands.

They finished the mail run to FOB Fenty. On the return trip, the driver that caused the accident was still there complaining to the ANP, demanding money for the damages we supposedly caused. Samurai paid a fee to the ANP so they could get out of the valley.

This was typical of the corruption in Afghanistan. If foreigners were in the vicinity of an accident, the Afghans blamed the foreigners. The goal was to get more money.

One time, I bumped a vehicle on a run to Jalalabad. There was minor damage. The driver wanted $200, so I told him I would pay it, but first I was going to do $200 worth of damage to his vehicle, starting with his windshield.

We agreed on $20.

Another time, in the spring of 2011, Team III with Craig Smith was on the J-Bad run when they were ambushed on a hairpin turn near the bottom of the valley. The high ground on both sides of the road made them sitting ducks. An IED was the initiator followed by small arms fire and they downed one of the mail trucks.

Craig went to work to cross deck the mail as they returned fire on the ambush. I called and told him to burn the truck if he had to. He dropped in a couple of incendiary grenades and the team carried on. The ambush was over and they were moving again without the damaged truck.

Mr. Suleiman, an Afghan-Canadian businessman whose specialty was running trucks, contracted cargo vehicles and drivers out to various companies in Afghanistan. Unable to recover his truck, this mission was a bust and would cost him.

The Four Horsemen ran so many cargo trucks and tankers, the convoy length was one - two kilometers long. The guard force had to drive up and down the length of the stack to provide protection and maintain line-of-sight with the convoy. Sometimes they staged a vehicle at a certain point and watched as it passed, functioning as their own QRF whenever they found out a truck was hit. Losses were staggering. When that many vehicles were moved at a time, FHI must have considered the amount of cargo that was lost on Ring Road acceptable versus the amount that made it to the destination.

Most drivers were hired by Mr. Suleiman, who had a vested interest in SOC-A. A few were hired by Mr. Timor, but he was dirty. We never knew what to expect. Every time we used his guys, we got hit.

When Cookie's team pushed out, they made it through Logar without incident. Once, when they passed Qala Khan, Cookie noticed one of the cargo trucks swerving all over the road. He called "all stop" over the radio and the convoy pulled over to the side of the road.

Aside from being high on *khat,* the driver had a hidden cell phone on him. He was talking to someone while he was driving. The mission was compromised, and Cookie was pissed. He slapped the shit out of the lethargic driver to get his attention. He asked Chase to look him over for sobriety.

Chase reported his eyes were red, and he could barely stand up, let alone walk a straight line. According to the terp, his response to questions was inappropriate and incomprehensible. Cookie contacted the TOC and gave Matty an update. They made the decision to push forward.

The dumbass was probably high on a mixture of *khat* and hashish.

Khat or "African Salad" contained the alkaloid cathinone, an amphetamine-like stimulant. It caused agitation, loss of appetite, and euphoria. Found in countries like Yemen, Ethiopia, and Somalia, it was also prevalent in South Africa, Sudan, Kenya, Madagascar, and Afghanistan.

Among communities where the plant was native, *khat* chewing had a history as a social custom dating back thousands of years. A couple of hours after use, a person experienced depression, sluggishness, emotional instability, insomnia, and a lack of concentration.

One of the LN gunners jumped in to drive the cargo truck the rest of the way to the drop site. The other translator took up his position on the PKM to stay attached to Cookie's rig. The wasted driver was left standing on the side of the road, twenty miles from the middle of nowhere.

If Mr. Suleiman received a complaint about any of his drivers, they got shit-canned immediately. Mr. Timor relocated his drivers to different positions, which never really solved the problem of OPSEC.

As if Afghanistan wasn't dangerous enough, running a mission in the mountains bordering Pakistan with cargo drivers all juiced up on *khat* was putting our lives on the chopping block and risking our operational security. We were asking for trouble we couldn't afford to pay.

CHAPTER TWENTY-NINE
The Tera Pass
DATE: November 16, 2009
MISSION: Convoy Security for C-1 client to Camp Chapman
LOCATION: Khost Province

Fucked up drivers, ambushes, roadside bombs—Ring Road was its own treacherous reality. Missions to Gardez and Khost went through the Tera Pass. Some areas were much safer to drive through due to the expanse and isolation of the terrain. It put life into perspective when I realized how small we were in such a vast area.

The drive from Logar to the bottom of the Tera Pass took thirty minutes. While we never let our guard down, we had the opportunity to eat, drink, and prep for the trip to the top of the mountain ridge.

The Tera Pass crossed a rugged mountain ridge with nearby peaks topping out at 11,000 feet. The pass itself rose approximately 3,500 feet from the lowest part of Logar and descended approximately 2,000 feet into the Gardez river valley to the south. The pass received heavy snowfall during the winter months, often to the point of being impassable. Snow tended to persist into the summer months on the north-facing side of the mountain ridge.

The narrow road through the Tera Pass was under construction and barely wide enough for one truck. Driving was a bitch. Moving too close to the mountain meant getting a flat tire from sharp jagged rocks. Getting too close to the edge meant flirting with a 1,000-foot drop.

Despite the perils, I liked being in the mountains. They were strikingly beautiful. I considered going through the Pass, which ran south of the Hindu Kush and parallel to Mount Sikaram, a reprieve. As the sun rose, it was surreal to see such beauty in dark times. Afghanistan could be hypnotizing. If we weren't careful, the scenery could suck us in, and in the next moment, the ugly side of war reared its head.

Team II rolled past a small village on the left side of a hill that showed evidence of an earlier attack. Sure enough, a US Army convoy was hit the day before. Cookie called back, telling the team to stay frosty.

Adobe huts were adorned with Hesco barriers, which indicated the military convoy had been ambushed. The Taliban had salvaged the spoils of that battle. They used the barriers to fortify their own mud huts. As our convoy turned the corner, a black hat stood up on a huge rock and leveled an RPG in our direction.

Cookie had just passed the rock, but before the Tango could fire the rocket, Andy took evasive action and swerved right, dropping into the riverbed. Chase yelled, "Contact!" but the radio mic didn't cue up, so no one heard the call.

He thought, *oh shit* and braced for impact. Adrenaline shot into his body. He became hyper-aware of their surroundings. All this went down in real-time, but it must have seemed like slow motion.

Chase tried to talk to Andy in a calm voice and prayed he wouldn't roll the vehicle. But the fear in his voice was readily evident. Andy said it scared the shit out of him too, but he was too seasoned to display any fear. Either that or he just didn't give a shit. They tried contacting the rest of the team to give them a heads up. Andy told Chase to track any movements and watch the perimeter for any signs of an attack.

It was definitely an adrenaline rush.

As luck would have it, the Tango ducked back undercover.

The team split. Cookie went on the high road and Chase took the low road. The road construction forced the rest of the team into the riverbed. They rode approximately eight kilometers to pass all the traffic jams of individual cargo trucks lined up for miles.

Things got worse when they hit the bottom of the pass. The rest of the road was completely shut down. The entire convoy lined up behind several bongos and cargo trucks moving about ten miles per hour. It took over an hour to drive the short distance.

Everyone was nervous about driving so slowly. We were an easy target and were very lucky that no one attacked us on that run.

Cookie and Chase arrived in the eastern Afghanistan city of Khost but were not allowed on FOB Chapman to drop their load. Located about ten miles northwest of the border with Pakistan, I knew security was tight, but thought the directive strange since Cookie had a secret security clearance. After an hour of trying to negotiate their way through the gate, they were still denied access and were instructed to leave the cargo outside the gate. The BW Cobras retrieved it.

A month after that mission, the CIA were hit hard by a suicide bomber-turned-triple-agent at the base.

Humam Khalil Abu-Mulal al-Balawi carried out the attack on December 30, 2009. Seven American CIA officers, an officer of Jordan's intelligence service, and an Afghan working as an interpreter for the CIA were killed when al-Balawi detonated a bomb sewn into a vest he was wearing. Six other American CIA officers and contractors were wounded. The bombing was the most lethal attack against the CIA in more than twenty-five years.

FOB Chapman forever became ingrained in all our memories. Why had they let that son- of-a-bitch on the base and not allow *The Pony Express* access? Trust no one.

I remembered the BW Cobras complaining that they were not allowed to search any client sources. I'm sure that directive was in writing, so it covered the BW Cobras when the bombing went down. I'm also pretty sure that after this incident, the policy was changed to allow for searches.

The team headed back to Logar but got lost just outside of Sedaq. Cookie was in the lead, but he was trying to navigate by memory and not GPS. The convoy drove straight for the border of Pakistan. There's really no clear crossing into Pakistan. The border is said to fluctuate about five to ten kilometers in either direction. This time, the Pakis set up their checkpoint just outside of Sedaq.

When the team approached the checkpoint, the Pakistan National Guard opened fire. Rounds just cleared over the team's lead gun truck. It was a good thing the top gunners didn't return fire. Cookie made a tight 180-degree turn and the team pushed their way back to the main road. The results could have been a disastrous international incident, but they got out safely.

On the return to Kabul, Team II got caught up in a huge traffic jam just prior to the Tera Pass, near a village called Serai. The trucks were 1,500 meters back behind a long column of cargo trucks who were jammed up on a curve overlooking a cliff.

Cookie ordered Chase to run up front to see what the holdup was. Chase saw a large convoy of ANA traveling in the opposite direction. The ANA commander was on foot, yelling at the convoy leader. The convoy leader was yelling at the mountain. The road was too narrow and there was no room for anyone to back out or pass them. The only thing to do was to have the ANA dismount, have the driver of each vehicle fold in their mirrors, and pass on the cliff-side of the curve.

It was a slow and painstaking process. All the expats knew it was an easy fix, but this was Afghanistan. Tera Pass tested us with many close calls on the treacherous twists and turns. That entire mission took a day more than planned because of all the delays.

That was the nature of the business: expect the worst and hope for the best.

CHAPTER THIRTY
Calling All Wives

No one wore wedding rings on deployment. For some, it was a symbolic act of temporary separation. For others it was a means of survival in case of capture and torture, still with the harder seasoned veterans, it was all about tactics, being able to quick draw, eliminating snags, etc.

After so many close calls, we needed a different reality check. But sometimes that left us even more vulnerable than the war zones.

We always talked about our wives, how much we loved them, how much we missed them, how beautiful they are, but we lived in a parallel universe. We could not communicate with them on a regular basis. We had internet access while in Kabul, but when we ran three-day missions, there was no time to e-mail, call, or write home. We thought about what it was like having our kids raised in absentia, but we had a job to do that was unforgiving.

The life of a contractor's wife couldn't be easy. It took a lot of love, patience, and understanding to deal with the traumatic psychological impact of war that we brought home.

Hindsight is twenty-twenty. We could have done a better job of communicating with our wives, considering everything they had to deal with. Maybe put ourselves in their shoes.

I met my wife, Toni, while still in the Marine Corps. We dated for about a year before we got married in 2003, right after Operation Iraqi Freedom. We were married for nine years, which surprised me, because I was contracting during the most dangerous times in Iraq and Afghanistan. She knew the dangers of the job and the risks involved. I was always honest with her about whenever we got hit or lost some guys from all the attacks and ambushes. But she never asked me to quit or give it up. But for seven of those nine years, I was gone, and we drifted apart. We ended up getting divorced in 2012.

Money's wife Brenda knew what he was doing, but she never fully understood the dangers involved until Money got hurt. She worried about him more after that, but distance and lack of communication drove a wedge between them. At home, Money kept things bottled up, and that didn't help matters. Money and Brenda stayed together, but not without having to work through a lot of problems.

With Chase, his wife Janie always worried about him. She could tell when Chase tried to downplay his role on the teams. She watched the news intently, listening for events in Kabul or anywhere in Afghanistan, just to get a feel for what was going on. If she didn't get any calls or e-mails from him after a couple of days, she began to freak out. She held it together for the sake of their three kids. That might have led to the strain between them. Janie was the disciplinarian, the father figure, and mentor to their teenage son, Keenan.

Some guys never told their wives anything. They figured the less they knew, the better off everyone was. Big Dan said if his wife knew what he was up to, she would've had him pop smoke in a heartbeat. They talked quite a bit, but Big Dan never let on to the dangers of the road. He always kept things to a bare minimum, discussing the weather, how the food sucked and how the gym was rudimentary.

Ryan Bennett wasn't married but he had a daughter named Karina who lived with her mother and grandmother while he was deployed. She was ten at the time and knew nothing of his exploits. It wasn't until she was older that she learned of the dangers of the job. When she told Ryan she wanted him to quit contracting so she could live with him, he did. Karina was his world. He would've done anything to make her happy.

One of the other guys wasn't married, but his girlfriend was always inquisitive. She wanted to know everything up to and including mission specs, timings, routes, and more. The way she constantly asked for information, made her look like a damn spy for the Taliban. He knew better and always skirted the questions, but the more evasive he was, the more she pressed him for answers. It seemed like she didn't believe what he was telling her, so he quit calling her altogether.

Cookie's wife, now ex (his third) was a Belgian national. She also had that mentality. She loved him when he was gone, but they clashed when he was home. Being pushed away was one thing. It was another to be close to home while having something deep inside you driving you back to contracting.

Rector's wife Angela was astute. She knew he had a tough job. She was accustomed to him being gone for long periods since Rector had spent a great deal of time in Iraq. Rector avoided the heavy questions, especially when Angela received news of events in Afghanistan. She was probably on to his minimal responses, but eventually, his absence took a hard toll on their relationship. They argued over money, time, and distance, and lived two totally separate lives. Rector's own injuries were the proverbial straw that broke the camel's back. Two months later, Angela served him with divorce papers in the baggage claim section of the airport when he came home on leave.

Drew was another operator who had an exclusive relationship. He and his girlfriend Ashley married soon after his return from Afghanistan. Drew said she was somewhat aloof but not naïve. She knew of the common dangers of being in Afghanistan, but not to the extent of the classified missions of some of the contracts he was assigned to. Ashley and his mother hated that he was gone all the time but saw the truth when he showed them a video of one of his IED contacts. They're still together with a new family and living happily in Texas.

Jeff Bedford was in a common law relationship, but his wife wasn't his better half. She constantly complained about him being gone so much. The problem was that Jeff was a serious operator. He put his team first when deployed. He knew how to prioritize. It was tough for him to concentrate on the task at hand while having a she-devil on his shoulders compounding the situation, adding to the stress levels of the job. They split up. Eventually he met and dated a beautiful, more compatible girl named Charity.

Out of all the guys I worked with, I felt bad for Arnie Campbell the most. He was married to Yolande for five years before he found out from a neighbor that she was seeing someone else. He had no choice but to confront her over the phone. She didn't deny it. Instead, she blamed Arnie for being married to SOC. I think the only saving grace was their two beautiful daughters, Gabby and Xarya. They finally divorced in 2013, but Arnie maintained a civil relationship with Yolande and saw his girls as much as he could when he was not deployed.

Calling our loved ones could be a challenge. We had marginal access to the internet. With email, Skype, and other social media, it wasn't hard for us to contact them if we had a signal, but often when we tried to call home, we couldn't get through. I remember Chase tried calling home and had to climb on a rock on the side of a mountain about one hundred feet up just to get reception.

On the other end of the spectrum, it was damn near impossible for our loved ones to contact us. It was a tedious waiting game of fear, anxiety, worry, and doubt that we all accepted. We never realized the toll it took on our families over the years, until we finally returned home for good.

Whether we were married, had girlfriends or not wasn't the issue. Some guys just had the itch. Others couldn't deal with life back home. Some couldn't adapt to the two very different lives they straddled. But we had one thing in common: all of us were called to something bigger than ourselves. No matter the risk, the sacrifice or the toll it took on our loved ones, we were brothers on a mission. We had to ride *The Pony Express.* And prayed we'd make it home.

CHAPTER THIRTY-ONE
Clearance

Getting into Gardez was like pulling teeth. There was never an *expat* or soldier at the gate, so we sometimes waited outside the wire for hours while the team leader with security clearance dealt with the third country national static security guards. They never seemed to be able to make a decision on their own, even when they knew who we were

FOB Gardez was an American outpost/firebase near the city of Gardez, Afghanistan, in the Province of Paktia. Located near the Pakistan border, Gardez was a strange-looking city. The modernized buildings stood unoccupied. The building centers were hollowed out by bombing sorties flown earlier in the war.

The firebase was one of the first Taliban strongholds taken over by US Special Forces. It was rumored that the 9/11 attacks were planned with Osama bin Laden present in one of the qalats located on the FOB.

An Afghan cemetery sat in the center of the base. The unique feature was sacred ground and—one of the reasons the FOB had only been attacked once in five years. Before that, the base was hit by indirect fire.

The rocket had landed in the cemetery, destroying several graves and tombs of a tribesman's family buried there.

The tribesman who owned the land was very angry. He found the perpetrators and had them beheaded. There were no attacks after that.

At SOC, we respected the cemetery by driving around it and not letting our teams go near it. It was like the Indian burial grounds seen in westerns. If anyone trespassed, they tempted fate and trouble followed.

The need to access military FOBs and the need for clearance was brought up several times. All expats needed to have security clearance in case something happened to the team leader while on mission. The Assistant Team Leader or medic would need to push into the FOB.

Since SOC had secured the contract with DGI, one of the other requirements for deployment was US citizenship. Chase was Canadian, and that brought a slew of headaches.

One day, Rector confronted Chase. "My office. Now."

Chase followed him inside and inwardly strove to control his reaction to whatever the man was about to say. He was completely unprepared for what happened next.

"You need to provide a urine and blood sample," Rector informed him.

Chase's head snapped up and he looked at the man in disbelief. "The hell I do. What for?"

Rector folded his arms across his chest and looked at him smugly. "Because you're juicing, and you know it's against the rules."

Chase had been working out really hard, had gained some weight, and looked physically more muscular than when I had seen him last in 2008.

Chase shook his head and argued, "No way. First, I'm not juicing. Secondly, any sample I provided would be invalid."

"Not true. I'll see that it gets sent off to the right place," Rector fired back.

"And where is that? We don't have the right equipment here to test samples on-site, nor do we have proper chain of custody set up for those types of samples."

"You let me worry about that."

"Not likely. Are you asking everyone else to provide the same samples?"

"We're not talking about everyone else. We're talking about you.

Chase grew furious. "What you're asking me to do is unfair and you know it." Chase felt he was being singled out. He had a valid point. Some steroids can remain in the system for up to eighteen months. There really wasn't a way to prove or disprove whether he was actively using steroids.

After leaving Rector's office, he told me what had occurred. "I'm telling you, Rector wants me gone."

"Well, you can't be pushed out for refusing to do his test, and there's not a clear policy on the use of steroids," I told him. "Illegal drugs, yes. Steroids...that's still a gray area."

I figured something was up from the beginning. Money told Chase to watch his back as soon as other folks got to Afghanistan. Rector was on his shit about everything. He told Chase that he couldn't purchase any Red Bull from the op funds. He tried setting him up on the juice issue, and he even got on his shit about Dragon and Saso getting drunk in Herat. Regardless of my input, there was nothing I could do. I really felt sorry for him.

Chase's assessment that Rector wanted him gone proved to be true. With Chase's Canadian citizenship, he pulled the secret clearance card. The highest clearance he could get was a Medium Risk Public Trust (MRPT) clearance.

Chase's contract was terminated because he couldn't obtain a security clearance. I don't think it would have mattered because Rector was all about business. He would've found a reason to kick Chase off the teams.

Rector offered him an option to stay on board, but he would have to move to a shooter/driver slot and take a huge drop in pay, equivalent to what the Serbians and Macedonians were getting paid. He would also be stripped of the team medic position.

How messed up was that?

Shortly after running a few more missions with Cookie, John Pickett-call sign Buddha— arrived in country to take the torch from Chase. They did a quick left-seat/right-seat transition and Chase was sent packing.

According to Rector, it wasn't personal, it was just business and despite their differences, they were brothers, although distant. I have no doubt that if the shit hit the fan, Chase would have Rector's back and vice versa. It always came down to tribe mentality.

Chase was missed. A lot of guys were sad to see him go. He was a damn fine medic, but he would eventually return to *The Pony Express* in the summer of 2012.

I preferred working with guys like Buddha and Chase because they maintained their skills on a regular basis. Chase cut his teeth working 911 in Oakland, California. Hell, they used to call that place the knife and gun club back in the day.

The other issue was the security clearance, although the argument about obtaining or needing one was a moot point. It didn't make the contractor a better operator, nor did it make the client any safer. Special Operations did not make a Security Specialist.

Many unsavory incidents in Iraq and Afghanistan were committed by security contractors with clearances. A BW operator killed Raheem Khalif, a security guard of Iraqi Vice President Adel Abdul Mahdi. The armorer was a former Ranger with the 82nd Airborne Division of the United States Army. Many Armor Group guys who were vetted to provide security and close protection at the US Embassy in Afghanistan failed. Fourteen operators were fired for misbehavior.

It must have sucked for Chase to be singled out over a freaking piece of paper. No matter, it was over, and Chase was fortunate enough to still be working. Instead of going home, he picked up a gig in Basrah, Iraq with Unity Resources Group (URG) as an Assistant Team Leader/Medic. URG was contracted to provide close protection for RONCO, who was tasked with mine-clearing operations in Majnoon, Iraq on the Iranian border.

The one thing that has proven true throughout the ages, politically minded decisions and considerations were not always conducive to effective military or security operations. It was similar to a ground controller in a tower telling a pilot of an aircraft what to do from thousands of miles away while ignoring the screen visual that he may have in real-time.

Micromanagement of field operations from the safety of a well-insulated building far away was not practical. In fact, it proved deadly. The division of duties could be simplified: issue the op order, trust team leaders to fulfill the mission, have team leaders submit the after-action report. They needed insight from the field. They needed us for security clearance and intel.

Chase's experience was not uncommon...in Afghanistan. It seemed people got jobs and were promoted for no good reason and others lost jobs over the same. It all depended on who the "boss" was. There were no HR offices to register complaints. That's how it was in Afghanistan.

CHAPTER THIRTY-TWO
Dust-Off
DATE: November 18, 2009
MISSION: C-1 Convoy to Herat
LOCATION: Senjaray, Helmand Province

Picking up my new team brought new challenges. Everyone was anxious because this was our first run together, with me as the team leader. The men were solid. Among them was Dave Thomas, an Army veteran and sniper, and my Assistant Team Leader. Buddha, who had replaced Chase, was my medic. He was an Air Force veteran, former cop, and paramedic instructor.

Our first drop in Kandahar went smoothly. On the second day of the mission, the US Army was performing a cordon and search operation near a village called Senjaray on Ring Road. They had the road blocked. They directed us to take a detour through the village to the south by following a dirt road.

On the detour, Buddha and I looked for a safe path for the trucks to pass. We had just cleared the mud huts when Alex pulled the lead vehicle forward to turn around. As he was beginning the maneuver, the right rear tire of the gun truck hit a landmine.

The loud blast was deafening.

"Oh fuck!" I yelled and hit the dirt.

The explosion covered the rear of the gun truck. A huge cloud of dust and smoke rose instantly.

Buddha was in the ditch next to me. "You okay?" I shouted. He confirmed he was good.

A dopamine dump of adrenaline pushed me forward. I scanned the area thinking it was a complex attack. I geared up for the possibility of a firefight.

Nothing came. I was actually relieved that it was just a landmine with no secondaries. It made it easier for Buddha to take care of the injured.

Since Big Army was in the area, I knew we could link up with them for more support. We began to move to the downed vehicle. I yelled at the gunners to cover our movement, but they had a WTF look in their eyes. The rear bumper from the gun truck was on the ground. I ordered everyone to "Hit the Ping" to let our TOC in Kabul know we had a problem.

Buddha yelled, "I think we're in a minefield!" We slowed our approach to the gun truck.

Dave and Alex came walking out from the driver's side toward the back of the vehicle and didn't trigger another mine strike, so we followed in their footsteps.

The driver and two gunners were injured. The recovery gear in the back had been tossed around the box like pinballs. The gunners were buried under the gear in the back of the truck, moaning. Having a ten-ton floor jack and a couple hundred-pound tires, guns, and ammo flying around in a confined space had done extensive damage.

Buddha went to work immediately on the injured local nationals. He began to assess, triage, and treat the casualties.

Both gunners had multiple lower extremity fractures and also suffered pelvic fractures.

Neither of them would ever walk normally again. "Fuck, they're spitting their teeth out!" I said.

The reality was, we had stopped at a roadside market prior to this incident where the gunners had purchased some pomegranates. The red and white pulp resembled broken teeth and it was all over their faces and bodies as a result of the explosion. Despite the circumstances, I couldn't stop myself from cracking up on the inside.

As we began to extract, I gathered up everything that was blown out of the vehicle and tossed a couple of thermites inside to destroy it. I found a dusty flashlight on the ground that seemed to work half-ass. It was peppered from the blast, but the lens was still intact, so I figured I could repair it and use it as a backup. It eventually found its way into my Gorilla Box war chest.

We began to retrograde back to the hardball to link back up with the US Army. They set up a landing zone so we could MEDEVAC our casualties out. This was our first experience with the Army's All-American Dust-Off Team. Blackhawks leave a helluva lot of dust on takeoff.

When we got there, the medics gave Buddha a hand with casualty care. This particular unit of theirs was green. The young soldiers could not have been out of school more than a year, but with Buddha's help, they treated the Afghans as if they were their own wounded comrades in arms, doing their jobs to the best of their abilities. We were able to splint and stabilize the gunners. We loaded them onto the awaiting Blackhawks for transfer.

I spoke with the tactical air control party via comms. He had two Bell OH-58 Kiowas do a fly-over to take a look at our gun truck. From the air, they said it was not a complete burn. I requested the vehicle be hit with rockets. The Army was more than happy to oblige. They fired two rockets into the already burning gun truck, blowing it to oblivion.

The link-up with the Army was a huge money-maker for us. We got our casualties evacuated, and we confirmed the destruction of the downed vehicle. When we arrived at Kandahar, we set up billeting and waited for another team to bring us a new gun truck and replacement gunners to complete our mission.

While there, we visited Camp Hero, a MASH unit for the Afghan military where our gunners were being cared for. They had to wait for their turn in the operating room.

During this time, we had to change billeting because an SUV with three suspicious guys were casing out the Kandahar Hotel. This prompted me to move the expats to the base. I arranged for the LN gunners to stay at a different hotel, but they moved back to the Kandahar Hotel because of the access to the Internet and TV.

It was a way to remain connected to the outside world. They kept up to date on current events in the country, and shared important information with our interpreter who, in turn, shared it with us. Open-source intelligence was unclassified and sometimes inaccurate, as a lot of media generally was, but any information was better than no information at all.

CHAPTER THIRTY-THREE
Ambush Shkin
DATE: November 19, 2009
MISSION: C-1 Convoy to Shkin
LOCATION: Shkin, Paktika Province

The Taliban ambushed Team II several times during a mission to a remote outpost known as Firebase Shkin. Located on a high plain in the Paktika Province of Afghanistan, the firebase sat six kilometers from the Pakistani border, right in the middle of a major infiltration route for the Taliban. In the early days of the war, it was a hotspot of insurgent activity and was dubbed "the evilest place in Afghanistan." Contact was inevitable.

Making matters more difficult was the ambiguous loyalty of the Pakistani border guards and armed forces in the area. The remote location meant help was a long way off if things took a turn for the worse.

Shkin Firebase was named after the village and then was renamed Firebase Lilley to honor Master Sgt. Arthur L. Lilley, a US Special Forces soldier who was killed in a gunfire exchange there in 2007. The heavily fortified military base looked like the Alamo or a Wild West cavalry fort ringed with coils of razor wire. A US flag rippled above the three-foot-thick mud walls. Anyone working the watchtower could scan the expanse of forested ridges that rose to 9,000 feet. They marked the border. When there was trouble, it usually came from that direction.

The firebase saw a great deal of enemy contact, and not just in the form of IEDs or rocket attacks. Actual direct fire came from the enemy. The unforgiving landscape gave them an opportunity to hide at close range, remaining invisible.

Since 2002, Firebase Lilley had housed mostly American

Special Operations Forces and the units that served there had taken more casualties from enemy fire than any other location in Afghanistan. Soldiers lived near the front lines and were constant targets for Al-Qaeda and Taliban fighters who launched frequent strikes from nearby Pakistan.

The constant bombardment of fight or flight took an exacting toll on the mind and body. We suffered headaches from the rollercoaster flow of adrenaline and the subsequent dopamine dumps. We fed off each other's strength and courage just to stay alive. It was difficult to make sense of that kind of stuff, but if anyone communicated their fears, it only served to weaken the team.

One mission had to deliver three refrigerator trucks from Orgun-E to FOB Lilley. Cookie augmented Team II with an additional gun truck and crew. He positioned his gun truck in the rear of the convoy behind the team leader, the assistant team leader, and the three cargo trucks they were escorting. They arrived at Shkin late in the morning having only incurred some minor equipment problems. Due to poor road conditions, several tires from two different vehicles went flat after sustaining cuts from rocks.

After the trucks were unloaded and we prepared to depart, the team leader from Team II asked Cookie if the route he had taken in August 2009 was any better. Cookie recalled the road conditions to be superior. The team leader also asked Cookie if he could lead the route. Cookie hesitated. He had only traveled the road once, and that was when he had been injured in an RPG attack. The team leader said they would take the route known as Dodge from Shkin back to Orgun-E.

They left Shkin with Samurai in the lead vehicle, the team leader was in the second followed by the three cargo trucks, and Cookie's gun truck. The medic's (Jimmy Smith) vehicle brought up the rear.

During the return trip, Cookie was able to pick out two terrain features that looked familiar to him. His GPS quit working shortly after they left Shkin, due to poor quality batteries. After darkness set in, their worst nightmare occurred.

Enemy forces fired on them. Unseen in the night, the Taliban brought it all: RPGs, PKMs, AK-47s, and pen flares. Top local national gunners blasted back at the hostiles with PKM and AK-47 fire. They fought their way through each skirmish, holding their own. They made it back to FOB Orgun-E later that evening weary from battle, but without casualties.

Based on the nature of the attacks, the level of intensity, and the number of times that enemy contact occurred, Cookie recommended that any mission to Shkin be augmented with a local national Afghan familiar with the route. They could be recruited by SOC-A human resources in the same manner as our interpreters were hired. He further stated that a "remain overnight" should be factored in so the convoy team could return during the safer light of day.

Management ignored the ideas.

After the Shkin mission, Team II, led by Sam Samano, brought down our new truck, so we were back up to mission specs. Our route had changed to a new location and we went to Spin Boldak and Lashkar Gah—Lash—for our drops. Lash was located in Helmand Province and was a hotbed of Taliban militant activity.

In 2008, Taliban forces attacked the city heavily but were held off by the Afghan National Army and the Oregon Army National Guard. After training and equipping Afghan security forces, the foreign armies transferred security responsibility to the Afghanistan military and the ANP in 2011.

The Taliban continued to attack the city. The proximity to the Pakistani border remained a significant issue for convoy operations because of the well-documented enemy activity in the area of operation. Taliban, Afghan militants loyal to the Taliban regime, Al-Qaeda insurgents from Pakistan, Mujahideen freedom fighters, criminals, and bandits, as well as the Pakistan military were all out for blood.

The more active we were, the more chance we had of running into enemy elements. They always lurked there, watching and waiting. We ran a few more missions and faced contacts and ambushes with direct fire weapons. The gun trucks held up well, but things began to change for SOC when the enemy figured out the effectiveness of IEDs against our vehicles.

Winter was fast approaching, and we all had mixed emotions and concerns. Business would decline. Many of us were worried about being sent packing. The rest of us looked at it as a reprieve and an opportunity to decompress, a chance to get off the rollercoaster and far from Firebase Shkin.

CHAPTER THIRTY-FOUR
The Compound

SOC had outgrown the villa. Jon Wertjes and Ryan Bennett scouted out a new location and we made the move to a compound called the Kabul Program Management Office (KPMO), just on the outskirts of the city.

We nicknamed it "The COCK" (Convoy Operations Center Kabul). Clearly designed for the austere and hostile environment, the nine-acre compound was completely surrounded by twelve-foot reinforced concrete T-walls. An additional six-foot translucent barrier fence with razor wire on top extended the perimeters. There were twenty-four single room or wet *CHUS* (barracks) and four dry *CHUS*. Two additional *CHUS* held a laundry facility. The main building had a basement with a full gym, MWR, and armory. The walls were adorned with flags representing the countries of each contractor.

Plaques with slogans were everywhere. They built up our confidence and reminded us of our duty and risks.

- Train Hard, Fight Easy

- The more you sweat, the less you bleed

- Slow is smooth, and smooth is fast

- The only easy day was yesterday

- Pain is weakness leaving the body

- War means fighting, and fighting means killing

The second floor was used for the administration offices, a small non-functional DFAC, Tactical Operations Center, and conference/training room. The top floor of the three-story building was used mainly for storage.

On the rooftop, a perimeter parapet sandbagged for defensive purposes in the event of an attack. There was also a large maintenance building that housed a pressure washer, engine overhaul, vehicle body repair shop, mechanics office. Parking was large enough to accommodate twelve-gun trucks and four smaller B-6 limos. Concrete walkways were laid including a large aggregate parking area.

The primary and secondary entry control points, including all structures, gates, and barriers were manned twenty-four hours a day, three hundred sixty-five days a year.

The medics hated it because the gravel and large rocks and stones were everywhere, making it difficult to cross from the *CHUS* to the main building. Team members twisted their ankles trying to take a short cut to the gym. The docs handed out Motrin like it was candy.

It was a commonly accepted stereotype that corpsmen offered nothing to Marines outside of hydration, Motrin, and sock advice. It was always fun to kid about it until you got injured, then they were a godsend.

Despite the blessing of a good medic, none of them could perform an exorcism.

CHAPTER THIRTY-FIVE
The Mystic

At the new compound, rumor had it one of the guard towers was haunted. When a tower guard discharged his weapon on one of the other guard towers, at first, everyone thought it might be a negligent discharge, and the guard was playing it off. But the guard was adamant he had seen something.

Security guards began to complain that the guard tower was haunted. They refused to work in that particular tower. Rumors began to circulate, and other guards added their ghost sightings to the mix. It started putting a strain on the guard force rotation.

The Afghan Security Supervisor said the only way to get the guards to go back to work was to have a Shaman Mystic brought in to perform an exorcism on the guard and a blessing on the tower. The entire compound was put on hold until the ritual was completed.

Afghans are very superstitious; before any trip, water is thrown on their vehicles. They buy naan and give it to the poor. Before entering a compound, someone would burn coal in a wheelbarrow and fan the smoke all through the villa, clearing the house of any spirits.

The Muslim mystics and mendicants of modern Afghanistan, some of whom were referred to as *Malang*, practiced a variety of exotic techniques that had clear affiliations with shamanism. The healing and magical powers possessed by these individuals was either inherited or acquired through discipleship under established mystics. Considered holy men, they were believed to be touched by the hand of Allah. They were supposedly able to communicate with *jinn* spirits, help cure illness, foretell the future, and combat the malicious influence of evil spirits.

All Afghan shamans, irrespective of affiliation or title, acquired their powers through the control they exercised over the supernatural entity. In Afghanistan, there was a near-universal belief in jinn, malevolent spirits that haunted buildings, graveyards, and lonely highways, and attacked humans. There were two types of jinn. The white jinn were seen as benevolent. Black jinns haunted houses and played all kinds of mischievous tricks on people but could also turn violent, wrathful and cruel.

The stories filled our days.

The jinn had the power to cause humans to suffer in many different ways. Afghans believed they took the form of snakes and scorpions, and bit and stung people. They were capable of frightening people so badly, their souls fled from their bodies. They seized people, causing them to suffocate. They were able to enter a victim's body and make him or her go insane.

Many natural diseases, which failed to respond to normal medication, were attributed to the actions of such jinn.

In the end, *The Pony Express* riders didn't give a shit. Aside from living under the supposed umbrella of protection the guard force provided, we had a job to do. I'm not sure how much money we paid the holy man, but we paid the dude and got on with business.

War was business and business was good.

CHAPTER THIRTY-SIX
The Rollover
DATE: February 27, 2010
MISSION: C-1 Convoy to Shkin
LOCATION: Ghazni Province

With all the evil spirits expelled, we started up the convoys again. Afghanistan was a combination of the occult, the Wild West and the *Sopranos*. Every mission could be our last. We knew our job and our worth.

We officially called ourselves *The Pony Express* in homage to the short-lived mail service that connected California with Missouri before the Civil War. From April 3, 1860, to October 1861, the original Pony Express delivered messages, newspapers, and mail and was the most direct means of communication between the East and West before the transcontinental telegraph was established.

It was only fitting to continue *The Pony Express* legacy in the new Wild West of Afghanistan.

The Pony Express had a solid reputation for delivering the mail successfully. On this mission, not only were we moving cargo for a C-1 client, we were also handling mail delivery for the US Postal Service and the Department of Defense.

Delivering mail was not a priority for military convoys, but we could take the same load and deliver it in four to six hours. The contract was good for us and allowed us to support the US military at the same time.

The military liked having us on contract. The headquarters team augmented the C-1 runs.

They ran everything from local PSD missions to mail runs. Rector was the Director of Mobile Operation, which put him in charge of the convoys. To his credit, he made sure he knew the lay of the land. Even if enemy activity was deemed high threat, many times we weren't made aware that a route had been blacked out. We managed to push through the ambushes to get the mail delivered. The only time we didn't make drops was if the roads were impassable.

No one could say Rector wasn't out there on the runs dealing with all the bullshit.

He had control of the budget and the final say on hiring and firing personnel. If there was a problem, he was responsible for solving it. If someone created too much friction, then he launched them. The way he solved some problems also created friction among the guys.

To Rector, it was his way or the highway. But his word was gold, so it was another catch-22 for the teams.

For this mission, I was as an augmentee with Team II, filling the void as a vehicle commander and shooter. This was a tough one, a C-1 to Orgun-E and Shkin, located on the Pakistani border. since the route took us through what we nicknamed the "Valley of Death." It was a perfect spot for ambushes, I later found out the hard way.

Sam Samano was a retired team master sergeant with the US Army Special Forces with a wealth of knowledge to share with us, so he was a welcome addition. As the team leader, he utilized aggressive vehicle tactics in order to protect the convoy. This included increased speeds where possible, spacing, and the provision of a heavy overwatch position from either the front or rear of the convoy so we could dominate the high ground. In addition to movement, each two-gun truck team was mutually self-supporting and able to function independently in the event of an attack.

The team was split between the front and back, two vehicles each, making us evenly and mutually supporting. In effect, we rolled as two fire teams.

I was in the back with a medic named Siri Kalsa, a Sikh. I learned a lot from him about the Sikh religion and how the Sikhs and Muslims didn't get along. He also taught me the history of the Sikh Regiments who fought with the British Army. It was a good lesson about a culture of warriors who happened to be farmers. According to Siri, more than 50 percent of the commissioned officers in the Indian National Army are of the Sikh religion.

We also utilized time and darkness for our moves. We arrived at Orgun-E and set up to billet for the night and rolled out the next morning at 0300. However, sleep was not to be had. A unit was rotating out and going home, and they weren't too quiet about it.

To keep the Taliban militia from amassing forces against us, the plan was to move without anyone having eyes on us when we pulled out. We'd do a quick off-load and turn around at Shkin.

Unfortunately, it had rained a lot that day and it took us nearly twelve hours to arrive at the site.

Samurai and Ziko were in the lead vehicle. The trail we were on ran parallel to the river. At times, we had to cross flooded areas at the lowest point. We bounded one vehicle at a time. At one point, water covered the entire hood of Samurai's gun truck.

We traversed goat trails and streambed routes laid out by Special Forces. I was talking with Siri at the back of the convoy waiting for the trucks to clear the hill. As we reached an upward degree plane, the one cargo truck started to slide off the road. The tires began to spin. The more the driver accelerated, the more the truck slid. It began to roll back.

Siri shouted, "Oh, shit! Look at that!" I yelled, "There it goes! It's gonna roll!"

The driver bailed out before the truck went off the edge of a hundred-foot drop.

It was a miracle no one else was injured or killed. Despite the potential for disaster, we were both laughing. The drivers and the gunners were laughing, too. Then reality struck. I said, "Hey, Siri,

I guess you get the honors, brother. Let me know how pissed Sam is."

Siri radioed to Sam that one of the cargo trucks rolled. Sam wasn't too pleased that he had to burn the cargo.

The truck was lodged in a crevice about 100 feet over the edge. Sam carefully navigated his way down, pulled the pins on a couple of thermite grenades, and burned the truck, He came back up the steep and rough terrain barely breaking a sweat. He was a pretty tough son-of-a- biscuit.

I found one of the thermite grenade pins, stuffed it in my pocket and saved it for the war chest in my *CHU*. It would be cool to use it as a keychain. I was beginning to have a decent collection of war memorabilia that I could share with my grandkids someday.

We learned a lot from the run, especially the point of contact for coordination and support. We also saw problems with the Afghan gunners. Some of them had dropped into the trucks and hid instead of returning fire. Money, Cookie, and Chase had seen this before with their gunners, but remedial training was not a substitute for having a pair of balls.

The route to Ghazni was the most dangerous of them all. After that run, the teams always pushed to Ghazni at night. But rolling blacked out was so eerie it made the hair on my neck stand up.

Buddha was wide-eyed. Money had a hard-on. Cookie grinded his teeth.

The Taliban must have taken up residency on that part of Ring Road, near a hamlet called Qal 'eh-ye Mollā Ghāzī (Ghazi Town) because there were different sets of blown-up rigs, blast holes, burnt up tankers, and similar shit every time we rolled through.

The hamlet was a ghost town with no imaginable right to exist. It rose from the lifeless earth with derelict huts clustered together on both sides of the cracked asphalt. Even at night, we could see black dirt everywhere, evidence of roll overs and burning fuel tankers destroyed by the enemy. It was death squared and full of ghosts that lay under a blanket of sinister silence.

Hell, a cemetery had more charisma. At least a graveyard was built on reverence and sentimentality. This was pure evil.

It was a haunting memory I'll never forget. We rolled through as *The Pony Express,* trying to shake it off. In the darkness of the night, I was glad my brothers had my back.

CHAPTER THIRTY-SEVEN
Contact RPG Ghazni
DATE: March 05, 2010
MISSION: C-1 Convoy to Shkin
LOCATION: Ghazni Province

You never really get used to dodging hot lead.

Just south of Ghazni, we were ambushed. Caught in a crossfire in a complex attack, the Taliban opened fire. Gunners engaged both sides of the road, but our return fire seemed ineffective. We found out that the gunners were hiding in the truck, spraying the PKM in their general direction.

The lead vehicle took the first enemy shots. They pierced Big Dan's radiator and Codan antenna with a sound like a sharp crack followed by a loud hiss. We had to push them out.

My vehicle took a burst of fire along the right-side door. I flinched as the rounds bounced around inside the door panel. It was a cinematic moment.

"Are you okay?" yelled my driver, Perica Jaric. "Just keep driving!" I yelled.

It sucked to be in a defensive posture. I wished we had portholes so we could suppress the enemy with effective return fire.

As we pulled up behind Big Dan, I tried contacting him on the radio but there was nothing. Dead silence.

He finally turned on his hand-held radio and we were able to communicate. "Keep pushing," I said.

"We have no power," he said.

"Get ready for a push-out. I'm gonna have Pero come up behind you and make contact." I told Pero to go easy, but it was rougher than we expected. Everyone was hyped up from all the adrenaline, but at least we were able to get off the X intact. We plowed through.

Buddha and Alek were in the trail vehicle. I noticed their gunners were trying to shoot at the Taliban Air Force. They were ducking in their turrets, shooting their PKMs straight up in the air.

Neither Buddha nor Alek were able to get to the semi driver to evacuate him from his truck and cross-deck into their gun truck. It seemed like the asshole was just sitting there without a care in the world.

Since our gunners were not on target, the Taliban were able to zero in on us at will. Buddha was yelling at Alek, "Go! Go! Go!"

Alek gave him a WTF look. He glanced down at his foot. He had the gas pedal pressed through the floor. Suddenly, at their two o'clock, they saw a man stand up with an RPG positioned on his shoulder.

Time often slowed in moments of terror. They could actually see the RPG track towards them.

For Buddha, knowing the projectile's trajectory would result in an explosion somewhere around his door was surreal. In those nanoseconds of waiting, rounds continued to strike their vehicle. "Ping! Ping! Ping!" Buddha's window took a round that penetrated the ballistic glass.

Their only focus was on the incoming rocket-propelled grenade and its inevitable outcome.

They braced for impact.

The RPG hit just behind the passenger door of the gun truck—but didn't detonate. The missile's fins scraped the side of the truck and deflected. It exploded behind them.

Now that was a close call! Buddha became giddy as a schoolgirl. "Yes! Check this shit out! I just saw my own death!"

"Dude, what the fuck?" I said. "What hit you?" Since I was in the middle gun truck, I didn't see the strike.

Buddha replied, "An RPG! The shooter had us dead to rights. Either the rocket didn't arm or the angle was bad."

"Holy shit, you're one lucky fucker. How's Alek?"

"We're both good. Let's get the hell outta here. This place sucks!"

We consolidated the team at the ANA compound, and then made a move to retrieve the trail vehicle that had remained on-site with one of the flatbeds hauling an SUV. Its fuel line had been cut, so it stalled out.

A Taliban insurgent walked up on us to do a battle damage assessment. He was a really cool customer. He must've known we wouldn't react, considering our location and circumstance, coupled with the fact that he was unarmed and older.

My interpreter, Fawad, came up to me with his gear on. "Come on, sir, we are ready."

We bounded up to the gun truck, which provided overwatch support. The Taliban militia let loose a final burst of fire toward us. The rounds skipped across the road and picked up dirt. I turned and leveled my M-4 in their direction but they quickly ran off. The ANA came up behind us and I figured they didn't want to engage the additional manpower on the scene.

We secured the truck and cargo and Fawad got it running again.

Fawad was awesome. He had worked for the National Directorate of Security, an organization founded as the primary domestic and foreign intelligence agency of the Islamic Republic of Afghanistan in 2002. It was considered the successor to KHAD, the intelligence organization before the Afghan Civil War. It was the lesser equivalent to the CIA.

When I asked him why he wanted to work for us, he said he wanted to make more money. He was tactically proficient and spoke English very well. I liked him and he was a solid addition to the team.

Before we pushed off, I was standing next to my gun truck, looking down. A smooth, oblong gray stone caught my eye. It was split in half at an angle. When I reversed the two pieces, they came together in the shape of a heart. I pocketed it for another keepsake.

I began to sense things were changing for me as I went over the contents of my footlocker. I was never really all that sentimental, but this was something unique and it had a strange effect on me. Cool stone, bad memory.

We set up a tow for Big Dan's gun truck and then proceeded to Ghazni, where we linked up with Sam and Team II, then made our final push to Kabul. My vehicle was in the lead, doing the tow. This left Buddha as the reaction/recovery vehicle if something happened.

During debrief, we were asked why we had left the cargo truck and driver. The driver's story began to unravel, and it was readily apparent that he was not on the level. Mr. Suleiman fired him on the spot.

Another issue of concern revealed that the gunners were not engaging the enemy properly. We knew this was a remedial training issue and we told them they would be replaced. Everyone was scared, but there was a huge difference in being afraid and not being willing to fight. These guys were lazy and cowards at the same time, and it only served to bring everyone down not to mention increasing our chances of getting killed.

While the debrief was going on, Jon and Money were in Herat for a protection detail. They had received permission from the TOC to allow their client to visit the Herat Citadel that was built by Alexander the Great. They were one of four groups allowed to go inside for a tour. It definitely made points with the client.

The Herat Citadel, also known as the Citadel of Alexander, was a large fort located in the center of Herat. Built around 330 BC when Alexander the Great invaded, it had been a military stronghold for two millennia.

While they walked around, they came to a small hallway. They looked at each other and the realization hit them. They were dressed in full kit and weapons, ready for battle, just like Alexander and his men. Walking on the same historical ground was a rush for both of them.

They seemed to connect with the ancient ghosts of history.

When Money and Jon returned from their mission, we met at the SOC villa. Money went on and on, bragging about what he learned on his easy assignment. When I told him about getting whacked south of Ghazni, I could see his heart drop. Knowing Money, he would rather have been on our trip instead of the cakewalk he and Jon ran in Herat. There's something to be said about the rush of combat versus being laid back on a routine mission.

Even though there were too many close calls around Ghazni, I think I got the last laugh.

CHAPTER THIRTY-EIGHT
Quick Reaction Force
DATE: April 03, 2010
MISSION: QRF for DGI Mission
LOCATION: Wardak/Gardez Province Arch

Our next mission was a mail run to Ghazni and then to Gardez. Since Team II was going down range—south—at the same time, we made it as a single move, combining the two teams. This proved to be fortunate.

My assistant team leader was Scott Brown, one of the toughest men I ever met. A former Army infantry scout, he stood about 5-foot 11inches, was built pretty solid and knew his way around the gym. He worked for DynCorp on the ANP training program and was familiar with the territory. He told me about the time they were in a firefight with the Taliban and one of the ANP fired an RPG without checking his six. Scott was knocked out and it burned half his beard off.

We joked about whether his hair would grow back the same. But the fact of the matter was, it came back with a vengeance. He looked like a red headed Brillo pad.

We drove through Sheikh Abad in the Saydabad District of Wardak Province. Known for its agreeable climate and beautiful green scenery that included tall poplar trees, hillside vegetation, streams, and orchards, I enjoyed the drive. It was visually appealing. I'm not sure if it was the thought of being closer to Kabul that put my mind at ease, or the scenery itself.

The city of Saydabad served as the district capital. It was the most populous district of the province with 114,793 residents, mostly Pashto. At one time, the district was a popular retreat for Kabul residents—until an increase in ISAF vs. Taliban violence broke out from 2008-2012.

Heading south, the trees didn't seem as tall and the landscape became baron and drab. A couple of miles before we reached the bridge, Samurai broke in from the lead vehicle. "Ambush front!"

And then it was on.

Samurai could see the Taliban setting up on the right-hand side of the road. We had the advantage of elevation and could see some of the village rooftops, off the road. Normally his local national top gunners called out any threats, but these guys were seasoned gunners. They opened fire without hesitation. They did a great job laying down suppressive fire.

One of the black hats shouldered an RPG in our direction. Samurai had been through this several times before and maintained his cool.

PAPAPAPAPAPOW! PAPAPAPAPAPOW!" His top gunner opened fire to suppress the tango. The first RPG went high and missed the convoy. The insurgent ducked for cover.

Then the grenade made impact with the dirt 600 yards on the other side of the road.

I got on the radio to check on Buddha and Scott, "How are you guys doing back there?"

Scott said, "We're okay. We saw two RPGs fly ahead of you and two more that flew right over your vehicle."

Buddha jumped in, "It looks like they were gunning for you."

I could hear them both laughing and it kinda gave me a chuckle too.

It turned out the ambush was spread out over a one-kilometer front. Eight RPGs were fired at us. The entire town was being used as a death trap. Amazingly, none of our guys got hurt. We kept the convoy moving.

When we reached FOB Ghazni, we proceeded with the mail drop, and I debriefed the TOC about the ambush, so the Army could update their status board. We continued to FOB Sharana to do another drop, then headed north to the cut-off road into

Kajiki, also called the Tangi Valley.

This was the same valley where on August 6, 2011, a US Boeing CH-47 Chinook military helicopter, call sign "Extortion 17" was shot down while transporting SEAL Team 6, a QRF attempting to reinforce an engaged unit of Army Rangers in Wardak Province.

Located in the south of Wardak Province, the valley had no central government presence and was renowned and feared as resistance to invasion for more than 2,000 years.

The resulting crash killed all thirty-eight people on board. Fatalities included twenty-five American Special Forces personnel, five US Army National Guard and Army Reserve crewmen, seven Afghan commandos, and one Afghan interpreter, as well as a US military working dog.

It was considered the worst loss of American lives in a single incident in the Afghanistan campaign, surpassing Operation Red Wings in 2005.

The Army told us this was a green (safe) route, but events proved otherwise. The entire valley was a kill zone, with cliffs on the left and a river on the right. We had no room to maneuver. I thought, "Oh shit, this is going to suck bad."

The only reason we didn't get hit was that they had just attacked the US Army ahead of us.

While we waited for Big Army to clear the road, I picked up a small ceramic souvenir from one of the village shops for my footlocker. I wanted to balance out the evil that was beginning to dominate my mind with something good for a change.

When we linked up with the Army, we fell into their security bubble until they could clear the road. One of their MRAPs was cut in half by a culvert IED, but no one was killed.

We pushed out of the valley and did the mail drop at FOB Shank and FOB Gardez, before returning to Kabul. After that run, we never went down that road again.

We disseminated the information, so no other teams would

make the same mistake. I told Rector, "You know that shortcut that looks good on the map? It's actually a kill zone."

Rector replied, "How so?"

I went over the details of the terrain and explained the reaction by locals. "When we drove through the village, parents grabbed their kids off the street and locked up shops. They scattered like they were clearing the area for a gunfight. The only reason they didn't hit us was because they hit the Army unit in front of us."

Rector asked, "How bad was it for the Army?"

"They cut an MRAP in half."

Rector shook his head and agreed. The road was off-limits.

We did a couple more mail runs and a QRF mission for the DGI team trying to get to Herat. DGI was trying to stimulate the economy and enhance the business infrastructure of Herat Province. The hope was, once everyone saw there was money to be made, the insurgency would die down.

Our team was pre-staging with three gun trucks at FOB Saydabad. We awaited the arrival of the DGI team to pass us and get to Qalat. If they made it without incident, then we would return to base in Kabul.

That was not the case. I called the TOC for an update. The DGI team had been hit, ambushed north of Ghazni, near the arches that separate Wardak Province from Ghazni Province. Several Taliban opened fire on the two B-6 Limos as they passed by.

The lead limo was hit in the engine block and went down hard. The enemy shot out the tires of the trail vehicle, with Matty and Ritchie inside. Luckily, their Run-flat Insert Systems were made out of lightweight polymer material and engineered to prevent breakage or shattering under ballistic attack or road hazards. It was strong enough to support the full load of the B-6 armored vehicle and could sustain speeds of sixty kilometers per hour for a range of 100 kilometers on road, or fifty off-road.

The team got off the X and contacted the TOC at Kabul to let them know what had happened. I called J.J. for an update. Matty had given him details.

"Dude, they got hit just north of Ghazni," he said. "Both vehicles are down. No casualties. They're out of the vehicles and hiding right now."

We got ready to roll out.

I told my team, "Matty pinged hot! Get ready to roll! He's north of Ghazni. Both vehicles are down!"

Scott asked, "Where exactly?"

"Standby."

J.J. told me, "Right by the arch at the Wardak/Gardez Province line." I relayed the information to my crew. "I want to roll blacked out!"

"That's not a good idea, Hammer," Scott said. "That's gonna slow us down and we don't have night vision goggles. Neither do the gunners."

"Ok, fuck it. We'll go with lights on."

We rolled out with lights on. Matty confirmed their coordinates, just south of the arch at the Ghazni/Wardak border. I got my data dump on the move. We should have been informed about the mission through SECURO, the provider for our Track-24 locators. This was not the first time they let us down.

I briefed my team on how we would deploy. The lead element, with Scott, would push to the first downed vehicle. I would push to the second downed vehicle and Buddha would set up on the high ground for overwatch in the trail vehicle. Buddha would also man the lead PKM on his gun truck, which was comforting to me. I knew he was a good shooter and would look for targets.

If I said it once, I'll say it a thousand times. There's nothing quick about a Quick Reaction Force. For the DGI team, it must've seemed like a lifetime.

We established communications with the team. I told Matty

they had to stay down and find a defilade because we were coming in hot. If anything moved, we were going to see it and lay down some hate.

Enfilade and defilade described a military formation's exposure to enemy fire. A formation was "in enfilade" if weapons fired could be directed along its longest axis. Defilade shielded a formation from enemy fire by using natural or artificial obstacles.

We arrived and called for Matty and Ritchie, another Serbian driver, and linked up with the team. The terrain rolled gently, with waist-high grass, so Matty and Ritchie hid easily. We were still on high alert because we didn't know if there was another insurgent cell hanging back to ambush our QRF.

Matty confirmed there was no activity in the area.

We set up security while Ritchie did a tactical tire change on one vehicle. The other downed SUV was set up for a tow by the lead vehicle. We pushed to FOB Ghazni to drop off the downed vehicle and linked up with Team II to return to Kabul.

Although we were the QRF for DGI, Team II was on notice to be *our* QRF. It seemed like every time we rolled out or got hit, Team II was always there to back us up. Although we joked about it, we were damn lucky to have Team II covering our asses.

CHAPTER THIRTY-NINE
Mine Strike Orgun-E
DATE: April 20, 2010
MISSION: Phase I - C-1 Convoy Orgun-E Phase II – Resupply at Shkin
LOCATION: Paktika Province

The stretch of unpaved road between Sar Hawza and Orgun-E was known to be Taliban country. In fact, there were several hamlets along the route where ANA simply refused to enter. Yet here we were. The next C-1 mission to Orgun-E didn't sound like fun.

The problem with our missions was that we took all the risks and were exposed to all the dangers, but we had no support. Oh, we had promises of support including rescue, MEDEVAC, QRF, and Intel, but they never came through. They didn't see the urgency. QRF wasn't quick enough when teammates lay dying or needed surgical care.

On this mission, we needed them all. But we also reverted to our own team of experts.

Buddha's job as a medic was simple. Keep everyone alive. Many military units bugged out and had remaining medical supplies they didn't want to box up. So, with a little trade, he got enough equipment to handle three critical patients, and six to seven moderate walking wounded.

The problem was time. With no hope of rescue or MEDEVAC, patients stayed with Buddha until we could reach a safe haven to continue their medical care. Trying to get a MEDEVAC wasn't an option unless an ISAF or US military force was on the scene, and they wouldn't launch unless a landing zone was established and secured. Our security could not provide perimeter cover for the military.

It seemed like we were always just one step behind, always looking over our shoulders, praying for QRF and more.

I headed to Camp Phoenix to get the latest intel update, while Scott and Buddha made sure our trucks were ready. We sorted out our gear, M4s, AK-47s, PKMs, and enough ammo to piss off any bad guys. As always, we filled our units up with pogey bait not generally available to soldiers in the field: Red Bull, sunflower seeds, cigarettes, and of course, lots of chew. Once all our trucks were ready, I briefed the operation orders to the team, and we set off for a quick email or nap until muster time.

The mission was scheduled to launch on the evening of April 18th. However, the trucks all had problems, so we aborted, returned to the KPMO compound, and fixed them.

At 0200 hours on 20 April, our gunners showed up. We completed another equipment check, took a smoke break, and a piss. This was always a good indicator of the "oh shit" meter. I had tried to quit smoking, but after the first few attacks, the cigarettes were back. When I was smoking them like crack, Buddha knew I was worried. This time I was sucking them down.

Final checks were in place. Body armor on, weapons loaded, radio checks complete, and we were off. We were located in an industrial area full of contractors, but at this time of night, we were the only ones moving, except for the occasional donkey cart racing into Kabul center.

The first part of the trip we had made several times, but the final destination was new to us. We were going to turn off our normal route four hours in. This area was ramped up with IEDs and insurgent activity.

The beginning of the mission was always quiet. The local national half of the team slept, and the other half of us mentally prepped for what might come. We drove modified Ford F-550s with steel plated body armor, bulletproof glass, and two gun hatches in the rear tub, each manned with a PKM and an Afghan gunner.

Our thirteen-man team consisted of three expats, three Third Country Nationals, six gunners, and one interpreter. All our drivers and assistant team leaders were from Serbia, military-trained, and ready. Scott was the Assistant Team Leader/Navigator in the lead vehicle. Pero, his driver, had driven the Bernal route to Shkin before. They had an extra man, our interpreter, Fawad.

I was in the middle vehicle of the convoy with Maric as my driver. In the trail vehicle, Buddha was the medic and Alek was his driver. They brought up the rear.

This was our normal configuration. Buddha and I secured the convoy. It allowed Scott to push ahead as the rabbit. The rabbit always had a short life expectancy. All of our KIA and WIA were members of the rabbit unit.

As we moved through the city, there were several checkpoints, and most of the time the guards waved us through. On a few occasions, one particular ANP yelled at us to stop and pointed his AK-47 in our direction. That stopped pretty quickly when our lead gunner swung his PKM in the guard's direction and yelled a few obscenities at him.

It was open season on anyone who dared roll on Ring Road.

About forty-five minutes past the south gate, we arrived at our favorite village of Sayad Abad. There had been multiple enemy encounters in this village, and we were pumped as we approached.

There was nothing.

We sailed through, pleased and disappointed at the same time. Nothing woke you up like a gun battle. Everything seemed to be going fine until about an hour from our turning point, in a place called Salar, located toward the southern end of Wardak Province. Then one of our cargo trucks broke down.

The truck driver had fallen asleep and hit a crater in the road. We had to leave the truck behind because of the extensive damage and the inability to extricate it. At daybreak we passed through Ghazni, FOB Sharana, and entered into the valley that led to Orgun E.

Afghan truck drivers asked if they could get into our convoy for protection, but we told them no. They could roll behind us. If anything happened to them, we would get their bodies back to their families. This provided a buffer between us and anyone that may be following the convoy.

The trucks we rode in were pretty tough since they'd been in several IED strikes and complex ambushes. They could take a beating, but if our weak spot was hit, it was all over.

The bottoms of our trucks were flat, not angled. Any hit from the bottom, and we were royally screwed. We learned that the hard way. On our first mission we received a mine strike in soft soil, and Buddha had to MEDEVAC two of our gunners who sustained multiple fractures.

Anxiety was high. There was no turning back.

What did we see as we turned onto the new road? Culverts spaced 100 meters apart.

The road ahead wasn't littered with blast damage or burned-out vehicles like those found on Ring Road. There were many homes, roadside businesses, and farmland on both sides of the road. That didn't diminish the butt-clenching every time we drove over a culvert.

Despite the many culverts, the road was passable, but the last part of the trip required us to use a section of unpaved road. The trouble was, it was labeled Route Jeep, a major supply trail traditionally used by the Taliban to smuggle goods from Pakistan into Afghanistan. After about an hour we came to the end of the paved road. American military tracks stopped. As we drove through the checkpoint, heading into the valley, there was confusion in the soldiers' eyes.

"Who the hell went into that valley without mine sweeping engineers, over-watch, and predators clearing the way?" I asked.

Mmmmm. Let me guess. We would.

At approximately 1030 we moved slowly along the rough terrain, traversing thirty-degree inclines and drops. Then all chaos broke loose. A loud crack sounded. An IED ripped into our lead vehicle. A cloud of smoke and dust rose up. I grabbed the radio. "Lead, this is Hammer! Lead, this is Hammer!"

We turned the corner. The lead vehicle was down hard. "Oh fuck!"

The back door was blown open, so I activated my panic button and had Buddha hit the pings, as well. Adrenaline hit the bloodstream again.

I dismounted and ran up to the blast site. I called J.J., the communications supervisor at the TOC, to let him know we had men down.

"Hit the panic button," JJ instructed me.

"I already did! Activate the MEDEVAC plan."

The gun truck was bent about thirty degrees between the gun tub and the cab. I could hear Buddha moving behind me. I spotted a brown-colored object on the ground and prayed. "Please God. Let it be a sleeping bag."

It wasn't. It was my interpreter, Fawad.

I grabbed his shoulder and rolled him over. His eyes were open. I looked down at his legs. They were amputated at the knees. There was no blood. He was dead before he was blown out of the vehicle.

Buddha shouted, "Fuck him, he's gone!"

I must have had that stupid look on my face like, "Hey doc, can you fix him?" But Buddha snapped me back to focus on saving the lives of the injured.

Buddha directed his driver to move to the right. He shouted commands out to the gunners to kill anything that moved. "Scan the cliffs and find those bastards!" he yelled.

We rushed toward the lead vehicle. There was movement inside. The right front door popped open, and Scott stumbled from the passenger side of the vehicle. He grabbed an AK-47 and started moving up the hill to his right.

We didn't know it at the time, but he had a broken back and fractured pelvis. He got about a hundred meters up the hill when I chased after him.

When I caught up to him, I told him to stay put and instructed him to pull security in case of a secondary attack. He told me he was fucked up and running on pure adrenaline. His face was dripping with sweat and he looked pale.

He was in shock. I needed to get word to Buddha to check him out as soon as he could.

I ran back down the hill to the damaged gun truck and helped Alek and Buddha pull Pero out of the vehicle. He was coughing up blood.

All I could think was, "Sorry, brother. I'll see you on the other side." Maric was setting up security with the top gunners.

What was even more fucked up was Scott's adrenaline was beginning to wear off. There was no way he was getting off that hill on his own. Buddha grabbed him in a fireman's carry and headed down the hill.

I was at the bottom getting the convoy ready to move. Buddha got Scott as far as he could, then stopped. He yelled, "I'm smoked! I can't move him anymore!"

I moved in and threw Scott over my shoulder and got him to the recovery vehicle. When I reached the gun truck, Buddha told me to put him on the bumper, but to be careful.

By now I was winded from carrying Scott. When I put him down, it was harder than it should have been and he screamed in pain.

I kept repeating, "Fuck! Sorry, bro."

We carried Pero to the trail vehicle and Buddha began to go to work on him.

I heard him say, "Fuck, dude, this is the second time we've been decimated in less than six months."

"Just do what you can for him," I said. "If nothing else, make him comfortable." Our Afghan gunners had already moved the remains of our deceased interpreter into Buddha's gun truck. We extricated the remaining gunners and began working on Pero, Scott's driver. His airway was a mess. Blood gushed from his mouth. He had likely blown a lung from the blast.

Buddha intubated him and assisted bagging him outside the gun truck. Pero lost peripheral pulses. Both chest walls decompressed. Buddha yelled if Pero was to have any chance of surviving, we needed to get help quickly.

We relocated him to the unit and Buddha's driver continued to assist with his respirations.

I contacted the TOC and gave Marty an initial assessment and casualty count. We had four wounded and one dead, but it wasn't over yet. We were still on the X and needed to exfil pronto.

CHAPTER FORTY
Exfil
DATE: April 20, 2010
MISSION: Phase I - C-1 Convoy Orgun-E Phase II - Resupply at Shkin
LOCATION: Paktika Province

With one dead and four wounded—two critically—we needed to get the fuck outta Dodge. The injured gunners were placed in my truck, and we lifted Scott into the rear gunner's spot in Buddha's vehicle. Buddha treated the local national gunners enroute.

He was losing Pero. Buddha yelled out he needed surgery. Only a surgeon could fix his internal injuries. The second gunner was stable. Buddha told my top gunners to keep an eye on their buddy the best they could and call him if he got any worse.

I turned to leave and saw that our interpreter was strapped with cargo netting to the inside wall of the gun truck. Someone had found his legs and placed them with his upper torso. The feet were at opposite angles next to his head.

Buddha saw his lifeless eyes staring at him, square in the face. After everything we had just been thru, he almost shit himself.

That image fit into any A-rated horror movie, for sure. The memory would sear us for the rest of our lives, but we had to shake it off and take care of the others.

I studied my GPS to see how far it was to the nearest safe haven. "Fuck it. We're going to Orgun-E!"

My training took over. Everyone remained calm and acted professionally. In crisis situations, you never rise to the occasion, you always fall back to your training. Decision making in this kind of situation was instinctive.

We didn't have the luxury of military support to blow the gun truck to smithereens like before, so I sanitized our comms, maps, and intel, then tossed two thermites into the rig. The armor plating would have been salvageable, but there was nothing I could do about it. The damaged vehicle burned.

I ordered the cargo trucks to move forward. Buddha settled into the back of his truck and started an IV on Scott. He wouldn't lie down due to the pain and refused the morphine because he was intent on manning the rear PKM and didn't want to be drugged up. Buddha reminded him of the harsh road ahead and convinced him otherwise. The morphine didn't come close to taking the edge off his pain.

Turning back to Pero, Buddha tried to revive him for ten minutes, taking turns with CPR. We couldn't lose another man. Pero was only with us for three months. We couldn't lose him.

But we did.

Buddha conceded the awful reality. He sat back on his knees and pronounced Pero dead at 1132. Pero was gone and there was no time to mourn. There were other injured and wounded. Their cries and moans forced us to delay our grief. We had to focus on getting our wounded off the X.

We held our grief in check. Buddha stabilized the casualties. I called Matty and JJ, with a situation report. "Matty, this is abackmmer. We have a change in the casualty count."

Matty replied, "What happened? Did you get hit again?"

"Negative," I said. "We're now at three wounded and two KIA."

"Shit! Who did you lose?"

"Pero," I replied, my voice thick with grief that surfaced out of nowhere. "We lost Pero...he didn't make it."

I looked over at Maric and said, "Sorry, man. He was a good dude."

Maric punched the steering wheel and swore in Serbian. He looked over at me. "Let's get the fuck out of here."

I called my point of contact, a woman call sign "Mud Flap," informing her of the situation. We had hit an IED and a vehicle and men were down. We needed an immediate MEDEVAC. When she realized the gravity of the situation, she transferred me to the BW Cobras security team who prepared for our arrival at the FOB.

I again requested an air MEDEVAC, but no one was willing to go out. Guardian Medical was our contract air, but they never launched. There was some incomplete documentation and administration, so the contract was not completed, and no funds were committed. I also requested a QRF from the FOB to come meet us. They deployed, but never left the hardball (asphalt).

We were about halfway out of the valley when Bismullah, our back-up interpreter and top gunner spotted what appeared to be wires on the ground.

"What's going on?" I asked.

"Sir, the people are not going near it," he said in broken English.

We both dismounted and he ran up to the wires. "See, right here." He pointed to the wires coming out of the ground.

Sure enough, the locals were avoiding that exact spot. An old man looked at me and shook his head. I decided we would follow the civilians. "Okay, Bismullah, let's follow the other drivers. Tell them to hurry up and we'll take their route."

Bismullah said, "Very okay, sir."

I went to the trail vehicle and let Buddha know what was happening. Scott moaned from the gun tub.

"Hey bro, you gotta hang in there," I told him. "We are gonna get the hell outta here. I don't know how long it's gonna take, but we will get there. You have to suck it up."

Scott moaned and gave me thumbs up.

In times like that, the men didn't want lies or sugar coating. I had to tell it like it was.

As we began to move, with every bump we hit, Scott screamed. Buddha thought it sure scared the hell outta the bad guys. It sure as shit sent chills up our spines. I stopped calling Buddha on the radio because all I could hear was Scott screaming in the background and it was screwing me up.

We had to slow our roll even more to avoid jarring Scott unnecessarily and protect him from sustaining further injuries. We tried to stay in the streambeds to avoid any more IEDs in the road.

It took over three hours to move seven kilometers.

I finally made contact with the receiving client who said a QRF was on the way. As we moved through the valley, every now and then, we saw an MI-8 overhead, and hoped it was our MEDEVAC.

"Yeah right," Buddha said as the chopper kept going. "I should've known that wasn't going to happen."

Finally, we saw the QRF sitting on the hardball just where the road ended, about 800 meters from the camp. There they sat, the "high-speed low-drag" Afghan commandos, our QRF.

They refused to enter the valley because it was too dangerous. They might as well have been the United Nations. We met up with them and proceeded to the FOB.

As we entered the camp at Orgun-E, Buddha escorted the wounded to the waiting MASH unit. We took the casualties into the Battalion Aid Station.

Scott was in extreme pain and unable to move. It took a while to extricate him from the gunner's position and then they carried him into the operating room. The second gunner was less critical and was placed in a bed in the emergency department.

We stopped by a make-shift morgue, which was a large freezer. Buddha stayed with the KIAs to get them ready for transport.

He and the gunners washed and prepped the bodies for Return to Base and processing. There was something to be said about the care and preparation that Buddha provided for our deceased interpreter.

He took great care in trying to follow Afghan traditions in preparation for burial. The Islamic faith had a unique set of beliefs towards death and dying from what we witnessed. It was crucial that the body be completely cleansed at least three times. After the three attempts, if it was still not clean, it was washed as many times as necessary—but it had to be an odd number of times.

There was also a particular order in which the body was cleansed. It began with the upper right side, then the upper left side, lower right side, and ended with the lower left side. The body was then shrouded in three white sheets. The sheets were first spread out and stacked one upon the other. The body was placed on top of them. The left hand of the deceased was placed on the chest. The right hand was placed on top of the left. Then the sheets were brought over the body one at a time. Finally, a rope was tied at the top of the head and another below the feet. One or two ropes were tied around the middle of the body.

I was impressed with Buddha's knowledge of Muslim traditions and the Islamic faith. It was a huge benefit to the teams because it showed our SOC-A counterparts that we cared about them and, in turn, they showed mutual respect towards the expats.

Once the cargo and team were secured, Buddha and I went to the client's compound and met with their rep and Paladin. We got our debrief from the US Military Paladin team. They informed us how the tactics, techniques, and procedures for this valley were the use of Italian T-6 mines.

The Paladin teams were the counter-IED experts in Afghanistan, and they used every strike as a training tool in order to better counter the effects of IEDs. Paladin assessed we likely were hit with a triple stack Italian mine, resistant to mine detection. They were surprised we were on this mission alone and said we should have been doing these missions with the military when coming into that particular valley.

This was news to me. We never thought they did convoys, but we would coordinate with the Army and time our runs going into Orgun-E going forward. This way we had route clearance assets and air support if needed.

I got on the horn and called Matty at the TOC to answer any questions. There were a lot.

We were then stood down, meaning the mission to Shkin was aborted and we would not be pushing to that site.

Afterward, we made our way to the combat surgical hospital to check on our injured comrades. The Afghans were knocked out and Scott was laying on a gurney. It was a pretty somber moment.

There we were: Buddha, Mudflap, me, and two of the Blackwater security guys, standing around, talking to Scott. Then the doctor came in and started to examine him. He did a pressure check on his lower spine to confirm his injuries. Scott let out a scream

Right then and there we all looked at each other and then it began—every joke known to mankind came out.

"Poor Scotty, he can't buck back anymore."

"Sorry Scott, no more playing Captain Bottom Boy for you."

Everyone started to laugh and the brief beauty of it was, Scott couldn't stop laughing either. They took him into surgery with a smile on his face.

That night, Buddha was flown out to Bagram with the casualties and we stayed on the FOB.

Despite our losses, I was proud of my team for their actions that day. To see friends perform to that level of quick-thinking professionalism during an actual worst-case scenario was something only a handful of people in this world can understand or appreciate.

The next morning, we made sure the trucks were locked up, gathered up whatever gear we could take back, and headed up to the landing zone (LZ). I saw Fawad's shemagh in the back of Buddha's gun truck. It was tattered and torn from the blast and had been used to clean up some blood from one of the injured gunners.

I folded it as best I could and placed it inside my vest next to my heart. It was a somber moment, and I was sure the feeling would remain with me for the rest of my life. Our retrograde to Kabul was via air. We retrieved the bodies from the morgue. The Afghans carried Fawad. While Alek, and Maric, and I carried Pero. We put them on the MI-8 and flew out to Bagram.

At Bagram, we sat on the tarmac for about forty-five minutes. It was hot, which made it uncomfortable. The two bodies with us were beginning to decompose and smell. No one wanted to say anything because they were our friends who died for us, so we sucked it up and dealt with it.

We got to Kabul and were met by Rector, the rest of the HQ staff, and some of the client staff. Apparently, when Rector got the message about my team getting hit and the number of casualties, his team did the drop at Herat, rested up for a few hours, and drove straight through to get back to Kabul. His team was the third team on *The Pony Express* to make it on the 1000-km Club.

We debriefed some more, and the end result was that we needed to time our runs into the valley with the military. We had to stay off the roads and in the stream beds whenever possible. Pero's body was flown home, Fawad's was brought back to his family for immediate burial. The gunners took a few days off.

I went back to my *CHU* to get some rest. I was exhausted, but at the same time, I couldn't sleep. I laid there thinking about Fawad and Pero. What could we have done differently? What could we have done better?

I spent a great deal of time going over the events of April 20th trying to figure out what went wrong, if anything. Intelligence, communications, navigation, counterassault, first aid. All played a factor at one point or another. I was not second-guessing anything, although I felt a sense of guilt. Was it survivor's remorse or something else?

I sat up and stared at my footlocker. It was cold and black and reminded me of that fucking route. I grabbed a silver sharpie and began to mark a broken center stripe down the middle of the footlocker. It put me in a trance as if I had white line fever. I finally snapped out of it and opened the box and placed Fawad's bloody shemagh inside and sealed it up.

The next week, I flew out to Dubai for a week to decompress. I needed it badly and ended up getting drunk. Not a smart thing to do when feeling emotionally crushed, but it was all I could do to maintain my sanity. I knew a lot of guys post-mission who turned to the bottle or worse, drugs, but I never really went that far. I stayed by myself for the most part and ended up sleeping for two days straight.

Buddha also needed time to think. He took his downtime in conjunction with his upcoming vacation. As the senior medic, his insight into the event was paramount to the After-Action Report because it offered another eye-witness account of the incident through his actions and treatment of our casualties. His perspective revealed weaknesses in our contracted MEDEVAC services and the difficulty of obtaining any timely QRF response.

When I returned to Kabul, I was faced with another harsh reality. The fighting season was picking up. We would soon return to the "Valley of the Shadow of Death."

CHAPTER FORTY-ONE
Contact: IED
DATE: May 01, 2010
MISSION: C-1 Convoy to Spin Boldak
LOCATION: Qalat, Zabul Province

When I returned from Dubai, the fighting season was heating up. Another mail team had been attacked on the way to Sharana, at the Four Corners, near Janur District, southeast of Ghazni. This was a strange place to carry out an attack. The four corners intersection was flatland for miles, punctuated with an elevated refueling tank, a haji shop, and a billboard. There was no place for the enemy to hide. Any IED would have been detonated by a pressure plate or command-detonated from a distance; otherwise, we would have lit that building up and killed everything inside.

In the ambush, one of their truck drivers bailed out and took off running, so the team medic jumped in and drove the truck to the FOB. The driver was found a few days later in a ditch with a couple of bullet holes in his head. Who knows what would have happened if the medic hadn't taken the wheel? Each team member had to be ready for just about any job.

We made it a point to know how to drive the trucks in case something like that happened to us. It was good to see the training pay off.

Even so, gunners were continually unreliable and problematic. Anytime we made contact with the enemy, they ducked down and hid in the gun truck instead of returning fire. In response, we made a couple of runs with only US expats and Serbians. The gunners got the message: they were replaceable. The idea worked. We got a new bunch of gunners from Panjshir Valley.

Known as the "Valley of the Five Lions," Panjshir Valley was located in north-central Afghanistan, about 150 kilometers north of Kabul, near the Hindu Kush Mountain range. Divided by the Panjshir River, it was the site of the Panjshir offensives fought between the Democratic Republic of Afghanistan and the Soviets against the Mujahideen during the Soviet-Afghan War from 1980 to 1985.

Local commander Ahmad Shah Massoud successfully defended the valley from being taken. They witnessed renewed fighting during the 1996-2001 civil war when the Northern Alliance, under the command of Massoud, defended it from being overrun by the Taliban.

Our new gunners came from this volatile war zone, confident, well-trained, and deserving of the job.

As a prime example of their tenacity and grit came on a run with Money and Buddha.

We had stopped at FOB Apache for the night to do some repairs on one of our gun trucks before we moved on to Tarin Kowt and the Aussie FOB. One Afghan gunner who always wore sunglasses had a big problem that we were unaware of.

Our terp asked Buddha if he could take a look at the badass gunner's eye. He said it was hurting. Buddha went to their tent and got a firsthand look. When the gunner removed his sunglasses, Buddha stepped back. The gunner's eye was missing.

He had suffered an injury and the eye had been removed only a few days earlier. The dry socket wasn't healing well. He had failed to mention this little problem before the mission, but even with just one eye, he was still a far better gunner than the others who had fled. Buddha took care of him.

Money was my ATL on the next C-1 mission to Kandahar and Spin Boldak—with our new gunners. There was little warning of the dangers ahead. The Taliban insurgent had laid his ambush with great cunning, near a place called Shahjoy.

Hidden along the side of the road, the bomb looked like any

other piece of trash. The IED exploded near the right front of my gun truck.

The massive boom sent shockwaves roaring over us. I could feel the concussion roll through the vehicle like a wave. When the hood buckled under the pressure, a wall of heat penetrated the cab.

I felt a thump in my chest. My eyes burned and teared up. Despite wearing ballistic glasses, I could barely see. "You okay?" I yelled. The ringing in my ears was deafening.

"Yeah! Yeah!" Petko shouted back. Then he started cussing in Serbian. He inhaled deeply and spit on the floor of the cab. He hung onto the steering wheel and kept his foot off the gas to avoid rolling the gun truck. He did an awesome job of keeping control of the vehicle.

After a good hour, my ears began to clear to a dull roar. I spit out the dirt that had lodged between my teeth. We continued to push through, snot and blood trailing from our noses.

The translator was the only one hurt from the explosion, with several cuts on the left side of his neck. Money patched him up and radioed the Doc to examine him the next time the convoy stopped. Money was concerned the terp might have sustained an air embolism to his neck from the blast pressure, something that was common as a tertiary effect of blast exposure.

Within a few miles of the IED blast, one of the gun trucks started to overheat, so we did a quick-stop and hooked the gun truck up to another F-550.

Since we were down, Money had the Doc take a look at the Terp, but when he showed up to Money's rig, he didn't bring any of his medical supplies. Money was pissed off and asked where his med bag was. The Doc didn't think he needed it. Money made him run his ass all the way back to the front of the convoy to get it.

After the terp was tended to, we got back in line and started to roll. We had only made it a click when all of a sudden, another

IED went off on the right side of Money's vehicle. It stalled out from the vacuum created by the blast pressure. The fuel pumps in the F-550-gun trucks were designed to shut off with any kind of impact, to keep any residual fires to a minimum. Money had to hit the restart button located behind the glove box to get the gun truck back in service.

We were trying to establish communications when Money finally confirmed they were okay.

Then a third IED detonated.

I immediately ordered everyone to hit their panic buttons. I thought we were going to have a repeat of the Orgun-E run.

We pulled up and did another quick check. It was a good time to catch our breath and check for secondary injuries. There were many times when an operator was wounded but didn't know it until the effects of the adrenalin rush had worn off. We looked each other over and did a quick walk-around of the gun truck to check for damage. Everything checked out okay.

They got the vehicle going and we continued south until we got to Qalat. We stopped for fuel when one of the truck drivers complained his truck was broken.

I told him to fix it, or we would leave him behind. This was commonplace. Some drivers expected us to pay for repairs to their vehicles. Enough was enough. I refused to help him out. Miraculously, his vehicle repaired itself and made it to Kandahar.

After a round of drops at Spin Boldak, and Lashkar Gah, we began the drive back to Kabul. We came up on the rear of an Army convoy that was stopped. The road had been cut by another IED.

We turned around and found billeting at FOB Apache in Qalat until the road was repaired. After three nights, we safely returned to base in Kabul, with no other IED contact.

We had to remain vigilant of our surroundings. Contact IED was the real deal. We couldn't lose any more men. Everyone had to carry their weight—and then some.

The guys on *The Pony Express* had zero tolerance for stupidity when it came to staying alive.

When the Doc was ill-prepared to care for the injured terp, he was clearly out of his element. He could have compromised the entire team's safety.

Money had Rector cut the Doc loose for incompetence. It was easier once he was cited for a negligent discharge in his vehicle. He threatened the Serbs not to say anything, but eventually, we found out.

It was better to know the incompetence and cut it off at the knees than find out in the middle of an ambush or IED explosion where all our lives were at risk. Zero tolerance.

CHAPTER FORTY-TWO
Funny Money Mike

Money and I always had a good time running missions together. Hell, everybody liked working with him. He was serious when the time for seriousness was needed, but he cracked us up with his jokes and stories. Money was a walking holiday who shined light in the many dark places we traversed and brought us joy. He was always messing around when we had downtime.

One of the funniest things he ever told me was about a mission they ran to Gardez. They had already passed FOB Shank and were headed towards the Tera Pass when one of the drivers just pulled off to the side of the road.

Not knowing what was going on, Money ordered the convoy to continue onward to the next rally point. He stopped his gun truck to see what was up with the truck driver. Money walked up to the cargo truck, climbed up on the running board, and saw the cab was empty. He spotted the driver at 3 o'clock through the window about 100 meters away, squatting down to take a shit. A nearby row of mud huts known as qal'ahs or kalats were surrounded by berms and brush.

Then all hell broke loose.

The two rigs came under direct attack with small arms fire by Taliban militia who were hidden in the huts. Rounds plinked off the cargo truck as Money made his way back to his gun truck. The top gunners were laying down cover fire. The whole time this was going on, the squatter remained steadfast and undaunted. Money said, "That son of a bitch was bound and determined to finish taking a shit."

What cracked me up the most was when he said, "Who the

hell was gonna explain that to his wife—that something happened to her husband while some Nanner was taking a dump?"

He kept going on and on about how the guy lit up a cigarette or turned the page to his favorite magazine *Bachi Baazi Boys*. We all laughed our asses off every time he told that story.

Money was in rare form when the contract started to pick up and SOC brought in more operators. One of the new guys was a skinny medic. Money charged up to him, got right in his grill and asked, "What is your name, boy?"

"Jim," the timid medic replied.

Money scowled. "Look, you bleeding-heart, liberal pansy. I don't know what boat you just got off, but as your TL, I never call any of my men by their first name. It breeds familiarity and leads to a breakdown in authority. I refer to the guys on my team by their last name only— Chase, Langley, King, Babbitt, Ford—that's all! Do I make myself clear?"

"Yes, Sir," snapped the medic.

"Good, now that we have that straight, what is your last name?"

The medic looked less than happy about the request, but after only a brief pause, he sighed and said, "Yastorozhdestvenskaya. My name is Jim Yastorozhdestvenskaya. Sir."

"Okay, Jim. The next thing I want you to do is..."

We all busted out laughing at the same time. It was typical Funny Money Mike.

One time on a split mission back in late August 2009, Money and Chase ran a short hop from Kandahar to Spin Boldak with only two trucks and no gunners. Chase took up the rear PKM in the follow-vehicle. Halfway to the firebase, he heard gunfire coming from somewhere on the right.

Chase opened fire with a short burst on the PKM. At the same time, about three hundred meters out, a donkey reared-up and fell over dead. Money was pissed.

"What the fuck, Chase?" Money shouted.

"Dude, I heard bullets whizzing by." "Did you see anything?"

Money asked, "No."

Money just stood there shaking his head. He dipped into his pocket and paid some poor farmer a couple hundred bucks for the loss of his mule, which was his only means of making a living. Then he gave him a couple hundred bucks more not to say anything about it.

He leaned into Chase and gave him a stern ass-chewing, they continued on without incident. Money said it was the most expensive piece of ass they ever had to pay for without getting anything in return.

Chase asked Money not to tell Rector. He was already on thin ice and swore him to secrecy. Money's word was gold and he promised to keep it on the down low.

Buddha, Scott Vaughn, Yastorozhdestvenskaya and I had to fly back out to Orgun-E from Kabul to retrieve our two-gun trucks from the previous IED attacks.

We linked up with the client and coordinated with the next Army convoy coming to Orgun-E to escort us back to FOB Sharana. The personnel were put in the MRAPs and the gun trucks went on the heavy haulers. Everyone knew we were the easy target.

While waiting at FOB Sharana, Buddha flew out for leave and Yastorozhdestvenskaya resigned after pulling one mission and went home. Scott Vaughn and I brought back the two-gun trucks after linking up with a mail run team.

Money said, "Good, I was starting to run out of names for Y'ass-tore-zee-dust-off-vent-a-caca."

We laughed for days after that.

CHAPTER FORTY-THREE
Small Arms Fire
DATE: August 11, 2010
MISSION: Phase I - C-1 Convoy to Orgun-E Phase II - Deliver Generators to Shkin
LOCATION: Shkin, Paktika Province

Due to the close proximity to the Pakistani border, the routes we drove on saw significant enemy contact. This was not just in the form of improvised explosive devices or indirect rocket attacks, but actual direct enemy contact with small arms fire.

After getting our guts busted by Money, I was assigned another C-1 mission and a new ATL. Chris Vaile was a Marine combat vet who fought during Operation Iraqi Freedom in Fallujah, Iraq, 2004-2005. He was a solid dude and would have made an awesome team leader, but fate saw otherwise.

I gave him a quick brief on how the Taliban operated and how they were different from the Iraqi insurgents. The biggest difference was when the Taliban attacked, they stood and fought. The Iraqis tended to set off an IED and run. They never engaged us on open ground. I'll always remember his reaction when I told him.

"So, they're worthy adversaries?" he asked.

In his young days, Chris listened to his father and grandfather, a Korean war veteran who retired after twenty years in the Corps, talk about the brotherhood shared in the Marines, and the stories about their experiences. His father, Duffy, was also a Marine with 1/8 during the Beirut barracks bombing in 1983.

When it came time to open the door to life after high school, he chose the Marines. Chris loved being a Marine. He completed three tours in Iraq, rising to the rank of Sergeant. He was awarded the Purple Heart, Distinguished Army Medallion, and the Combat Action Ribbon.

After the Marines, he struggled with fitting in and finding work. He needed to get back to what he liked most—helping others. Eventually, he arrived at SOC. He was at his best and happiest with the guys from *The Pony Express*. The rest was history.

My first C-1 mission after returning from leave was going to be back to Shkin. I almost shit myself when Rector told me. I tried to keep my cool, but the flashbacks hit hard.

This was the same route we took when Pero and Fawad were killed.

Chris and I went over to Camp Phoenix to coordinate with the Army about their convoy and route clearance moves through the valley. I called the platoon commander in the TOC at FOB Sharana using a secured encrypted phone line.

It turned out they had an ongoing operation in the area during the same time we were going to be there, so I knew the routes were cleared and air support was available if needed. This paid huge dividends when we launched. Chris told me I had a whole different demeanor afterward.

Yeah, I felt a whole lot better going in knowing the US Army cleared the route.

The makeup for the mission was Chris in the lead, me in the middle, and Buddha in the trail vehicle. We got to the vehicles, double-checked all our gear, and began to push out while it was still dark. As we entered the valley, I met up with the platoon commander.

"Good day, sir. My name is Ed Ford. I called you earlier on SVoIP to discuss the route." "Ah yes glad you made it safely. I'm going to have a couple of Apache's fly overwatch.

I'll let them know to look for you and provide cover."

"Awesome," I said. "Thank you."

"No worries, glad to help."

We shook hands and departed.

We were to pick up two generators from Orgun-E and deliver them to a Firebase in Shkin. They were huge and were originally placed on the wrong-sized trucks, which were the smaller Hinos. The previous team that was sent down to make the delivery couldn't get them to the site because one of the vehicles rolled off the road due to the overload.

We passed the rolled truck. Sitting off to the side of the road, we spotted our old lead vehicle that had been burned and destroyed by the mine strike.

I got a shiver up my spine when I saw it, then settled back in my seat and said a quick silent prayer for Pero and Fawad.

"Uh... Lord...Looks like you got yourself a couple of good souls..." I paused for a moment and then continued, *"I don't know if they prayed or to whom, but please keep them...They made our jobs easier and I'm thankful to have known them. Dust to dust. Till Valhalla Brothers."*

The two heavy-duty cargo trucks were waiting for us when we pulled in to Orgun-E. One was a Mercedes and the other, a Kamaz. We rented a crane and an operator and got the generators switched over to the cargo trucks, then pushed to Shkin via the Barmal route.

There were two main routes from Orgun-E to Shkin. Route Jeep was the shortest and hilliest. The Barmal route was longer but flatter, so we were able to move faster. The benefits of each route didn't offset the opportunities for attack. An ambush could easily be set up on Route Jeep, and on the Barmal route, the enemy could see us coming from a distance and set up a complex attack. It was a catch-22 all over again.

One of the truck drivers knew the Barmal route well, so I promised him some extra money if he led the way. I was hoping for an uneventful trip but halfway through, we started to get a number of flat tires. One of the truck drivers forgot to bring a spare. When the tire went flat, the generator and cargo shifted, and we constantly had to stop and readjust the load.

Normally, we made the drive in three hours, but this trip took eight hours to complete.

We pulled into Shkin at 2345 hours. We were lucky because the contract stated delivery no later than midnight and everyone was happy. We beat the clock by fifteen minutes. It would have been funny as hell if the damaged truck had rolled onto its side the minute we made it into the client's holding yard.

I got a call from Cecil Corbin, the in-country manager, and Rector, telling us we'd done a good job. Since we were running parallel to the Afghan/Pakistan border, the client told me they were prepared to launch a QRF if we needed it, but saying that after the mission brought little comfort since we had been let down in the past.

After the offload, we prepped to head back to Orgun-E. The driver who had forgotten his spare tire asked if we could load his truck onto the Kamaz. This was his third mistake and we got tired of picking up his slack.

I told him, "Fuck off! It's not my fault you forgot your spare!" We left the truck there at Shkin.

On the way back to Orgun-E we had to go over a series of hills where Taliban Militia and criminal activity took root. In the village at the foot of the hills, we made friends with some of the kids. We stopped and handed out a bunch of snacks and pogey bait, thinking if the kids liked us, maybe Dad and Uncle Achmed wouldn't launch any RPGs at us. We were desperate to make friends and a little goodwill went a long way. In other words, "Hearts and Minds" at work.

My lead vehicle with Chris Vaile got a flat tire and we had to stop to fix it right there in the hills. The trail vehicle stayed low and covered the rear 180 degrees. I pushed my vehicle past the lead to cover the front 180 degrees.

We were hit by incoming small arms fire. "Load up and get ready to move," I called.

Chris radioed me. "The lead vehicle is still on the jack."

That wasn't the news I wanted to hear, but it was the situation I had to deal with. "Everyone hit your pings. Deploy. Secure our perimeter."

I moved toward Chris. He was scanning the area when a burst of fire stitched the ground between us. We hit the deck. We both saw the firing position and returned fire. I'll always remember the look on Chris's face. "You mother fuckers! How dare you!"

In the middle of the attack, Rector called. "What's going on?"

I could hear the gun truck behind me engaging to the left front while I gave Rector an update and directed the gunner's fan of fire. I spotted my terp, Timor Shah, kneeling behind a tree returning fire, so I helped him out with suppressive fire.

Four or five criminal insurgents worked through the defilade to the left front of the convoy, so we engaged them. Between Timor and I returning fire and suppressive fire from the PKM's, a couple of insurgents left the area in haste. Unfortunately, a couple of their shooter buddies weren't so lucky. We laid down the hate and sent them to their 72 virgins. It's God's job to forgive the terrorists, it's our job to arrange the meeting came to mind.

The attack came from three sides. Buddha's truck was engaging to the enfilade to the left rear, too. By then, Radamir, the driver of the lead vehicle, had fixed the tire.

We rolled off the X.

I joked with Chris: "Fix your shit or I'll fucking burn it and you can walk!"

As he drove past me, he got on the radio and told me he was up. When I looked out, he flipped me off. Yeah, he was a fighter. He later said he would rather be shot than let the guys down. He really solidified the team dynamic.

It was one thing to be cool and another to be Marine, but Chris was definitely a cool Marine. I liked that about him. He also had a deeper perspective of our situation. One of the things he liked the most was making the run to Jalalabad.

Driving through the mountains on the Mahipar Pass was an eye-opener for him and for many of us. It was beautiful but extremely dangerous. We had to push through, despite small arms fire—and worse.

CHAPTER FORTY-FOUR
The Mahipar Pass

During the war in Afghanistan, the Mahipar Pass was a major route for resupplying military armament and food to NATO forces. In August 2011, coalition forces halted activity at the Pass due to the number of attacks from extremists. The US and its allies took losses during a large number of assaults on the trucks heading to the frontier line.

The Americans built this engineering feat in the 1960s. The road dropped down more than a mile. In those few kilometers of zig-zagged highway that is carved and tunneled into vertical cliffs with one-hundred-meter-high waterfalls, temperatures went from freezing at 7,000 feet to subtropical at around 1,700 feet. The sides of the gorge were so high and steep, it was impossible to see the road below. On the hairpin route, there was no shoulder, only a crumbling low stone wall in certain places.

Taking our eyes off the road, even for a second, was never an option.

The next deadly portion of the route was the road at the Tang-e Gharu gorge. It ran directly between the Kabul River and 600-meter-high cliffs. The Taliban took several opportunities to attack our convoys, having the tactical advantages of surprise, elevation, cover, and concealment.

The forty-mile stretch at the peak claimed so many lives so regularly that most people stopped counting. Cars would pass a convoy on a turn and flip over, flattening out. Trucks often soared to the valley floor. Buses loaded with passengers would play chicken with other buses and collide in a massive onslaught of mangled wreckage and death.

The Mahipar Pass was historically famous. Rudyard Kipling

wrote about it and Afghanistan, in general, during the days of the British occupation. The Soviets learned the hard way that the pass was a dangerous place when the natives got restless. It was notorious for traffic jams on both sides, leading to many angry ANA and ANP.

There was nothing anyone could do to explain to an Afghan policeman who was pissed off and waving his AK-47 around like an idiot that we needed to get our job done. He wasn't hearing it. We could not move anyway. It reminded me of someone pushing the up or down elevator button twenty times as though it would somehow get there faster. We were all sitting ducks and extremely lucky we didn't get ambushed while waiting for hours for the traffic to clear.

Any runs through the Mahipar Pass were missions to FOB Fenty in Jalalabad. The base was named after Lieutenant Colonel Joseph J. Fenty, Jr., a founding member and first commanding officer of 3rd Squadron, 71st Cavalry (Recon) that built the organization from the ground up. He took command on September 16, 2004, trained the unit, and led the Titans on their first deployment to Afghanistan, in support of Operation Enduring Freedom VII.

On May 5, 2006, nearing the end of Operation Mountain Lion, Lt. Col. Fenty personally oversaw a high-risk night extraction of one of his Cavalry scout teams located high in the mountains above Chalas Valley. During the extraction on the hostile rugged terrain, the Boeing CH-47 Chinook helicopter that he was in crashed. Everyone aboard perished.

The route to J-Bad was dangerous for a number of reasons. First and foremost, it was the only route to J-Bad and it was a long trip. Once a team passed Sarobi, the battle switch was turned on.

There was nowhere to turn or go if your convoy came under attack. That meant driving during the day and night. Trying to be time and place unpredictable minimized the team's exposure on the worst part of the route known as Psalm 23— "Yea, though I walk through the valley of the shadow of death, I will fear no evil: for thou art with me..."

Psalm 23 was also called the Voodoo Highway after a song written by Ray Gillen and Jake E. Lee from the 1990s rock band Badlands. *"Wake up on a Sunday mornin', heard a voice in my head... He's tryin' to take me down before I'm dead. Oh, down that Voodoo Highway. Oh, down that wicked road."*

The turnaround time for mail drops at J-Bad was notoriously slow. It was common practice to bring back outgoing mail to Kabul to be sorted for transport to the United States. A team arrived on time but would still have to wait for a KBR Fobbit to show up with a T-Rex to offload the mail trucks.

The team would split up and stop by the DFAC for a hot meal, then bring back a couple of extra plates for the guys who stayed back with the trucks and mail. Pretty routine, but the long wait times put the team in jeopardy for the return trip for two reasons.

Even though the convoys moved at night and had the advantage of darkness, movements were slower. Secondly, the enemy was always watching. They might not have known when we were rolling to J-Bad, but once we passed their lookouts, they knew we would return on the one and only route back.

When running missions to J-Bad, we learned about the Coca-Cola vs Pepsi wars. West of Sarobi was Pepsi country. Bloody battles between Mujahideen guerrillas and frustrated urban militias occurred there. Yet, we were never ambushed next to a Pepsi advertisement. The closer we got to J-Bad, the more Coca-Cola ads appeared—and we knew we were in the badlands—and would likely be attacked.

The real Coca-Cola-Pepsi war began in 1990. Pepsi was smack in the middle of the historic invasion route to Kabul. It was awarded two large loans from Kabul to boost sales of the new generation cola. Coke had the disadvantage of being located right next to the conspicuous Ministry of Defense building, a frequent target for rocket attacks and the site of bloody fighting in past coup attempts. Both franchises faced the problem of production slowdowns due to guerrilla rocket attacks and house-to-house street fighting.

Either way, I didn't give a damn because nearly half the military and two-thirds of *The Pony Express* team drank Red Bull, despite Rector's directive. With such high demand, it became a regular "morale staple," and was included on trips and convoys alongside food, water, and bullets. Caffeine and war went hand-in-hand.

We needed all the caffeine we could handle as we maneuvered our way through the Mahipar Pass. Attacks were inevitable. And we needed to be on high alert.

CHAPTER FORTY-FIVE
General Matiullah Khan
DATE: August 15, 2010
MISSION: Resupply to FOB Hadrian (to stand up the static site)
LOCATION: Uruzgan Province

With Red Bull in hand, we headed out on our next mission to FOB Hadrian in the Uruzgan Province, a mountainous badlands that was a Taliban stronghold before General Matiullah Khan beat the insurgents back in 2001. The camp was located south of Camp Holland, a Dutch battle group known as Task Force Urozgan, in Tarin Kowt. In June of 2007, in the Battle of Chora, a Taliban offensive and a Dutch counterattack proved to be the heaviest fighting in Uruzgan Province since ISAF extended its area of responsibility to the south.

The data dump provided by the S-2 intelligence officer revealed that the local police force had been recruited by the Army. The police commander was General Matiullah Khan, a known drug dealer who controlled the opium trade in the south. Apparently, the deal was as follows: If nothing blew up on the road, the Army turned a blind eye to his dealings. If anything blew up on the road, the Army would take the drugs.

Fair enough, I guess.

Matiullah was America's go-to man in Urozgan. His presence was equally important to the US military, which viewed Urozgan as a linchpin in southern Afghanistan. It relied on Matiullah to support US Special Forces and to secure the crucial supply road from Kandahar to Tarin Kowt.

Like other Afghan strongmen supported or tolerated by American forces, Matiullah had the gunmen and the iron fist to hold off the Taliban, even at the cost of undermining the very government institutions the US was trying to bolster. Despite attempts to sideline warlords, men like Matiullah remained in power because the weak and corrupt central government had very little authority, especially in remote areas.

US forces needed strong military allies and the Afghan army was unreliable.

For a decade, Matiullah's gunmen secured the winding dirt road, earning the chief millions of dollars in fees from trucking companies that contracted with ISAF to deliver supplies to Tarin Kowt. Some sources said Matiullah paid 1,200 gunmen, in addition to his cops stationed at posts along the road, to protect the convoys. That meant he was making a profit from the security provided in part by government-paid police.

Matiullah was at the center of the coalition military presence in the area. A base for a US Special Operations Task Force was just 200 yards from his expansive compound, which was powered by an enormous generator in a province with no electrical service.

Ten years earlier, Matiullah had been a lowly highway cop. He built a power base through guile and savvy, and via his hereditary role as a leader of the powerful Popalzai tribe. He protected Hamid Karzai, a fellow Popalzai who took refuge in Urozgan when the US-led invasion was toppling the Taliban regime in 2001.

Matiullah had commanded a mountain militia that waged guerrilla warfare against the Taliban in Uruzgan, the birthplace and former power base of the Taliban's spiritual leader, Mullah Mohammed Omar.

The chief was also close to Karzai's half-brother, Ahmed Wali Karzai, the political boss of Kandahar who was assassinated in July 2011 and had been described by US officials and others as flagrantly corrupt.

That interesting fact got us to Tarin Kowt without incident.

We made the next push from Tarin Kowt to FOB Hadrian. When we arrived, we met the SOC site security manager and did the offload, refueled the vehicles, and left immediately. We got back to FOB Tiger without incident.

It was the holy month of Ramadan, the ninth month of the Muslim year. Strict fasting was observed from sunrise to sunset. I wanted to depart FOB Tiger when all the Afghans were breaking their fast and eating. This way we could get a head start before any of the spotters and triggermen were out.

Maybe it was a solid plan to have allies like Matiullah on the treacherous routes. But that never meant we stopped looking out for ourselves. "Trust no one" rang in my ears.

CHAPTER FORTY-SIX
Left Behind
DATE: September 06, 2010
MISSION: Phase I—C-1 Convoy to Orgun-E Phase II—Resupply to Shkin
LOCATION: Gomal District, Paktika Province

Mobility was a game of cat and mouse. We were always trying to out-guess the Taliban so we could move while they didn't have observation on us. When Team V secured a mission to Orgun-E and Shkin, I temporarily loaned them Chris, my lead navigator and ATL who knew the route to the drop sites. He would command their lead vehicle.

I was just beginning to break into the operations side of the job, so I got to know some of the guys better since I had access to their personnel files. Matt Attalai, who I assigned to Team V with Chris, was the only other Canadian aside from Chase to roll with *The Pony Express.*

Born and raised in Toronto, Ontario on November 1, 1983, Matt moved to the States after high school and joined the US Army. He served as an infantry soldier with 2nd Battalion, 3 Infantry, also known as the Patriot Battalion, from 2004 to 2008. He had one deployment to Iraq.

Matt was honorably discharged and was hired by SOC in February 2010. His favorite thing to do was to take long walks on the beach, literally. The guys teased him all the time about it until he finally had a patch made that said he liked taking long walks on the beach. It was pretty funny, but Matt was serious.

On the run to Orgun-E, Team V was hit. An IED struck the lead vehicle, killing Chris and Matt.

Two gunners and the interpreter were also injured in the blast.

Matt was blown from the vehicle and his body was immediately recovered. However, the team leader did not seem to think it important to recover Chris's body. They left him on the X without confirming his death.

It angered and hurt me to think that the last thing Chris could have heard before he died was the sound of a gun truck pulling away.

We were at the KPMO compound when notification of the hit on our team came through. Rector put the units on lockdown, with no Internet or phone calls, to keep the news from getting out until we got the full story.

B.J. Tooker, my earlier relief at Chapman, had since bumped up to SOC corporate. He had just arrived from Minden, Nevada and was sitting with Rector in his office when the situation report from the team leader came in. A thermite grenade had detonated as a result of the IED blast, the unit was on fire, and they were unable to recover Chris's body.

B.J. had his start with the teams in Iraq and when he came to Afghanistan, he ran the roads with us. At least this way, we had someone in Minden who knew what we were talking about.

He was under the impression they were under secondary attack and so a decision to move quickly off the X in order to save the living would have been understandable.

At the Camp Phoenix TOC, a representative from the combat surgical hospital at FOB Sharana stated that when Team V rolled in, the medic told him they only had one set of remains. Why was Chris not with them?

The team leader said the vehicle was on fire and Chris was not recoverable. This did not sit well with us. It wasn't until the next morning that the stories didn't match.

Rector coordinated with the C-1 client and sent an Operational Detachment-A (ODA) to the site. Samurai's team did the recovery on what remained of the TL's crew. They extricated Chris and then burned the vehicle.

Rector and B.J. headed to Bagram AFB to view and confirm the remains. Neither body had indications of being burned.

Everyone was pretty shaken up and confused. The team leader had real problems trying to reconcile what he had told us on-site and what actually happened. His explanation changed. He said due to the stressors of combat and the fog of war, he had to leave Chris behind.

I reminded him that I was also hit in that same valley and lost two good men, but I didn't leave anyone behind.

Rector and BJ pointed out to the team leader that they had to explain to the client why an American body was left behind. There was a protocol in place when an American or ISAF member went missing, dead or alive. The priority went to the rescue/recovery effort of that member. The team leader backpedaled, trying to justify his bullshit actions.

All I wanted to do was hurt him. Badly.

I remembered the curb stomp scene from *American History X* and pictured my foot on the back of his head. I lost a lot of sleep over this because I was so full of rage. My anger overshadowed my sorrow for Chris and Matt. It truly robbed me of my grief. There was no way to let my anger out. I had a glass of chai in my hand and slammed it against the wall.

Finding the largest broken piece, I stuffed it in my footlocker and carried on. I wasn't alone.

Other members of *the Pony Express* felt the same way when they found out what the team leader had done. "Frag that fucker" they whispered, over and over.

One thing about tribe mentality. It's not like a stone hitting the water and leaving a ripple effect. The loss of Chris and Matt wasn't close to a ripple, it was a fucking Tsunami.

For his incompetence and inability to handle the situation on the site, the team leader was relieved of his duties and was reassigned to FOB Hadrian. As far as I was concerned, he was lucky to keep a job. He should have been fired.

Rector tried to have the team leader fired, but corporate was concerned about opening a retaliation lawsuit. This was another good example of the business side of war. Any other time, the team leader would've been fired, but for this case, it was more beneficial to protect corporate interests.

I told Rector, "We should have taken that mission. This shit never would've happened." Rector replied, "Every team is required to do all runs and the team leader is no exception to the rule,"

Rector also added. "He fucked up big time and it cost us two lives!"

It pissed me off to think the shithead got a pass. If he had stayed in Kabul, it would have been a different outcome.

It was sad to think about life and death, even though it was all around us, all the time.

Why did good guys have to die, and assholes get to live?

At this point, I realized my prized footlocker was becoming something more sinister, something I wanted to avoid. Bad memories could drive you to the brink of insanity and that was a place I didn't want to go. I needed time to get into the right headspace before I could deal with the risks, the tragedies and betrayals. I had to take charge of my own rate of progress even if it meant switching off temporarily.

Although Matt was Canadian, he had served in the Army and as an American expat providing a valuable service to the Department of Defense. The Army decided to keep him and Chris in the military system to get them home.

We mustered at the Bagram mortuary affairs hanger. Their caskets were draped with the American flag and placed on a Bier rolling-system-type gurney. We said a few prayers, then loaded our friends onto the box trucks that were backed up to the hanger. We locked them in and rode in convoy to the C-17 Globemaster.

I tried to get "Knocking on Heaven's Door" by Guns and

Roses to play, but the damn CD got stuck, so we rolled in silence.

It was a somber moment for everyone. We all had mixed emotions about losing close friends, men we considered brothers, in battle. Still, we knew all too well the dangers in running missions on Ring Road.

It must have been difficult for Rector, who was responsible for the repatriation of the remains. The notification process was extremely informal and detached, but the goal was to notify the family before the news was released on the Internet and social media. I can't imagine finding out your loved one just got killed by reading it on the Internet.

Once there, we loaded Chris and Matt onto the aircraft where they received full honors from the flight crew. SOC's human resources and legal departments were immediately engaged and contract agreements were carefully reviewed for authorization and release. Because of the initial misinformation by the team leader, both Chris and Matt were cremated at Dover AFB upon arrival. Both bodies could have had an open casket if the team leader had only sent the correct message.

Rector said SOC corporate then contacted the local police agency to knock on the door and inform next of kin with the death notification. It would have been more respectful to have a SOC representative accompany the law enforcement officer, but that didn't happen.

About a year after the incident, Rector spoke with Chris's mother. She had a lot of questions and wanted to know all the graphic details. In the end, they were both in tears, but she felt much better knowing the truth. She appreciated hearing it from one of the guys on the ground. For years, the aftermath of dealing with so many losses, especially since he knew everyone on a personal level, took a toll on Rector.

Another hard pill to swallow was that a police officer had to notify Matt's parents at their home in Toronto, not a SOC representative. They drove to Delaware to pick up his remains and all the items he was wearing, like his parachute cord bracelet. They said driving home with his remains was absolutely devastating.

He was given a flag ceremony by the US Army with a three-gun salute and taps in Michigan's upper peninsula. Some of his ashes were buried there in Eagle River. Some of the remaining ashes were spread around the world in different places that he loved.

Matt had told his family that when he died, he wanted a Viking send-off. He said it jokingly, but not completely. He wanted the whole Viking Valhalla funeral. Ha! Only Matt! He was loved so much, they all said, "Okay, Matt, sure thing."

A year after he died, they had the Viking funeral.

They built a Viking boat, and family and friends came from all over, including Arnie Campbell, all the way from Scotland. They wore Hawaiian shirts and aviators and placed letters, flowers, a pack of smokes, and more personal items next to his ashes on the boat. They accompanied him on his journey to the next realm.

Matt would've loved it. They set his boat on fire with a flaming bow and arrow.

Everyone raised a cold glass of beer and toasted to Matt. A warrior, hero, son, and friend.

Our brother.

CHAPTER FORTY-SEVEN
The 1000 Kilometer Club
DATE: September 20, 2010
MISSION: C-1 Convoy from Kabul to Herat
LOCATION: Ring Road

The losses tore me up. The clock started ticking for me. I needed a change of pace, a break for my body and my sanity.

My last mission as a team leader was a long one mentally and physically. We ran from Kabul to KAF to Spin Boldak, to Lashkar Gah, and ended in Herat, which was approximately 883 kilometers, but with detours it was closer to 997. kilometers. Quick turn-around times were instrumental for SOC to make more money, so they had to love us for this. A typical run to KAF took eight to twelve hours. However, on the second day, our entire trip with stops at all sites lasted twenty-four hours. It was one hell of a run.

My new assistant team leader was Greg Swanson, call sign Proximo. Greg was an old convoy guy from the Cochise days. Cochise was a security company that did a lot of convoy and security work in Iraq. Greg was taking over as TL for one of the teams and needed to learn the routes.

The security contracting world was a small one. It turned out Greg knew Chase from their work at EODT in Iraq. They were both members of a motorcycle club called the Original Infidels MC. When Greg went end of mission in June of 2012, Chase was hired to fill the void.

They missed each other by a matter of days but remain brothers for life.

On the first day, we arrived at Spin Boldak and spent the night there, then proceeded to Lashkar Gah and dropped off two of the cargo trucks. From there we drove to Herat and did the offload then spent the night at FOB Arena. The cargo truck was staying with the client, so I knew we could get an early start.

The next day, we pushed from the FOB back to Lashkar Gah to pick up the trucks. Once there, we made the decision to push through to Kabul in order to get back a day early.

We got everyone fed and then pushed up to Kabul. Along the way, one of the trucks broke down, so we left it at the Polish Provincial Reconstruction Team and pushed to Ghazni. There we picked up a truck that had been left by another team. By the time the sun came up, I was wired out on Red Bull, nicotine, and beef jerky.

We got to Kabul by 0800. Completing the Herat to Kabul run in one push made us official members of the "1,000 Kilometer Club." Our team—Rector, Drew, Money, Cookie, Chase, Samurai, and some of the drivers and gunners—were now proud members of the club.

Other teams made the long haul, but there was no matter of record. Cookie and Chase made the run in 2009. Cookie was sick and it damn near killed them. Two of their gunners were pissing blood, everyone had back pain from wearing all that kit and one guy quit because they didn't stop at the Kandahar Hotel for the night.

Our team was special, hardcore. We got the jobs done. We were proud of what we did and how we conducted ourselves. Not just anybody could do our work. To join the 1,000 Kilometer Club was a feather in our cap, bragging rights, but we'd already gone the distance in other ways.

From the time we were awarded the USPS/DoD contract, we had been dubbed *The Pony Express*. Although the title was unofficial, we later had a patch designed by the teams and sewn together by a local tailor to commemorate the contract.

As part of *The Pony Express*, I held every position in the SOC Afghanistan program, from Site Security Manager (Khost) to Assistant Team Leader to Team Leader on convoys. I was looking forward to moving on to the next phase, to operations. It was different and meant more responsibility, but I could handle it. I'd been trained with the best and had my patch to prove it.

CHAPTER FORTY-EIGHT
Casualties at the Arch
DATE: May 25, 2011
MISSION: DoD Mail Run to Ghazni
LOCATION: Wardak/Ghazni Province Arch

Team I was returning from a mail run in Ghazni, when the lead vehicle hit an IED. The team was about 300 meters away, but the blast threw the eight-ton gun truck forty yards into the air and flipped it upside down.

The casualties and injuries were plenty.

The driver, a Fijian named Ben, was killed instantly when he was pinned under the vehicle. One of the top gunners was also killed. The other gunner was unconscious. The assistant team leader on that mission, Nenad Antic, aka "Ness" was alive but unconscious, he died shortly after. In the back of the gun truck, the terp, Timor Shah, was dead for a total of five KIA on that run. The team leader, Jeff Bedford, was in the second vehicle. His gun truck hit the crater and went down. Bedford was knocked out.

When he came to, his team was under heavy fire from insurgents. He grabbed his gun and fought back. His adrenaline masked the excruciating pain from two ruptured spinal disks.

The third vehicle, commanded by Clint Anderson, the medic, avoided the crater. They stopped, dismounted, and began to cross-deck the casualties from the lead into the trail vehicle. They pushed back into the FOB, but all personnel in the lead vehicle died from extensive injuries sustained in the blast.

Jeff and his driver Obren, another Serbian, stayed on-site with their gunners to provide security and protect the mail truck. Jeff called for help. He waited nearly five hours for a coalition QRF to arrive from Ghazni, about thirteen miles away. Ben was still under the vehicle and needed to be extricated.

Jeff would not leave him or anyone behind.

When the soldiers finally found the mail convoy, they asked Jeff if they could call in an Apache helicopter strike to destroy the two disabled gun trucks with a Hellfire missile. He wholeheartedly agreed.

Both vehicles were pulled off the road and destroyed by the airstrike.

Even though the attack occurred in close proximity to the FOB, Lt. Col. Miroslav Ochyra, a spokesman for the Polish military responsible for Ghazni province, said the QRF was delayed because it was deployed five times that day, including a mission to assist Polish soldiers who had come under fire.

What was done, was done. They estimated five hundred pounds of homemade explosives had been buried in a culvert. Definitely not amateur hour.

We had all the guys who were in-country at the time gather in the main office. Tim and I informed them Team I had taken a bad hit.

"We lost five men," I said. "We lost the lead gun truck and all five of our brothers.

They're gone."

The looks of disbelief and shock on their faces, especially the Fijians, took us aback. This was their first loss. Ben's cousin Oscar was also on the same contract and took it exceptionally hard. They all gathered together to spend time with each other and remember their fallen comrade.

The Serbs were more stoic. They had been through this before. When Team IV returned to KPMO later that day, I went out to notify Samurai of the incident. Drazen was given permission to pull aside the two Serbs and break the news to them.

Ziko had known Ness for a long time and was visibly shaken.

They had both served in the Serbian Army together and were used to death and losses because of their involvement with the civil war in then Yugoslavia. He already missed his brother, who had positively impacted all who knew him.

We were very tight with our third country nationals. Greg Swanson referred to his Serb drivers as his "Serbian Sons." I was with him when the attack went down. Ness had been a driver on his team for quite some time and he took the loss pretty hard.

"You okay, Brother?" I asked

Greg said, "You know, it's unfair how the good guys are always taken from us too soon, and us grumpy old fuckers seem to survive."

"Dude, we could do this shit for a hundred years and lose a hundred friends, but we need to carry on for them. It's the only way to keep their memory alive."

He remembered times with Ness.

One Christmas Eve—the first of three days running hops to Kandahar and the surrounding other governmental agencies drop sites—Greg teamed up with Ness and Dragan Vidovic aka "Galib." They left Kabul early in the morning but got stuck in a traffic jam.

Galib opened his driver's door to try to get one of the cars to move out of the way. A bus driver going in the opposite direction pushed forward and hit his door, breaking his arm.

Greg got out of the vehicle, boarded the bus, grabbed the driver and beat his face against the dash. Every passenger within the line of sight ran to the back of the bus to get away from the crazy American. There must have been a couple dozen Afghans all crammed into a space of about five feet.

Ness came in and dragged Greg off the driver. "We have to go, Boss!"

It was like Ness was Greg's very own personal bodyguard. Whenever Greg was out of the truck, Ness was right behind him, moving at a run to back him up at all times. A lifesaver.

Greg drove the rest of the trip for Galib. When they got to

Kandahar, nobody wanted to look at Galib's arm. Everyone was too busy celebrating the holiday and nobody cared about non-Americans or Third Country Nationals.

His arm was obviously broken, but he continued to roll on the mission until they returned home on December 26.

Greg took him to a French hospital where he received an X-ray, confirming the fracture. They applied a cast. To get him paid for loss of mobility, Greg worked the system. It took over a year through the Defense Base Act, but Galib was then able to take some well-deserved time off and built his home in Serbia.

When we won over the third country nationals, their fierce loyalty was steadfast. But I could say the same for my team. Greg missed Ness, his Serbian Son.

When the team was recovered, our human resources specialist, Amr Uddin, identified the bodies. He let me know we had recovered all the local nationals killed in the blast.

The local hospital had a morgue where Tim and I had to confirm the remains of Ben and Ness. I looked at their bodies and went through their pockets. It was a strange feeling for me. Not two days earlier, I had worked out with Ness at the gym.

His face and clothing were soaked in blood. The tubes were still in his mouth from where Clint had tried to save him. The blast trauma caused a lot of swelling on his body. My primary ID was the tattoo on his arm. A large chunk of glass was embedded in his skin just below the tattoo. I pulled it out of his arm and put it in my cigarette pack.

It was at this time I realized I had to get out of running convoys. I saw myself being the next body on the slab. It scared the living shit out of me.

I also wondered what was going through Clint's mind at that time. *The Pony Express* was a brotherhood and losing a team member seemed to hit him even harder, especially since Ness was his friend.

"Don't go dark on me, bro," I told him. "You can't second-guess anything. Trying to understand the ifs and the whys of combat...you'll never really come to grips with the answer."

I don't know if my words offered any comfort at all. It was in those moments, the demons' howls echoed in our ears, deafening out all other sounds.

Tim and I coordinated the recovery of the bodies from Jeff's team for repatriation. They were extracted by air from the FOB and a MEDEVAC flight brought them back to Kabul. A second convoy drove down to Ghazni to pick up the mail truck and the gun truck.

Our Afghan counterparts complained that we were not doing enough. In actuality, we had gone above and beyond what was required.

They feared for their friends not being brought back to their families and given a decent burial in the traditional sense. Many believers tried to have the burial take place within twenty- four hours of the person's passing. During that time, the body was never left unattended.

Muslims made sure certain pre-burial rituals were completed before the burial occurred. The sooner this happened, the better.

The third country nationals were returned home, but their family members were not too happy about them being shipped as cargo. The difference between how we sent Chris Vaile and Matt Attalai home and how we sent home the third country nationals was not lost on anyone. They took the same risks we did, and they deserved to have the same respect, honor, and traditions allotted to Americans.

We did the best we could under the circumstances. And said our silent prayers for them and their families, the loss hitting us more than they knew.

After the attack and so many losses, we needed to rebuild an entire team. Jeff went home to be checked for a traumatic brain injury. Obren went home for good. Clint ended up quitting. He legitimately suffered from undiagnosed PTSD and the pain of remembering how he tried to save five of his friends only to end up losing them all. I told Clint not to beat himself up over it, but they were merely words. He had a tough recovery for a long time after going home.

That night I stayed awake staring at my footlocker. That familiar glow was beckoning me. I must have looked at it for an hour, wrestling with the thought of opening it up to put the glass I had extracted from Ness's arm in with the other items I collected over the past two years.

I dragged the box over in front of me and popped the latches. As soon as I opened it, that's when I caved in.

There they were, piled together in this lifeless cold black box. A coffin of sorts, all my brothers, all my memories, all my epitaphs just lying there speaking to me. The pain I felt at that moment was staggering.

I placed the glass inside and closed the lid, forcing myself to push aside the pain and memories. I still had a job to do. I somehow knew that when the time came to open the box and leave it open, I would need time to process. Time to heal.

That time wasn't now. It took a long time to drift off to sleep.

Needless to say, I was apprehensive about rolling out again. Terrified was more like it.

But in order to keep the teams moving, I requested additional manpower for Team I. We got Mike Stegman in as a replacement team leader. We put together the HQ team to run more missions. I rode in the lead gun truck as the vehicle commander.

One of those missions was a run to FOB Shank in Logar Province. The ANA had blocked off the road. I made visual contact with one of the ANA soldiers who mouthed "IED" and pointed to his cell phone. The device was remotely controlled.

I made the decision to turn around. We let the FOB know what was going on. They took the threat of us getting hurt for their mail more seriously.

I was now at war with myself. Part of me wanted to quit while I was ahead but I still needed a job. Since I was going on leave in July, I put my name in the hat for the Panther program and was selected for it. The Panther program was another government agency gig providing close protection for case officers in Iraq, Pakistan, and Afghanistan. I was scheduled to attend training in September, so this gave me some time off to think about giving up contracting altogether.

Fortunately for me, the State Department stopped giving out diplomatic passports due to an issue involving another contractor who got into a shootout with two Pakistani criminals and ended up killing them. They had to pay out $2 million for reparations to Pakistan for the deaths, so that put all diplomatic passports on hold.

Again, the image flashed in my mind. I would be the next one to bite the dust.

That's when I decided it was time to get out. I remembered a quote from Lois McMaster:

"The dead cannot cry out for justice. It's the duty of the living to do so for them."

Suddenly, my love for life was greater than my fear of death

CHAPTER FORTY-NINE
Return to Hell

I ended up going back to Iraq as Operations Manager at Umm Qasr, offering oversight for static security at the base. It was safer and gave me more time to decompress before I transitioned out. It didn't last long. SOC asked if I would consider running convoys in Iraq.

I decided to give it another try.

This was a different set up than what we had established in Afghanistan, and I wasn't comfortable with it. Only three people spoke English. The only reason I was asked to work on the contract was simple. I was an American citizen with a security clearance and had a valid Common Access Card to get onto any of the bases in Iraq.

I only did one run with this program and went back to the static site at Um Qasr. When the contract came up for bid, another company took over the site. I went back to SOC and Afghanistan.

My return to hell was wrought with emotion. I had a different sense about me, almost like a disconnect. I had boxed up all the bad memories in my footlocker and sent the war chest home before coming back to Kabul. It was a welcomed relief, knowing it was thousands of miles away, along with all of the memories it held.

Still, there was trepidation. Initially, I filled in as Mobile Operations Director for Samurai, who was going on leave. I fell into the old routine of getting the teams moving and keeping track of the cargo delivered.

During that time, Team III, commanded by Craig Smith, had an incident when his trail vehicle rolled. Watching the video, we saw there was snow, black ice, and water on the road— and the vehicle began to hydroplane when the driver overcorrected.

We launched a QRF to escort a crane and a flatbed truck to the site for recovery and bring the team back to Kabul. Scott was in the lead with Jenkins as his driver, and I was in the follow-vehicle with Arnie Campbell as my driver. Of course, we had our gunners.

Since we had more security, we expanded the perimeter when we arrived. The crane operator put the rolled vehicle onto the flatbed truck. I was hoping to complete the mail drop, but it was getting late. The insurgents were taking to night-time ambushes in that area, so I informed the drop site and the contracting officer of the situation.

They agreed to abort the mission and we returned to Kabul.

It was difficult to gauge mission success, especially when one mission turned into two. We had rolled a gun truck and the mail drop was aborted, but we successfully launched a QRF and recovered our gun truck and, technically, we didn't lose any cargo, no one was injured and we delivered the mail on another day. In my book, that made the mission a success.

On December 31, 2011, Samurai returned from leave and I was deployed to FOB Hadrian via air—with $250,000 cash in hand. Due to FOB Hadrian's remote location, it was customary to deliver at least four months' worth of operational funds. A typical monthly op fund expenditure was about $60,000. Approximately $30,000 went for payroll and the rest was used for other monthly expenses.

The sun had set and we decided to use the back alleys as our route to get to the airport.

There were fewer ANP checkpoints there, and less likelihood of having to pay any get-out-of-jail bribery fees.

All told, I was rolling out with about $250,000 on my person, driving through back alleys in Kabul at night. This could have been an MTV video with the song "Indestructible" by Disturbed playing in the background.

Amazingly, I made it to FOB Hadrian without incident.

During my rotation at Hadrian, I found out that Chase was back in Afghanistan working with DynCorp on a task order project in Kandahar. We stayed in touch via e-mail and Skype and when the contract ended, Chase was picked up by another private security company in Kabul. He hadn't taken leave in over six months. The recruiter who called him said the job was extremely dangerous; that they had lost five guys in one ambush and nine guys within a year's time. It didn't register that it was SOC and one of the victims who was killed was his old friend Ness.

The Afghanistan government was charging outrageous amounts of money for vehicle registrations, weapons authority, and operational security licenses. SOC refused to pay the extortion/expedition fees to remain in business in Kabul. Another private security company that was still licensed picked up the gig instead.

The mission remained the same and *The Pony Express* was still intact. Same shit. Different day. Different T-shirt.

Then we realized we might be at risk in a bigger way.

The US drawdown in Afghanistan began July 13, 2011, when the first 650 US troops pulled out. Two Army National Guard cavalry squadrons left: the 1st Squadron, 134th Cavalry Regiment, based in Kabul, and the 1st Squadron, 113th Cavalry Regiment, which had been in neighboring Parwan province.

On April 18, 2012, the United States and its NATO allies finalized agreements to wind down the war in Afghanistan. Officially titled the "Enduring Strategic Partnership Agreement between the Islamic Republic of Afghanistan and the United States of America," it was signed in May and went into effect on July 4, 2012.

The plans called for the removal of 23,000 US troops by the end of September 2012. The Afghan security forces would take the lead in combat operations by the end of 2013. ISAF forces would train, advise, and assist the Afghans, and fight alongside them when needed. Finally, the agreement called for the complete removal of all US troops by the end of 2014, except for trainers who would assist Afghan forces, plus a small contingent of troops with a specific mission to combat Al-Qaeda through counterterrorism operations.

Without US forces in Afghanistan, we didn't have the backup we had before. This affected our teams and our reputations.

The Pony Express had a high turn-over rate after SOC lost five men in the May 2011 IED ambush. Word was out about the dangers in providing convoy security. In Afghanistan, no one wanted to take a gig with such a high-threat risk factor for the same amount of money an expat could make working on a FOB. Those guys were called "Fobbits," soldiers or other persons stationed at a secure forward operating base that rarely, if ever, left the relative safety of the base. They weren't looked at too kindly by the soldiers and contractors that spent most of their time outside the wire being shot at and dodging road-side bombs.

The few recruits who came to us were too green and inexperienced. My brothers Arnie, Jeff, Alek, Greg, Andy, and Ziko held the teams together, but new recruits made a lot of mistakes, which put us at risk.

Arnie Campbell left and accepted a gig with Cochise somewhere near Konduz. After he left, training suffered, money was tight, and morale was low.

Somehow, we held on. Everyone on *The Pony Express* became extremely efficient at tactical tire changes, pushing and towing off the X, and conducting vehicle recoveries.

With a new contract ownership, the situation improved over time and management brought on guys who had some actual experience.

All the teams had survived several enemy encounters, ambushes, and attacks. They had a solid reputation for getting the job done. Mike, Andy, and a couple of 18-Deltas worked hard to put together a clinic at the KPMO compound, so medical supplies were abundant. Andy was assigned to Team III as a paramedic. He had been outside the continental US for a few years and knew the routine and team dynamics well.

As prepared as we were at times, that never meant complacency in a place like Afghanistan.

What we had learned and knew to be true was this: Afghanistan was hell and took a toll on all of us. Letting our guard down anywhere on Ring Road was never an option. Movement was life.

CHAPTER FIFTY
Innovative Logistics: The End of an Era

The Pony Express knew what it was to keep moving. Our contract was re-drafted and acquired by Innovative Logistics. The owner, Todd Wilcox, was a former Green Beret and ex- CIA officer turned entrepreneur. The cool thing about having a special forces operative owning the company was like the old days when SOC started out in Iraq. Having an SF background with experience ensured *The Pony Express* wouldn't be operating in a vacuum. If anyone knew what it was like, it was Todd.

Todd was commissioned as an infantry officer in the US Army and served as a rifle platoon leader with the 101st Airborne Division during Operation Desert Storm. Upon promotion to Captain, he volunteered for a transfer to the US Army Special Forces branch and ended up commanding a Green Beret Special Forces A-team in a counterterrorism role in East Asia.

After eight years of military service, Todd resigned to accept a position as an intelligence officer with the CIA and joined America's global war on terrorism. He completed two years of Arabic studies and then served at various US Embassy postings in the Middle East and North Africa.

One of Todd's other companies, Patriot Defense Group, acquired Innovative Logistics, which provided expeditionary logistics to US and NATO Special Operations Forces clients, NGOs, and diplomatic organizations. It was imperative for SOC to pull out and beneficial for IL to establish a footprint in Afghanistan.

Todd was friends with the President and CEO of SOC. They both attended an executive education course at Harvard Business School. Based on that interaction, they learned Todd wanted to expand Innovative Logistics into Afghanistan and SOC wanted to focus on Iraq and get out of Afghanistan.

In 2011, they negotiated an asset purchase agreement. Innovative Logistics became a subcontractor to SOC and took over the operations of the postal delivery contract. All personnel, equipment, vehicles, and infrastructure were conveyed to them over a ninety-day period.

It was a good move.

The IL *Pony Express* in Afghanistan was featured on the front page of the *Wall Street Journal*. They threw a big party to celebrate the new contract.

Chase was assigned to Team II. On my way home from FOB Hadrian, we caught up. It was great seeing him again and although I was headed home for good, *The Pony Express* would continue with him and the rest of the guys. He met Jeff Bedford, who lived in Newfoundland, Canada, so they had some common ground.

Glen Witt remained on site for another month to ensure a smooth transition "left seat/right seat. Greg Swanson went end of mission, and Jeff remained at KPMO running one of four teams who continued to deliver mail on Ring Road for another three years. Jeff, Alek, and Ziko were on *The Pony Express* contract longer than anyone else during the operational period.

Innovative Logistics became a major player in the demobilization process of the 10th Mountain Light Infantry Division, stationed at Bagram Air Base. The goal was to help build the Afghan National Security Force's capability and increase the Afghan government's independence.

But the attacks continued to tear at them. The teams survived multiple ambushes on the missions to Logar and J-Bad at the height of the summer months in 2013 and 2014. Team III was attacked a third time on the Voodoo Highway near the outskirts of Ka Kas. No one was seriously injured, but they lost cargo. Enemy insurgents killed several civilians at the onset of the ambush, but Team III held its position, and the tangos suffered heavy losses during the battle.

One of the gun trucks was severely damaged on the way to FOB Fenty in Jalalabad. Two expats were injured when their team was ambushed on a mission to Ghazni. The team leader suffered a broken back during the attack. The assistant team leader and several of the local national gunners, including the translator, were also injured. Chase's former assistant team leader suffered some hearing loss and several local national gunners sustained minor injuries from shrapnel and barotrauma from the attacks.

The losses were hard to swallow. It took a serious toll on the team's morale.

The last significant attack resulting in injury was in late 2014 when Team I was ambushed just outside of Jalalabad. Their gun truck took enemy fire from a crew-served weapon, which turned out to be a Dishka. The attack nearly killed one of the top gunners—shrapnel pierced through his abdomen and groin.

Innovative Logistics sustained one employee killed in action bringing the total KIA to ten brave men and eight wounded as a result of enemy contact or IEDs from 2012 to 2016. The drawdown of US forces brought an end to the J-Bad and Logar missions. Due to the series of events, the Sustainment Brigade Commander and Innovative Logistics decided to end the long runs to Ghazni.

Innovative Logistics remained in Afghanistan until December 24, 2016. And *The Pony Express* rode off into the sunset.

CHAPTER FIFTY-ONE
Farewell Docs

Although not a member of the Pony Express, the contributions made by Sgt Eric Williams to the SOC Mobile teams, The US Army, coalition forces in Afghanistan, and America bare mentioning. Sgt Williams was instrumental in enhancing our medical response posture and overall contributed to the success of *the Pony Express's* mission outcomes.

Eric was one of the U.S. Army's premier flight medics with the All-American Dust-Off Team. He was attached to 3rd Battalion, 82nd Combat Aviation Brigade, 82nd Airborne Division, Company C and flew out of Ghazni Province. He would always hook Chase up with medical supplies and intel whenever they met.

Eric was KIA by IDF Mortar rounds in eastern Afghanistan on his return to the United States on July 23, 2012. Eric was twenty-seven years old at the time of his untimely death and hailed from Murrieta, California. The All-American Dust-Off Team flew more MEDEVACS in Afghanistan than any other air medical resources combined.

SSG Tiffany Kwiecinski was a Senior Medic with the Route Clearance Task Force Red Devils HHC 7th Engineer Battalion, 20th Engineer Brigade out of Fort Brum, New York and was stationed at the BAS in Shank. She also knew the flight medics from Ghazni and understood our needs too. It was an even exchange of medical supplies for pogey bait that her team was deprived of since they were essentially on 24/7 lockdown and rarely had any access to good sticks.

Cigars were key for their morale nights and the team would

gather around their wood burning stove in the shape of an engineer castle and drink Czech near-beer, smoke decent cigars and reminisce about home and the day's events.

Tiffany knew how to take care of her crew and was also saddened by the loss of such a stellar flight medic. That night they gathered by the fire, said a prayer, and raised a glass to toast Eric in US Army fashion.

Having a flight medic in your corner was a valuable asset, and Chase often spoke of the dangers they both faced on a daily basis outside the wire. Chase and Eric had a lot in common, both being flight medics and firefighters, they had a great deal of respect for each other. Chase had mentioned the need for reliable air rescue assets as KAM air and the fact that Guardian Medical, our contracted air rescue service sucked. Eric always said his team would always respond if ever needed. The All-American Dust-Off Team were all heroes in our book and his death hit Chase hard. Eric was half his age, but Chase always looked up to him even at ground level.

Nick Gurik was one of the last Paramedics hired by SOC who didn't have a military background. He was a great medic, but outside his element tactically, so he was assigned to Miroslav on Team 4. Miroslav took him under his wing and brought him up to speed. It was some serious OJT as the teams saw a lot of heavy enemy contact and they became very close.

Nick was soft-spoken and kept to himself most of the time but was well-liked by the crews. He stayed on contract for about a year but left suddenly without explanation. It was safe to surmise that it was stress related as a lot of guys were ambushed on several occasions and we were all rolling the dice with the Taliban. The last I heard was that he had gone to Iraq to work as a clinical medic for about a year and then finally home.

Samurai stayed in touch with Nick until late October 2011, after that we learned that he was found in a hotel room on January 17, 2013 from an apparent overdose. It was determined to be accidental, as Nick had dialed 911 when he knew something went wrong. What bothered us the most was we had lost another brother. Another Doc, and it was a sad state of affairs for all concerned.

"Not all battles are fought on the battlefield", sounds cliché, but it's true, more so, it sticks in my craw and it bothers me to think about having lost another brother to war. Sean Bland was one such brother whom I had the pleasure of working with on the Pony Express. He replaced Nick on the teams, but what I didn't know was that he was troubled by something from the start.

Sean Bland was the consummate warrior-medic, a man dedicated to his craft. He embraced the mission set like a true professional, always early, always there, he was one of those Docs who would give the shirt off his back. I know, another cliché.

He had already been in-country for some time when Sean was notified of the death of his older brother, Jim Bland. James Bland was a pilot who flew Leer Jets for celebrities and VIP's. He was killed on Friday evening September 19, 2008 when a tire blew out on takeoff.

Besides Mr. Bland, the other pilot and two passengers were killed in the fiery crash. Amazingly, two celebrity passengers, Travis Barker, a former drummer with the rock group Blink-182, and disc jockey DJ AM (Adam Goldstein) were also injured severely but survived.

Sean was flown home to attend the memorial service. According to his mother, Jocelyn Morland, they were very close and Sean never fully recovered from the loss of his brother by the time he began working for SOC.

Sean worked for SOC mainly on the short mail runs, but occasionally ran the gauntlet to Ghazni where his team had a lot of enemy contacts. He was a great medic and good at making contacts for sourcing medical equipment and meds, but things began to deteriorate for him over an extended period of time. He became increasingly agitated and short-tempered, and I think he knew it was time to get out of the game.

We stayed in touch online, as most of us were spread across the globe. A majority of the conversations he had with myself, Arnie Campbell, Chase, and his team leader, Matt Mac aka Samurai.

March 6th, 2020 was the last we heard from Sean. A year later we learned that he had taken his own life on May 5th, 2021. Several team members made inquiries to each other. It seemed the information was vague and fragmented. Others expressed their sympathies while some were concerned that we didn't do enough to reach out and help, but hindsight is 20/20 is just another fucking cliché...He is sadly missed and will always be remembered as Doc.

EPILOGUE
Stepping Off the Road of Death

It was the best job we ever had, but under the worst circumstances imaginable. It was a dream and a nightmare all rolled into one.

The only people on the planet who truly understand our *Pony Express* experiences are the brothers we ran with, who lived the dream and survived the nightmare. Those trials helped mold us into one of the United States Postal Service's bravest mail carriers in the world. Just about everyone I worked with on this gig was hit hard at one time or another. We were all some badass motherfuckers.

The Pony Express ran hard until 2016, and earned a reputation worthy of the historic name.

I often wonder if anyone would ever believe what we witnessed, what we did, and what happened to us. We suffered losses, received multiple injuries, worked through illnesses, overcame the technical: flat tires, mechanical failures, motor vehicle accidents. We survived countless attacks and ambushes.

Every one of us went home, recovered, and returned to do it again. Some people thought we were adrenalin junkies. Some argued we were crazy. Others said greed motivated us.

But I knew in my heart, none of those reasons had anything to do with it. Brotherhood was our common denominator. We did it out of respect for each other. We did it for the guy fighting next to us. We knew, without speaking a word, that they would do the same for us.

Ring Road tested us in ways we never imagined. It was more than a route. More than the Road of Death.

It was a pathway to the soul resulting in a deep sense of significance, where the true meaning of brotherhood was found somewhere beyond the pursuit of mission success. It generated a domino effect that positively impacted our lives.

It measured how we value life, purpose, and friendship. We served a cause greater than our own by sharing what we learned, not just what we earned. We made a difference in the lives of others. We gave back to the soldiers, sailors, marines, and airmen who served their country in times of war.

It all added up to who we were authentically, at the core.

If that doesn't speak volumes to the character of those who rode *The Pony Express*, I don't know what does.

When I left *The Pony Express* in 2012, I spent Christmas with my parents in Scituate, Massachusetts, and New Years with my brother Mike in Portland, Oregon. I began work as a fitness instructor and also worked for Lowes in Oregon, It was definitely different. No guns were required, and people weren't trying to kill me. Plus, I spent quality time with my girlfriend.

Chase returned to Texas and works as a medical technician for NLUC and a Firefighter Paramedic with Community Fire/Rescue. Money retired in Bay St. Louis, Mississippi, and makes rustic furniture out of distressed lumber. Buddha works in Abu Dhabi, U.A.E. Cookie became a police officer in South Carolina. The rest of the guys got by the best they could.

I take comfort in the fact that we call each other every once in a while and talk shit. We remember the brothers we lost: Chris Vaile, Matt Attalai, Nenand Antic "Ness," Perica Jaric "Pero," Peni Tirikula Tulovo Jr. "Ben," Ahmad "Fawad" Khalid, and Timor Shah.

We get online and chat or text and, on occasion, toss back a shot of whiskey, light a cigar, and toast some of the best times of our lives—and curse the worst that haunt us.

As I peer inside my footlocker, my war chest, the realization hits hard. The men of *The Pony Express* were the best of the best. We were human, not just warriors. We followed that Road of Death until it finally led our weary bodies home.

The Immortals

The horrors of war bond men together. Men who sacrificed their own safety for those who eventually became their brothers. This fact was driven home in a letter written to the guys by one esteemed fellow operator, team leader, Aaron Kirch. It was, interestingly enough, titled, "The Immortals."

> Hey fellas, we didn't really get a chance to have this discussion before we all split, so we're going to have it real quickly. Our project is by far one of the most dangerous in Afghanistan. For what's required of us with absolutely minimal support structures, equipment, and actual ability to apply any sort of MDMP (Military Decision-Making Process), it's absolutely incredible we all made it out without so much as a scratch.
>
> We work solely under the reaction and defensive, which creates even more risk and inability to control our environment or set any sort of conditions for successful outcomes. As I said in the very beginning, it was 90% luck and 10% skill, and I can honestly say, we only gave the enemy a small percentage of our skill factor.
>
> We just got damn lucky.
>
> In the military, there are exponential amounts of programs, briefings, and outpatient services available to the average Joe after he experiences life-altering events. Still, every unit from the Army to the Marines experience difficulties due to soldiers not accessing these and ALWAYS somebody post-deployment beats the shit out their wife, smashes a bottle of booze over someone's head, or runs his motorcycle into a ravine.
>
> As contractors, we have none of these programs, yet in this situation, we are expected to reintegrate into normal society,

which is bad enough having spent all summer expecting to get smashed up. It's a complete stress event.

What transgressed on our QRF is a perfect example of what I'm talking about. We launched a rescue operation to recover our friends. People we cared about were bleeding, and we hastily created a plan, executed, and recovered 100 percent of the folks that mattered. Then we were asked to sleep a few hours and go home.

Any number of emotions can be triggered after something life-threatening takes place. It won't necessarily happen Sunday morning or tomorrow night, but we've been through some incredible shit, and people process these situations differently. If at any point in time, you notice something different, if your spouse notices something different, or anything just doesn't seem right, don't fucking hesitate to call me.

I can promise you, after five combat deployments, the answers are not in the bottom of a bottle of whiskey. You aren't going to get anywhere from growing angry with your family. And more likely than not, your friends have no idea what it takes to wash someone's face out of the back of a gun truck.

I don't care how hard you think you are. We are only human. This year is going to be over before you know it, but please fucking enjoy it. You've earned it. Ride like it's your last ride, fish like you've never fished before, and play like you'll never see your kids again. In the end, that's the only thing that matters. Doing what you love, because you've worked hard to be able to afford what you normally could not and take comfort in the fact that the people who are around you, are damn glad your home.

If you need anything while we're back, at any time of the day, don't think twice. Call me. I'm proud to have been next to you all, and you should take pride in the fact that, collectively, we brought everyone home. Stay safe, travel well, and I'll catch you on the flip side.

AK

Men of the Pony Express

From dusk until dawn Ring Road is the route, we delivered the mail There was never a doubt

Guns loaded for bear we maintained our comms
Sixty pounds of gear dodging gunfire and bombs

Our actions, our tribute from Kabul to Khost
Been shot at and ambushed by the Taliban Ghost

Three hundred horses all armored and mean Through enemy forces we rode the machine

Names may be forgotten yet our fallen we claim
As their lives were boughten in the badlands of same.

Our oath to each other we would give our best From Brother to Brother, Men of the Pony Express.

Author Alan Chiasson "Doc Chase"

Lost But Not Forgotten

To our fallen comrades. We recognize the unthinkable pain that remains with loved ones of those who did not return home. This book is dedicated to you and your families in hopes that your memories live forever. We honor you for your unwavering sacrifice, courage, and selflessness. We pay tribute to the members of *The Pony Express* known to God, and never forgotten.

Perica Jaric "Pero" – KIA 4/20/2010 Mine Strike - SOC (Driver/Shooter)

Ahmad Fawad Khalid – KIA 4/20/2010 Mine Strike - SOC-A (Translator/Terp)

Chris Vaile – KIA 9/6/2010 IED - SOC (ATL/Driver/Shooter)

Matt Attalai – KIA 9/6/2010 IED - SOC (ATL/Vehicle Commander)

Nenad Antic "Ness" – KIA 5/25/2011 IED - SOC (ATL/Vehicle Commander/Medic)

Timor Shah – KIA 5/25/2011 IED - SOC-A (Translator/Terp)

Peni Tirikula Tulovo Jr. "Ben" - KIA 5/25/2011 IED - SOC (Driver/Shooter)

Mohammed Wares – KIA 5/25/2011 IED - SOC-A (Team Leader)

Azizullah Chase Haqim – KIA 5/25/2011 IED - SOC- A (Top Gunner)

Farhad Faizi – KIA 10/01/2012 IED - IL (Top Gunner)

Acknowledgments

by Edward "Hammer" Ford

Years ago, we embarked upon the idea of writing about our exploits as security contractors with *The Pony Express* on the most dangerous road in the world, Ring Road. We sifted through memoirs, journals, and after-action reports to piece together a tangible story that would explain in detail the horrors of combat, the heroics of those who survived, and honor those we lost in our efforts to deliver the US mail and other critical supplies to American and coalition forces in Afghanistan.

The support system we were contracted to provide was a godsend to those on the front lines.

First, thanks to my family for having patience with me for taking on this huge challenge, which decreased the amount of time I was able to spend with them, especially Trisha and Aden. They share credit on every goal I achieve. Thanks to all my friends for sharing my enthusiasm when starting this project and following with encouragement when it seemed too difficult to complete. I would have probably given up without their support and their example on what to do when you really want something bad enough.

I want to thank members of *The Pony Express* for their contributions and insight to this book. Without them, it would not be possible. Thanks to my medic, John Picket "Buddha," for being there for the team through the ambushes—demolished twice in less than six months.

Thanks to Mike Hearty "Money" for making the job enjoyable, and Scott Brown, who showed me the true meaning of being a badass.

I would also like to thank the Serbian and Fijian contractors who were on this program. Thank you for your perseverance, loyalty, courage, and friendship during the tough times; you have no idea how important that was to us.

Thank you to the families of the men we lost. Their sacrifice can never be replaced or compensated. Just know that when they were taken from us, they were with their friends. This book preserves their integrity. In my eyes, it is a testament to the bravery displayed by so many in some of the worst conditions and circumstances we faced every day on Ring Road.

Thanks to Alan Chiasson "Chase," my co-author. He took the lion's share of this project and made sure we were on the right track by placing everything in sequence, conducting interviews, and researching a number of documents, articles, and contributions from other sources.

Thank you to Scott Huesing, best-selling author of the book *Echo in Ramadi*. You told us what we needed to hear, not what we wanted to hear. That's what brothers do for each other.

That's how we made it here.

Acknowledgments

by Alan Chiasson "Doc Chase"

This book is the product of many men thinking back to some of the worst and best times imaginable in the midst of history's longest war, the war in Afghanistan. To some, *The Pony Express* was a job embraced by patriots to continue to serve. To others, it was a never-ending nightmare of attacks and ambushes that continued long after the mission was over. Finally, thank you to the men who lost their lives in the performance of their duties. They made the ultimate sacrifice and did so proudly, without reservation. They are not forgotten.

First and foremost, I would like to thank God Almighty for being my Lord and Savior, and for all His blessings throughout my life and with this project. I want to thank my awesome wife, Janie. From listening to war stories, reading early drafts and giving me advice, to keeping the dogs out of my hair so I could research and edit, she was as important to this book getting done as I was. She is truly my rock and salvation. She is my best friend and I hope that one day she can read this book and understand why I spent so much time in front of my laptop.

In addition, I want to thank my children, Krystle, Kyra, Keenan, and Brian for believing in me to get the job done, and to my Mom and Dad—I hope I made you all proud.

I also want to thank my friend and co-author, Ed Ford "Hammer" for being my mentor and sticking with me throughout the turmoil we faced in Iraq and Afghanistan. You are truly an inspiration in both combat and training. I learned a lot from you, and I appreciate your confidence in me and for allowing me to participate in this historical recollection of *The Pony Express*.

To my co-workers, especially Mike Hearty "Money," who showed me the ropes in Iraq and recommended me for the job with the SOC Mobile Operations Program in Afghanistan.

Without his knowledge and input, I would not be alive today. To Rob Cook "Cookie" for being a good friend and confidante and taking me to the battalion aid station in Gardez when I was all jacked up. You literally saved my life.

To Mark Mattson "Matty" for helping me put the SOC medical program together that provided valuable medical intelligence to our teams. To John "Buddha" Picket for taking the reins and carrying the torch, keeping our brothers alive. To Drew Babbitt for his friendship and for whipping me into shape. I'll never forget those rigorous workouts at Eggers and Phoenix.

I'd especially like to thank Sylvia Mendoza of Mendoza Communications as well as Kirk Chaisson and Liese Thompson for their editorial advice on this project. To Scott A. Huesing for the autographed edition of his book "*Echo in Ramadi*. You were our toughest critic and your guidance helped us immensely. I appreciate everyone who believed in me and provided me with support and encouragement to make this historical project a reality. Without them, this book may not have been written.

In the end, I believe that the team members of *The Pony Express* are all true heroes, each in their own right. From my team leader, Aaron Kirch, my drivers Dave Gengenbach "Racer Dave" and Jay Vitokai, who kept our gun truck on the road, and all the local national gunners who laid down the hate. To all my Serbian, Macedonian, and Fijian warrior buds—Alek, Saso, Blasko, Slav, Ziko, and Bill, Zack, and Jope—you guys made it worth the risk. Brothers for life.

About the Authors

Alan has been a Peace Officer/Firefighter/Paramedic, aside from being older than dirt, he's also a hell-of-a-good looking guy. He is currently an Engineer/Firefighter/Paramedic with Community Fire & Rescue in Houston, Texas serving the Alien/Mission Bend area and loves saving lives. A Former US Navy Corpsman, Alan spent most of his career in California, Arizona, and Texas. He spent 10 years as a tactical medic on SWAT and eight years in the Middle East providing combat medical support as a security contractor in Iraq and Afghanistan. Alan is also the co-author of the book Postcards Through Hell. He is such an optimist, he posted that it was an award-winning book on his website. Aside from writing his first book, Alan is a hopeless romantic and is writing his second book a work of fiction titled "Melody" also a soon to be best-seller. Optimism runs deep in his family.

Edward Ford is a retired Marine and former Security Contractor. He served for twenty years in the United States Marine Corp as an infantry and Force Reconnaissance Marine. His memoirs describe how he battled the Taliban through countless attacks and ambushes while he and his team delivered the US Mail and other critical supplies to military and coalition forces along the infamous Ring Road. After his retirement from the USMC, Ed worked for eight years as a security contractor in Iraq and Afghanistan on various programs, to include The Pony Express. In addition to being an author, Ed lives the sweaty life. He is currently a Fitness Trainer in Central Oregon, where his knowledge of physical fitness is put to good use. Ed also enjoys the outdoors, hunting, fishing, and of course working out. When Ed isn't working out, he's working out.

www.postcardsthroughhell.com

APPENDIX ONE

Maps

- Afghanistan – Route A01 (Ring Road)
- Afghanistan Provincial Map
- US and ISAF Medical Facilities
- MEDEVAC and Dust Off Capabilities

Afghanistan Provincial Map

US and ISAF/NATO Medical Assets

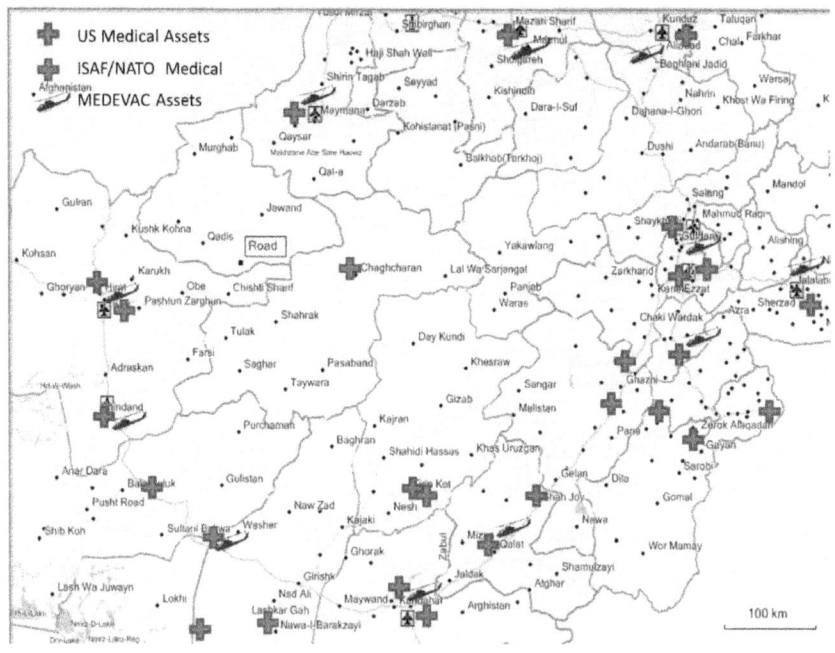

MEDEVAC Capability with Dust-Off Perimeters

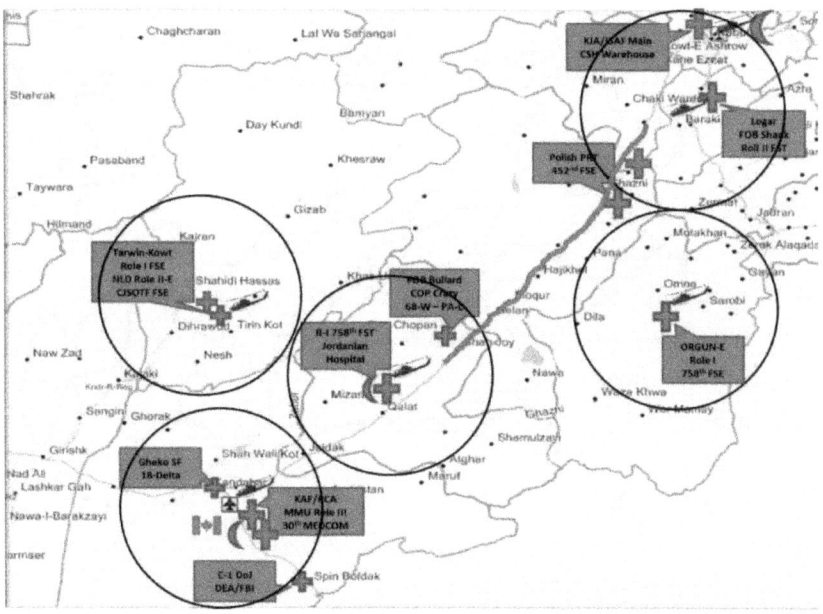

APPENDIX TWO

CPI-Operational Order

Date: 26 Feb 2008

OPERATION PLAN: 000-0210A

References: MHQ//KPMO

Time Zone Used Throughout the Order:
PST//EST//Afghanistan-Local

Task Organization: MHQ//KPMO

1. SITUATION
SOC-A has been awarded a contract to provide convoy escort teams to various locations throughout Afghanistan.

2. MISSION
SOC-A on order will deploy convoy escort teams of up to 16-man teams in four (4) trucks comprised mainly of Afghan local national's team members and drivers. These teams will be used for the purpose of escorting and delivering strategic and sustainment cargo to assigned locations. (Kabul-Khost)

3. EXECUTION
Intent: The intent is to provide an armed escort team of 16 personnel comprised of Afghan Local Nationals that have

been highly vetted and locally trained to complete the missions.

A. **Concept of operations:**
   I. Team assignments and responsibilities; all team members will be vetted and trained locally. They will be proficient and experienced in all aspects of armed convoy escort.
   II. All team members will be armed with an Ak-47 rifle with a full combat load. Vehicles will be equipped with radios for vehicle-to-vehicle communication and cell phone radios for communications between the convoy and the hard sites.
   III. Convoy will consist of four (4) escort vehicles for larger convoys, of five (5) cargo vehicles or more. Three (3) escort vehicles for smaller convoys, of under-five (5) cargo vehicles.

B. **Contingency Operations:**
   I. Escort Teams will coordinate with the ANP and the ANA checkpoints and bases along the Kabul-Khost route for any Extremist support and Safe Havens. Bases are in Kabul, Baraki, Gardez, and Khost.
   II. MEDEVAC will be done via ground evacuation to local hospitals located in the Kabul, Baraki, Gardez and Khost areas, utilizing the support from ANA and ANP. **Note:** Coalition Forces will NOT respond to LN MEDEVAC needs.

C. **Task to Operations Units:**
   I. Team Leader- will be overall responsible for the success and or failure of the mission. He duties will

include but are not limited to:
- II. The readiness of all team members, vehicles, communication gear, route assessments and the execution of the mission
- III. Assistant Team leader- Second in command and report to the team leader and fills in for him in his absence. His duties will include the inspection of all personnel their personal gear, vehicles, and all related items. He is to always support the team leader before during and after the mission.
- IV. Vehicle Commanders- Reports to the Assistant team leader. Responsibilities include the readiness of his vehicle, related items, and the personnel and or cargo in or on the assigned vehicle.
- V. Team Members- are responsible for their personal gear to include their assigned weapons. It is their job to protect the convoy during movements to assigned areas. They are to assist the vehicle commanders and or ATL when needed.
- VI. Drivers- Responsible for the overall condition of the vehicle assigned. Must maintain the vehicle and be ready to deploy the vehicle where and when needed. Also, must know the capability of the vehicle assigned.

D. Tasks to Support Units:
- I. KPMO will be notified of all movements at least 48- hours prior to the commencement of the convoy mission. SOC-A will have a "radio watch" to monitor any radio or phone traffic that may occur during the time frame that the convoy is outside of a secured location.
- II. MHQ will provide help as requested from KPMO and will be notified at least 24- hours prior to any

convoy mission.

E. **Coordinating Instructions:**
   I. TBD

4. **SERVICE SUPPORT**
   KPMO - Primary focal point/lead for all convoy planning.
   MHQ- In support of KPMO when needed.

5. **COMMAND AND SIGNAL**
   A. Command: Primary Chain of Command-TBD
   B. Signal/Communications

Primary: Radio (vehicle to vehicle)
Secondary: Cell (convoy to hard site)

Key Phone Numbers:
Lumpkin - 775-555-7765
Coleman -775-555-7764
Witt - 775-555-7349
Tooker - 775-555-1922

APPENDIX THREE

Attachment Alpha Convoy Configuration

Option 1

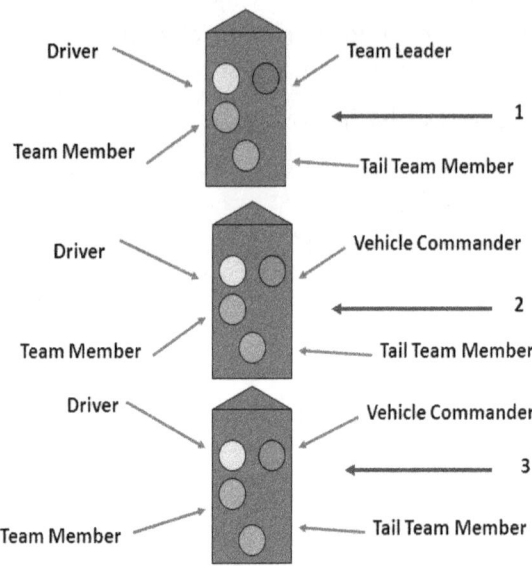

Option 2

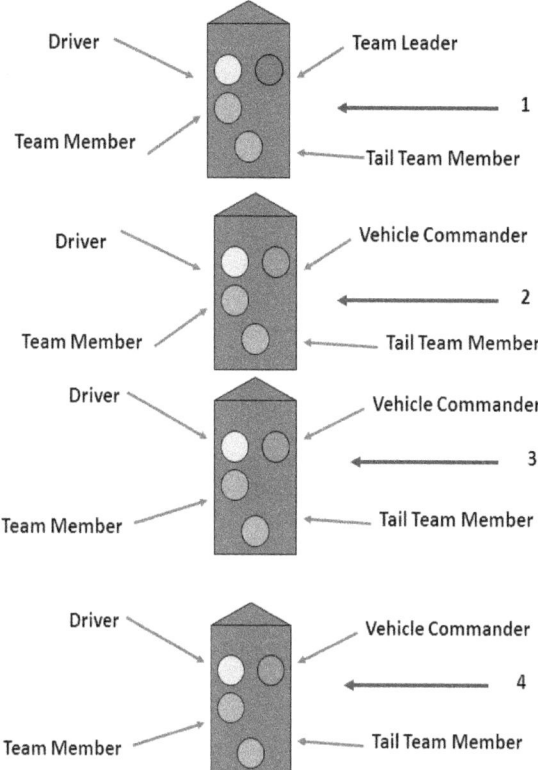

Attachment Bravo Convoy Configuration

Option 1

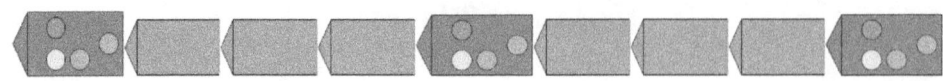

Option 2

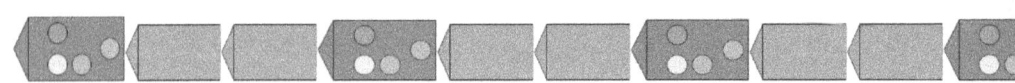

Option 3

Option 4

APENDIX FOUR

SOC-Afghanistan Medical Force Protection

Medics: Currently, three paramedics are sharing the bulk of responsibility in Afghanistan. All three medics have a total of sixty years of operational experience and come from extremely diverse backgrounds including prior military, SWAT, tactical/combat medicine, aeromedicine, and remote/isolation medicine.

Three other medics are in transit or are processing through orientation and/or transferring from other theaters of operation. They are expected to arrive within the week and will be immediately assigned to the convoy security teams to supplement ongoing operations.

Equipment: A comprehensive supply list has been approved and is scheduled to arrive via DHL freight carrier. This will allow us to fully stock the convoy security operations element and secondly place additional resources towards PSD as originally intended. The order is inclusive, as all the kits will arrive fully stocked.

We are developing a means to sign for issued equipment placing responsibility on the team medic. The plan is to maintain uniformity and even PAR levels for each team, should the need arise, to have another medic float into a vacant position for whatever reason.

Mobile Operations: Convoy operations constitute the bulk of contractual agreements in Afghanistan. All efforts have shifted towards supporting the mission accomplishment to include business development, PSD, some static, and logistics overall. As soon as the medical equipment and supplies arrive, the convoy will be entirely self-sufficient with respect to medical operational capability and staffing.

PSD: PSD Operations are an integral part of the "big picture" for SOC – Afghanistan. They handle most of the client transportation and employee movement within Kabul. To date, we have split their medical supply in order to assist convoy security operations and have done so at the risk of the PSD program. They do not have designated medics and two operators are trained in CLS. The intention is to have PSD equally stocked with BLS equipment and bring their staff up-to-speed on the current TCCC guidelines with a rotational training schedule that will accommodate their needs and staff.

Clinical: Plans for a 200 plus man-camp are in effect with a projected move-in date approximately 56 days from today. An RFP awaits to be submitted for approval, based on the medical program assessment, yet to be conducted by Dr. Jay Sullivan. A full-time dedicated medic with clinical and operational skills, as well as overall managerial skills will be needed to provide project oversight, write policy and SOPs, maintain PAR levels and medical inventory, channel documentation through the proper chain of command, handle sick call, fill in medic vacancies created through leave and attrition, schedule training, and serve as the patient advocate/liaison for CARE and other duties as assigned by the Program Manager.

MEDEVAC: SOC-Afghanistan has GPS tracking that, monitors vehicle movements throughout the AO. The IT company that uses the PDT 300i systems and Track 24 system, is known as SECURO, which is also partnered with Guardian Medical. The contract for GPS tracking is inclusive for MEDEVAC and QRF capability, although their services have yet to be tested under extremes. In order to maintain redundancy, we have conducted advances on PRTs, FOBs, OPs,

NGOs, COBs, Air Bases, and NATO/Coalition Force locations to enhance our independent ground medical capabilities as well as sought out information on air assets (both military and civilian) that have dust-off capability.

Medical Intelligence: We currently have solid relationships with CJTF Med, 30th MEDCOM, and UN/NATO Forces for up-to-date medical intelligence, JTF medical assets, Echelons of Care, POC's, and dust-off capability, which allows us to conduct operations in the austere environment in a safer manner. Our medics are absorbing the information, transferring data, and continually updating information into the GPS tracking capability for independent operations as a fail-safe.

The medics are included during route briefings and intel reports relevant to mission assignments.

Medical Force Protection: (MFP) means to provide medical expertise beyond the scope of conventional medical wisdom prior to, during, and well after the mission ends...The health and safety of a tactical team is a command responsibility, a part of risk management policies that cannot be abrogated. Manpower, maintenance, and appropriate medical support are essential to successful mission outcomes. The Tactical/Combat Medic serves as the team leader's medical conscience, focusing on reducing injury and illness associated with deployment against all potential threats. This is an on-going process through the pre-deployment, operational, and post- deployment phases of the mission.

Miscellaneous: Several programs, including SOPs, exist to support the medical start-up program for SOC-Afghanistan...They are:
- Medical Profile Cards
- Preventive Medicine
- CARE Document

Medical Profile Cards: MPCs are a means to acquire and maintain important medical history such as the current health status and immunization status of each team member to ensure the transfer of pertinent information to appropriate medical personnel to save valuable time during the treatment of injury or illness...This information is gathered prior to a team assignment and

serves to give a bird's eye view of the total medical/surgical history and health information of an individual team member.

Preventive Medicine: Concerns should be prioritized according to the nature of the mission, with the emphasis being placed on prevention NOT treatment. Team members are at risk if not prepared...Heat, cold, inadequate nutrition or hydration, and sleep deprivation can affect behavior and ultimately performance without the individual being aware of any changes...Safety is placed at the forefront during the entire mission.

C.A.R.E.: Casualty Assistance and Repatriation Evacuation (CARE) is a document designed to assist with the transfer and care of injured and/or ill employees, as well as employees killed during the line of duty or while in theater. It provides a clear guideline for notification procedures within SOC and the next of kin, and other representation to include casualty escort, family liaisons, and embassy contacts for *ex-pats*, TCNs, and LNs.

APPENDIX FIVE

Abbreviations

AO – Area of Operation
ATL – Assistant Team Leader
BDOC – Base Defensive Operations Center
BW – Blackwater
ATL – Assistant Team Leader
CAC – Common Access Card
CAG – Combat Applications Group
CAT – Counter Assault Team
CFC-A – Combined Forces Command–Afghanistan
CHU – Containerized Housing Unit
CIA – Central Intelligence Agency
CJTF – Combined Joint Task Force
CIVPOL – Civil Police
COB – Contingency Operating Base
CSH – Combat Surgical Hospital
CSTC-A – Combined Security Transition Command–Afghanistan
DBA – Defense Base Act
DEVGRU – US Naval special warfare Deployment Group
DFAC – Dining Facility (US Military)
DGI – Defense Group International
DI – DynCorp International
DOD – Department of Defense DOS – Department of State
EFP – Explosively Formed Penetrator/Projectile (Shape Charge)
EMDG – Expeditionary Medical Group
EOD – Explosive Ordnance Disposal
ETA – Estimated time of arrival
FHI – Four Horsemen International

FNG – Fucking New Guys
FOB – Forward Operating Base
FST – Forward Surgical Team
GPS – Global Positioning System
HDSOC – High Desert Special Operations Consulting
HQ – Headquarters
IED – Improvised Explosive Device
IFAK – Individual First Aid Kit
IL – Innovative Logistics
INTEL – Intelligence
IPLO – International Police Liaison Officer
ISAF – International Security Afghanistan Forces
IZ – International Zone
JTF – Joint Task Force
KAF – Kandahar Airfield
KIA – Kabul International Airport or – Killed in Action
KPMO – Kabul Program Management Office
LN – Local National
LZ – Landing Zone
MARSOC – Marine Special Operations Command
MEDEVAC – Medical Evacuation
MGRS – Military Grid Reference System
MOLLE – Modular Lightweight Load-Carrying Equipment
MRAP – Mine Resistant Ambush Protected
MRE – Meal Ready to Eat (US Military)
MSR – Main Supply Route
MWR – Morale Welfare Recreation
NATO – North Atlantic Treaty Organization
NCO – Non-commissioned Officer
NDS – National Directorate of Security
OCONUS – Outside Continental United States
ODA – Operational Detachment-Alpha
OEF – Operation Enduring Freedom
OGA – Other Government Agency

OIF – Operation Iraqi Freedom
OPSEC – Operations Security
PKM – Pulemyot Kalashnikova Machine Gun
PM – Program Manager
PMC – Private Military Company
POC – Point of Contact
PSD – Personal Security Detail
QRF – Quick Reaction Force
ROE – Rules of Engagement
RPG – Rocket-Propelled Grenade
RTB – Return to Base
RTC – Remote Training Center
RUF – Rules Use of Force
SAF – Small Arms Fire
SIR – Serious Incident Report
SOC – Special Operations Consulting/Securing Our Country
TERP – Interpreter
TL – Team Leader
TOC – Tactical Operations Center
TTP – Tactics Techniques Procedures
URG – Unity Resources Group
UXO – Unexploded Ordnance
VBIED – Vehicle-Borne Improvised Explosive Device
WIA – Wounded in Action
WPPS – Worldwide Personal Protection Specialist

APPENDIX SIX

Bibliography

Abi-Habib, Maria. "On Afghan Odyssey, Gifts to Troops Brave Ambushes, Bombs."

The Wall Street Journal. 2012.
https://www.wsj.com/articles/SB10001424127887324296604578179740347483934

McGirk, Tim. "Taliban Stepping Up Attacks on NATO Supply Convoys." Time. 2009.
http://content.time.com/time/world/article/0,8599,1928899,00.html

Micallef, Joseph V. "Afghanistan 2015: The View from Kabul." Huffington Post. 2017.
https://www.huffpost.com/entry/afghanistan-2015-the-view_b_8476964

Evan Wright, War could be fun "quote" Generation Kill
https://taskandpurpose.com/culture/generation-kill

www.ingramcontent.com/pod-product-compliance
Lightning Source LLC
Chambersburg PA
CBHW020833160426
43192CB00007B/632